D0045582

TRIBAL WARS OF THE SOUTHERN PLAINS

Tribal Wars
of
the Southern Plains

by

Stan Hoig

University of Oklahoma Press : Norman and London

By Stan Hoig

The Sand Creek Massacre (Norman, 1961)
The Humor of the American Cowboy (Lincoln, Nebr., 1970)
John Simpson Smith (Spokane, Wash., 1974)
The Battle of the Washita: The Sheridan-Custer Indian Campaign of
  1867–69 (Lincoln, Nebr., 1979)
The Peace Chiefs of the Cheyennes (Norman, 1980)
The Cheyenne (New York, 1989)
A Capital for the Nation (New York, 1990)
Jesse Chisholm: Ambassador of the Plains (Niwot, Colo., 1991)
People of the Sacred Arrows: The Story of the Southern Cheyennes
  (New York, 1992)
Tribal Wars of the Southern Plains (Norman, 1993)

To Mary Ann, with love

ISBN 0-8061-2463-6

Copyright © 1993 by the University of Oklahoma Press, Norman,
Publishing Division of the University. All rights reserved.
Manufactured in the U.S.A.

Contents

Illustrations

Maps

TRIBAL WARS OF THE SOUTHERN PLAINS

Introduction

DURING the latter half of the nineteenth century, the United States of America conducted a war to conquer the Indian tribes of the southern plains of North America, an area here defined as the land lying between the Platte River and the Rio Grande. This, however, was but the final chapter in a long history of warfare throughout this vast region—principally the western portions of present-day Kansas, Oklahoma, and Texas—a region that was once grazed by immeasurable herds of buffalo and populated by the Plains Indian tribes.

Most studies of Plains Indian warfare have dealt with the Anglo-American phase of this conflict and ignored the earlier history of intertribal warfare. A full understanding of the subject must also take into account what is known of tribal arrivals on the land and the wars the tribes fought among themselves for possession of it. Only by seeing this New World drama from the standpoint of the Indians as well as that of the conquering white civilization can the whole story be known.

Perhaps the American conquest of Indian lands can be justified by world history, which time and again repeats the conquests of nation areas and the overthrow of native residents by invading armies. The Plains tribes themselves originally won their right to the land by means of militant force. But it is also true that the modern Indian tribes occupied the plains before the whites—before the Spanish or the Mexicans established themselves, before the United States assumed proprietorship after the Louisiana Purchase, before the establishment of the Republic of Texas.

There was a unique quality to the American conquest. It was accomplished under the pretense of civilized law. From the beginning, the United States *legally recognized* the Indians' claim to the land on which they resided. Then, repeatedly, the government abrogated its promises and treaty commitments in order to invade and take over more and more of the Indians' homeland. Often, the rights to Indian lands were secured through bribery, duplicity, intimidation, alcoholic stupefaction, and other spurious methods.

The western historian Robert M. Utley quotes a Georgia governor, who stated the creed of many whites in regard to treaties: "Treaties were expedients by which ignorant, intractable, and savage people were induced without bloodshed to yield up what civilized people had the right to possess by virtue of that command of the Creator delivered to man upon his formation—be fruitful, multiply, and replenish the earth, and subdue it."[1]

Thus, to justify invasion and making war, the U.S. government often broke the rules that it had established as fair by so-called civilized standards. Today few Americans realize the extent to which solemn treaties with Indian nations were disregarded or the chicanery that was employed by the federal government, the states, and private citizens to dispossess the tribes.

It is not difficult to understand why the Indians too sometimes rescinded agreements or conducted themselves in war with less than Arthurian chivalry. They knew, even if the American public did not, that they were being victimized. They realized this well enough when surveyors and settlers began arriving. The U.S. citizen who built a cabin and fenced it round was often as much the Indian's enemy as was the soldier, the buffalo hunter, or the railroad builder.

When the Indians struck back in defense of their rights to the land, frontier whites judged them "barbarous" and "savage." And in truth, by any standard, in war they often were—just as were whites. Because such words have long been used to discredit the Indian, academics today are attempting to censor them.

To limit language is to limit truth. Consistently overlooked in comparisons between Indians and whites is the fact that during the nineteenth century American Indians underwent a phase of social development that Europeans had undergone centuries earlier. History reveals that in Europe, as well as in other areas of the world, human behavior had been as barbaric as anything exhibited by Indians.

Even as they resisted a better armed, better organized, and more numerous foe, the Indians were experiencing their first contact with formal language and writing, legal documents, commercial trade—a vast array of new goods and foodstuffs—and a formal religious morality that often seemed contradictory and hypocritical as practiced by the body of people who proclaimed themselves to be superior.

The bitter enmities among the tribes served them poorly in their conflict with whites. Intertribal hatreds prevented the tribes from consolidating against American intrusion. There were times when two or more tribes would join together to fight the common enemy. In the main, however, the wars involved independent tribes. Occasionally, individual bands, not a complete tribe, mounted some resistance. Ultimately, even a unified Indian alliance would probably have met defeat; divided, the tribes stood no chance whatever of holding back the American advance.

Promises made by the U.S. government to tribes uprooted from their native areas were fragile. Even in the Indian Territory (now Oklahoma), which was established as a repository for tribes from all over the country, the Plains Indians stood as a barrier to the American idea of a manifest destiny to span the continent. Whites soon came to covet this land just as they had all the other. In the end, the promised sanctuary became a final battleground for the basic concept of Indian independence.

With more than a century having passed since the end of the Indian wars, American history is still seen principally from the Anglo-American majority viewpoint, with little understanding or empathy for the Indians. As the Smithsonian ethnologist John C. Ewers has pointed out, white historians have long approached the subject of the Indian wars largely from an ethnocentric perspective, perceiving the Indians as obstacles to white expansion rather than seeing the whites as intruders and invaders of the Indian domain.[2]

It would be up to the social psychologist to determine if ethnocentrism is simply a natural, self-protecting inclination or if it also embodies a sense of national guilt. Unquestionably, it is difficult to admit historical wrongs and, in so doing, to violate our moral image of ourselves and our nation—a nation that, in truth, was created out of war with the Indians.

Still another difference between white and Indian perceptions is that whites see the Indian wars and Indian affairs of the past as separate from the present—as events that once happened but, right or wrong, are no longer pertinent. Indian people, by contrast, consider history a continuum, past and present being firmly connected by their "Indianness," their traditions, and their continuous subjugation in American society.

The reader of these pages will encounter many instances of atrocities both by Indians and by whites against each other. Crimes by soldiers and citizens against Indians were not reported nearly so often as those by Indians against whites. Nor were the acts of whites viewed with the same public passion or indignation. In the minds of most Americans, transgressions against Indians were simply not considered equivalent to those committed against whites.

"What the white man does to the Indian is never known," Major General John Pope noted in an official communication in 1865. "It is only what the Indian does to the white man (nine times out of ten in the way of retaliation) which reaches the public."[3]

Moreover, the reaction among the American public to a cavalry charge through an Indian village, in which tribespeople were killed indiscriminately, was far different from the response to an Indian raid against a white settlement. Nineteenth-century whites saw little comparison between the rape of an Indian woman and the rape of a white woman—or between the capture of Indian children and the capture of white children.

In truth, there simply was little understanding or recognition of human qualities in Indian people. Many nineteenth-century Americans believed that the best way to solve the Indian problem was to kill the Indians off along with the buffalo. Only a few whites even realized that Indian people loved families and children every bit as much as they.

Disturbing though Indian battle atrocities may be, we must remind ourselves that the world today is just as guilty of horrendous crimes in and out of war. Any judgment of right and wrong regarding the tribal wars must go beyond individual deeds and consider the merits of the opposing societies as a whole.

As a result of white bias, American Indian history has been, and probably will continue to be, subject to distortion. In the past it has been common practice for historians to accept government documents as a valid basis for research in part because they were "official," in part because they were the only detailed records available, and in part because they sustained the perspective of the white majority.

The Sand Creek massacre of Colorado Territory offers a prime example of an Indian conflict in which the white viewpoint was propounded by historical writers for many years. Testimony of the affair was fully given in both army and congressional inquiries. In these can be found damning eyewitness evidence against the white troops under Col. John M. Chivington. Though the affair was publicly denounced in its aftermath, it was nearly a century before this vital evidence was given proper historical credence.

As Gen. Alfred Sully once acknowledged, military commanders were prone to exaggerate the number of Indians their units may have killed. Seldom did they really know the count. After his attack on the Cheyennes on the Washita, Gen. George Custer made no battlefield count of the victims. Only after he had retreated for nearly twelve hours did he call his officers together for their best guess as to how many Indians had been slain on the different areas of the battlefield.

Though Custer grossly overglorified his Washita attack, describing it as a great military victory rather than as the hit-and-run raid it was, generally his books and newspaper narratives of his field activities contained good descriptive reports. Indeed, many military men gave accounts of their engagements with the Indians as thoroughly and honestly as their soldierly prejudices would allow. Also, there were other whites who were totally honest and sympathetic to the Indians and left behind valid reports on Indian conflicts.

Still, it must be recognized that much of the reporting of Indian affairs was done by ambitious officers, conspiring government officials, less-than-honest Indian agents and traders, and other whites who stood to profit in one way or another from their dishonesty. In short, most records of Indian conflict were written by whites, and seldom have these records had the benefit of contemporary Indian challenge.

In addressing the subject of tribal warriorship, we must note that American Indians have an outstanding record in the modern military service of the United States. Indians have served often on the front line in combat. Of those Indians serving in Vietnam, some 80 percent were volunteers. Eighty-four percent served in U.S. military combat units, suffering a 31 percent casualty rate.

The general conception of Indians as warriors and natural scouts sometimes works to their detriment. One veteran noted that in Vietnam, whenever a man was discovered to be an Indian, he would almost always be assigned to the dangerous task of walking point. "You might say," he added with a wry grin—illustrating another overlooked trait of Indian character, an irrepressible sense of humor—"that we were overqualified."[4]

American Indians have, in fact, fought bravely in all the wars of the twentieth century. The rolls of those who gave their lives or otherwise served with distinction in World War I, World War II, Korea, and Vietnam are replete with Indian names. The ethnologist Tom Holm notes:

> When World War II broke out, American Indians readily accepted these duties. They registered at selective service centers in the cities and at their agencies. There was little protest against the draft, and very few attempted to avoid service on grounds that it was a white man's war. In fact, many Indians refused to wait the prescribed time to enter the military and either requested early conscription or contacted a recruiter and volunteered. The Indian people, just as they had done in 1917, accepted their share of the burden of the war.[5]

As examples of Indians who fought with outstanding honor in World War II, Holm cites Kenneth Scission, a Sioux who led a special commando unit in Germany and personally killed ten Germans on one patrol; Robert Stabler, an Omaha who performed heroically in an American landing at Sicily; Ernest Childers, a Creek who won the Medal of Honor with the Forty-fifth Infantry Division; and Gen. Clarence Tinker, the famed Osage who died as he led an air attack against the Japanese fleet during the Battle of Midway. There were many others equally as heroic.

There is a direct connection between the tribal warrior of yesterday and the Indian soldier of today. The warrior tradition is still strong among Plains Indians. Tribespeople continue to hold the warrior in great esteem; as in the old days, a young male can find special recognition and attention among his people through wartime military service.

It is common practice for a powwow to be given in honor of a tribal member when he graduates from paratroop jump school, goes overseas, or returns home from war. The powwow dance and the sweat lodge are still looked on as a means of spiritually healing the returning tribal warrior.

Military organizations, such as the Black Leggings Warrior Society of the Kiowas, pay special homage to veterans, whereas the Intertribal Association of Vietnam Veterans works to help veterans with their problems. The latter group also sponsors an Honor Guard, which appears at nearly all Plains Indian ceremonies and hosts a National Vietnam Veterans Powwow each year.

But it is not tribal tradition alone that calls Indians to fight in the wars of the United States. Plains Indians are undeniably as loyal as any other group of Americans. No powwow or formal meeting is begun without an opening prayer and the pledge of allegiance to the flag of the United States. Indians are no longer the sole proprietors of the land of North America. But they love it just as much as other Americans, even though they may disapprove of the behavior of a government whose aggression their ancestors once fiercely resisted.

This book aims to provide an overview of the tribal wars on the North American plains south of the Platte River. It also examines the historical nature and character of the Plains Indian warriors, their fighting tactics, and the relationship of their warriorship to their sociological and cultural background. Its intention is to focus on a simple truth often overlooked by many Americans: in defense of their homeland, Indians were every bit as moral, courageous, and patriotic as the whites who were attempting to deprive them of it.

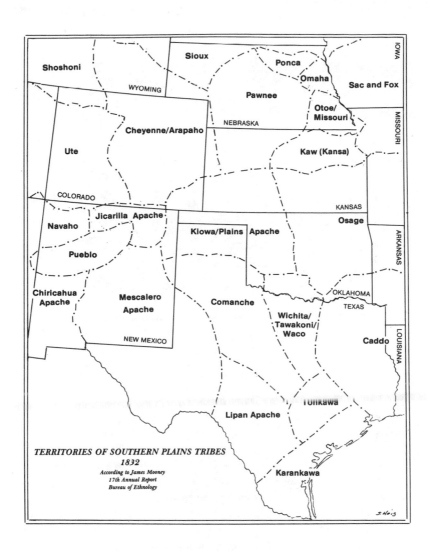

Shoshoni

Sioux

Ponca

Omaha

Sac and Fox

WYOMING

Pawnee

Otoe/
Missouri

Cheyenne/Arapaho

NEBRASKA

Ute

Kaw (Kansa)

COLORADO

KANSAS

Jicarilla Apache

Osage

Navaho

Kiowa/Plains Apache

Pueblo

Chiricahua
Apache

Mescalero
Apache

Comanche

OKLAHOMA

TEXAS

NEW MEXICO

Wichita/
Tawakoni/
Waco

Caddo

LOUISIANA

Tonkawa

Lipan Apache

TERRITORIES OF SOUTHERN PLAINS TRIBES
1832
According to James Mooney
17th Annual Report
Bureau of Ethnology

Karankawa

IOWA

MISSOURI

ARKANSAS

S. Heig

Typical of exaggerated military claims, this heroic view asserted that Custer attacked "over two thousand warriors" at the Washita. There were only some fifty lodges in Black Kettle's camp. (Richard Irving Dodge, *Our Wild Indians*)

CHAPTER 1

The Warrior Ethic

FOR over three centuries of recorded history and undoubtedly much, much longer, the great southern plains of North America was a warring ground. During that period, the region was dominated by bloody intertribal conflicts among native tribes and their defensive wars against outside intruders—namely the Spanish, the French, and the Anglo-Americans. Just as whites had done throughout time in Europe and Asia, tribes contested adversaries for territorial rights, for captives, for property, for food, and for the honor and glory of conquest.

Although the cultures of the various Plains tribes contained many characteristics in common, each tribe had its own traditions and its own personality structures that separated one from another.[1] Ewers, in stressing that every Indian warrior of the plains was passionately devoted to his own tribe, noted:

> The roots of intertribal warfare in this region can be found in the very nature of tribalism—in the common disposition of the members of each tribe to regard their tribe as "the people," and to look upon outsiders with suspicion. . . . The history of intertribal warfare in this region seems to show that

it was much easier to start a war than it was to end one, and that hostilities between neighboring tribes persisted from generation to generation.[2]

Cave pictograph drawings from Canada to Texas depict armed prehistoric warriors carrying round, leather shields large enough to protect their entire bodies. Many of the shields are decorated with drawings of animals and designs calling for assistance from the supernatural in battle. Some of the warriors wear feathered headdresses, and some carry sacred pipe stems for spiritual protection.[3]

Such warriors were often part of Indian armies that marched on foot to attack an enemy village, massacre its inhabitants, loot, and take captives at will. Usually, they were led by a head war chief, and war captains controlled individual battle units. Sometimes the target villages were fortified with ditches and palisades. On other occasions the attackers were met in the field by an opposing army of warriors, the two clashing head on in a bloody melee, with numerous casualties on both sides. Victory generally went to the army with the most warriors.

Gleanings of the earliest white contacts with the Indians provide narrative support for the pictographs. Accounts such as that of Father Couquart tell of an attack by 200 Assiniboine-Cree warriors on a Sioux village in 1742. In a four-day battle, some 270 Sioux, including women and children, were killed, and an estimated 200 more were taken prisoner.[4]

The explorer David Thompson recounted the story of a Chippewa revenge attack on a Cheyenne village before 1799. The 150-member Chippewa war party had no horses as did the Cheyennes. The attackers hid in a grove of trees and spied on the Cheyenne camp until most of the occupants had departed on a buffalo hunt. The Chippewas then raced across about a mile of open plain and fell on the village, killing twelve men and capturing three women and a baby. After burning the lodges, they decapitated the corpses and took the severed heads with them, fleeing in great haste lest they be caught on the prairie by the mounted Cheyennes.[5]

These prehistoric armies were far better organized and operated in a more regulated military manner than might be suspected. In 1806 the Canadian traders Charles Mac-Kenzie and Alexander Henry witnessed the march of a nine-hundred-person Gros Ventre–Mandan caravan on its way to a Cheyenne–Sioux camp. Though their purpose was to trade, the Indians held to a rigid battle formation in case they were attacked.

> The men were separated from the women and children and formed in squares of sixty four; there were eleven of these squares, making the number of warriors about seven hundred. . . . We continued our march all day in the above manner, the men at the head, at a slow trot, while the women, children and baggage jogged on behind. Their order of march, their weapons which consisted of bow and arrows, lances, battle axes, shields, would have reminded one of old times, when our forefathers made war.[6]

Intertribal warring had firmly established militancy as a significant part of the Plains Indian culture, an aspect that would be advanced considerably with the arrival of the European horse and explosive weapons. At first these enhancements were used by the tribes to gain superiority over one another and to invade territories previously impenetrable.

It was, in fact, only after the arrival of the Europeans in North America that the Dakota Sioux moved west and pushed the Crees, Assiniboines, and Hidatsas from present North Dakota and Montana; the Comanches and Kiowas overran the Apaches of New Mexico and Texas; the Cheyennes and Arapahos moved down from the Black Hills of present South Dakota into Colorado and Kansas; and pressure from the Osages of Missouri and others finally drove the Wichitas south from the Arkansas River to the Red River.

This fluctuation of military power and shift of populations took place largely during the seventeenth and eighteenth centuries, before white people arrived on the central plains in large numbers. However, there can be little doubt that the horse and the gun, which arrived on the plains ahead of these intruders, were critical instruments in the mass movements of tribal people and the creation of new conflicts and new alliances among them.

The long-standing intertribal wars prepared the tribes to wage a desperate fight to protect their homes and way of life from as alien an invader as might have come from some distant star. The white people's military power, vast population, and societal organization made them invincible, but they were too contradictory and too dominating not to be opposed by the Indians.

For the most part, Indians first received the whites with friendly hospitality. Soon, though, they found themselves ill rewarded. Not only did the visitors transgress against the occupants, but shortly there was an unending parade of intruders onto and across the land. Yet, while the Indians quickly had enough of white intrusion, they found that they had developed a strong taste for the goods of white civilization: tobacco, whiskey, sugar, metal tools, guns, textiles, and a large variety of other items. The one meant the other.

Beyond the surface causes of tribal conflict with whites, Plains Indians knew that they were fighting for their very survival. They resisted as best they could, but in the end they faced a hopeless dilemma. Should they follow the warrior's will, continuing a hopeless struggle against an enemy of overwhelming number and power until they were either starved or killed? Or should they give in to defeat, saving themselves by accepting white dominance and the loss of their way of life?

The first Spanish and French explorers arrived on the plains to find the Indians fractionalized into independent tribes, each living in a state of hostility with the others and maintaining an individual tribal society. Some wished merely to be left alone to pursue their activities of hunting and agriculture. But when threatened by other, more aggressive tribes with strong war cultures, they had been forced to develop defensive warrior systems.

While exploring present-day eastern Oklahoma in 1719, the Frenchman Bénard de La Harpe discovered a quasi–Plains Indian society residing there. These Indians were both planters and hunters and possessed a strong warrior culture as well. The encampment comprised Wichitas and several other Caddoan tribes, who resided in domed houses built of straw and reeds and covered with dirt. However, each October the Indians deserted their homes in the woods to hunt buffalo on the prairie, returning the following March to plant maize, beans, and pumpkins.[7]

These bands owned many fine horses, which they used in hunting and making war. The horses were equipped not only with saddles and bridles but also with breastplates for protection in battle. Only a few guns had made their way to these tribes, who warred regularly with the Osages of Missouri and the Comanches to the west, as well as with other enemies.

The significance of warfare in their lives was emphasized by leather shields above the door of each home. Bearing images of animals, the sun, the moon, and other objects, these shields constituted the personal coat of arms of a warrior family. The position of the war chief was very strong among these people. Yet, significantly, in La Harpe's first meeting with the Indians, Chief Touacara presented him not only a colorful eagle-feathered headdress but also two "calumet plumes, one of war and the other of peace . . . the most valuable gift that these warriors could make."[8]

The very desire for security and peace fostered the need for a protective military body within the tribe and gave rise to a dual system of leadership: one for peace and one for war. This arrangement prevailed among many tribes in North America, not only the Cherokees of the South (who had considerable experience on the plains after 1800) but also the Apaches, Comanches, Cheyennes, and other tribes of the central plains.[9]

Early battles between the Mandans and the Cheyennes are reflected in this Catlin sketch of a Mandan robe drawing. (George Catlin, *North American Indians* 1 [1841], pl. 65)

Normally the peace or political chief, whose role was to keep peace within and without the tribe, was considered to be of highest rank. But a war chief could recruit soldiers and conduct raids much at his own will, overriding the moral authority of the peace chief.

Because of the opposition by the militant war societies, as well as the personal risk involved in dealing with white people, Indian leaders sometimes found it more dangerous to seek peace than to make war. It is ironic, indeed, that probably more Indian leaders were killed while working for peace than while fighting in battles. This was especially true among the Comanches and the Cheyennes, both of whom had numerous peacemaker chiefs killed by whites. Some chiefs were assassinated by their own people for giving up land or assisting whites.

Chiefs who had been escorted to the east to visit the

white world and had seen the superiority of numbers and arms there realized that in the long run, their people could not defeat the whites. However, this insight did not always subdue the warrior elements of the tribe. Often the situation was akin to that of the Cheyenne war societies under Principal Chief Black Kettle. The attempt of this intelligent leader to make peace put him dangerously at odds with the Cheyenne war leaders.

After his efforts to seek peace were betrayed by Chivington's attack on his band at Sand Creek in November 1864, Black Kettle lost much prestige among his people. Much of his power to decide tribal destiny shifted to the Dog Soldiers war society, who now dared to threaten and intimidate him. Thereafter, his capacity to work out peaceful relations with the whites was severely diminished.

The ordeal of Black Kettle illustrates another critical factor of Indian life that white people seldom understood. In the dual form of peace and war leadership, the peace chief's authority rested entirely on the respect he carried within the tribe. He could make peace; but with little or no power over the war societies, he often could not prevent the young men from making war, particularly in times of crisis.

The inability of the leader to control the actions of those under him was a problem equally severe on the side of the whites. The agreements made by government officials were often negated by American citizens who intruded onto Indian lands against treaty stipulations and who could and did commit crimes against Indians without fear of punishment. In talks with the Cheyenne chief Lean (Starved) Bear at Washington in 1863, President Abraham Lincoln sadly acknowledged: "We make treaties with you, and will try to observe them; and if our children should sometimes behave badly, and violate these treaties, it is against our wish. You know it is not always possible for any father to have his children do precisely as he wishes them to do."[10]

The following spring, U.S. troops killed Lean Bear while he was leading a peaceful buffalo hunt on the plains of western Kansas. The peace-minded chief was shot from his horse as he was attempting to present his letter of recommendation from the president. His murder touched off the Cheyenne outbreak during the summer of 1864.

The military sector of the Plains tribes was formalized by the development of war societies and such warrior rituals as the sun dance. This rite, which was adopted by virtually all of the buffalo-hunting tribes and is still practiced by some, is an annual tribal celebration featuring initiation into manhood and spiritual commitment for young males. It is believed to be an adaptation of rituals practiced by the Mandans, Hidatsas, and Arikaras of the upper Missouri River.[11]

Most likely the sun dance developed among the prairie tribes after the arrival of the horse had made warriorship less of a mass undertaking and far more personal. The mobility that the horse provided had a profound effect on the character of the Plains warrior and on the entire nature of Indian warfare. Utley has observed, "massed encounters on foot, involving heavy casualties, gave way to mounted hit-and-run forays by small parties."[12]

The warrior no longer was confined largely to the defense of his home, and he no longer suffered being lost among his tribe's warrior legion. Now, in a small party with other warriors, he could range far from his village, attack an enemy, and receive individual notice when he returned home. Also, smaller war parties meant that the head tribal war chief was often replaced by the war captain, who organized his own forays.

Warring exploits were made far more romantic by virtue of being aggressive, vengeful, and subject to personal retelling. The Cheyenne chief Old Bark, or the Bear's Feather, admitted to such a retelling on one occasion. During a horse-stealing venture as a young warrior, he was befriended by an enemy Pawnee chief. The Pawnee and his wife fed him and gave him a fine white mule and a Mexican saddle. However, in order to appear brave when he returned home, he told his village he had stolen the mule and saddle.[13]

It became standing practice for warriors to be welcomed back with orgies of celebration by their entire village. The Canadian trader Charles MacKenzie described one such festivity held on the return of a six-hundred-man Gros Ventre–Mandan war party that had gone to avenge the death of some of their young men in the spring of 1806:

> The war party, who were absent two months, returned in triumph with three scalps! War parties generally content themselves with attacking the first enemy they meet, and return as soon as they have killed and drawn blood, thinking themselves entitled to equal laurels and equal honors whether the contest was severe or easy. This war party paraded the villages for several days, singing and dancing, with the scalps at the end of long poles.[14]

The Cherokee war captain John Smith described a similar event after the Cherokees of East Texas raided the Tawakonis on the Brazos River in 1829 and returned to camp.[15] The war party rode into the village singing war songs and toting scalps on the ends of long poles. Switch-wielding guards kept the camp dogs away from the dishes of food that the women had placed on the ground. All the villagers came forth to shake hands with the warriors. A feast was followed by a scalp dance that night.

This exultation of warriorship and victory was an essential part of tribal life. It celebrated and emotionalized the tribal existence, providing the people with a sense of unity, strength, and purpose. And, as in all celebrations, it was a time of joy and relief from the drudgery of camp routine. Even today the *dance fête* continues to be a vital force in Plains Indian life.

Conversely, the defeat of a war party or the death of a warrior was mourned to the extreme. During the Treaty of Camp Holmes near present Norman, Oklahoma, in 1835, Assistant Surgeon Leonard McPhail noted:

> A great wailing was heard last night. On inquiry understood it proceeded from the lodges of some Wich-e-taws en-

camped close by. They had just received information of the complete rout of one of their war parties and the death of many of their relatives in a fight with the whites of a Mexican settlement. Nothing in the way of mourning can exceed the demonstration of feeling made by the Indians on receiving intelligence of the death of a friend or relative. Has he fallen with honor in battle his exploits are sung with the lament for his death and the scalps of his slaughtered foes are exposed with the last memorials of his fame. The songs of the Indians on these mournful occasions are extemporaneous and sung with streaming eyes, indeed their emotion is strong and heartfelt.[16]

"It has pleased the Great Spirit to visit me with sorrow and trouble," the Comanche chief Pahauca wrote to Commissioner P. M. Butler in 1843. "I mourn the loss of my only boy, who met his death on the war path. I must cry and mourn till green grass grows; I have burnt my lodges [five of them], killed my mules and horses, and scattered ashes on my head."[17]

An intermingling of societal and sexual motivations was commonly involved in the warrior's psyche. He hoped to advance himself in the hierarchy of his warrior group and the tribe; in addition, no small part of his warring will came from his desire to win the pleasure of young women. These incentives were strongly reinforced by the total appreciation of the warrior's role by the tribe. Further, the horse held such great importance among the tribe that it became a valued medium of wealth and exchange. A warrior could conduct horse-stealing raids that would provide him with not only prestige but also the wealth by which to purchase a wife.

The tribal male's innermost self was programmed from birth toward his emergence as a warrior. Though it was usually his own choice to do so, becoming a warrior was psychologically predetermined. Bravery was stressed above all other virtues, and to die for one's people in battle was the highest honor. As a result, the Indian warrior was often a highly motivated and extremely fearless fighter.

Capt. John G. Bourke, who was with Ranald Mackenzie

in the 1876 attack on Dull Knife's village, later told of a daring chief who, wearing a beautiful warbonnet, rode his white charger along in front of a line of troops. The Cheyenne taunted his enemy until finally he was shot dead. Then, in an act of great daring, a gorgeously dressed warrior spurred his mount forward, protected only by his war shield. As bullets cut the air on all sides, he lifted his fallen chief onto his pony and dashed for his own lines. The warrior was almost to safety when he too fell to the fire of the troops. "They had been comrades in battle and in campaign;" Bourke wrote, "and in death they were not divided."[18]

The dreaded Taovayas, a branch of the Wichita Nation, were noted for their cruel treatment of prisoners, whom they often tortured to death. The Spanish lieutenant Antonio Trevino put up an especially courageous stand against them before being taken, badly wounded. In respect for his bravery, the Taovayas nursed him back to health and accepted him into their midst as a friend for two years before escorting him safely back to his home at San Antonio.[19]

As children, Plains Indian boys were seldom disciplined by whipping or other such physical abuse. Lewis Garrard, in his classic *Wah-to-yah and the Taos Trail*, describes how the trader John Simpson Smith dealt with his half-blood son in the style of the Cheyennes. The child threw a temper fit in his tipi before a gathering of chiefs on a cold winter day. When there was no quieting him by coaxing or "shu-ing," Smith sent for a bucket of icy water from a nearby stream. Cupful after cupful of the nearly frozen liquid was poured over the boy's head until finally the youngster's rage subsided, and he fell asleep in his mother's arms. "The Indians never chastise a boy," wrote Garrard, who spent the winter in 1846–47 in a Cheyenne camp, "as they think his spirit would be broken and *cowed down* . . . and they resort to any method but infliction of blows to subdue a refractory scion."[20]

Boys were trained from childhood in the skills of hunting and fighting and were indoctrinated in the values of physical endurance and sacrifice for the tribe. They were taught to ride at a very early age. It was not uncommon for a Comanche father to hang tiny archery bows on the cradle board of his son, gradually increasing the size of the bows as the boy grew.

Even the games they played as children cultivated male youths' martial skills. Sports such as wrestling, running, archery, throwing sticks, and other forms of boyhood play not only developed physical capacities but also established a taste for competition and conflict.

An observer at the Treaty of Comanche Peak, Texas, in 1846 noted a group of twelve Comanche and Kichai boys, twelve or fourteen years of age, who met on a prairie hill. Each "engaged in kicking his adversary side ways barefooted and legging and throwing his adversary, by combining sometimes on one, each party assisting until the first in contact was brot to the ground, by that time in a pile."[21]

At the Treaty of Medicine Lodge in 1867, a journalist watched as Arapaho youngsters cavorted. He noted: "Leap frog, and baseball after their own fashion, were the principal games. A few hurled the tomahawk at a target, while others practiced with headless arrows."[22]

The anthropologist George Bird Grinnell told of a sham battle in which young Cheyenne men and boys participated.

> Most of them were on foot, and many carried the imitation weapons of willow which they had brought in a short time before. Six or eight men, however, were permitted to go into this fight on horseback. The footmen divided into parties, usually by soldier bands, and indulged in the kicking game, the kickers springing into the air and kicking at the opponent with both feet. Sometimes in sport the willow weapons were used; but the men were careful in using them, no severe blows were given, and all were good-tempered.[23]

The warrior spirit was further perpetuated through the recognition and adulation given warriors, war captains, and chiefs. Young boys looked up to them as models, emulating them and hoping to join them in the war-council circle. Hunting excursions for small game were the male youths' first predatory experiences. Indoctrination into warfare usually came to them as teenagers on forays into enemy-occupied territory to look for buffalo or to steal horses.

The warrior's fierce commitment to the welfare of the tribe was enhanced by religious devotion to a tribal deity. This deity not only looked over the people in securing sustenance but provided empyreal assistance in war as well. Tribal religious belief was often expressed in strongly revered symbols, such as the Sacred Medicine Arrows of the Cheyennes or the "taíme" pouch of the Kiowas.

Thus the whites arrived to find the southern plains populated by native tribes whose internal peace and security were externally protected by a fierce warrior ethic. This ethic permitted the killing of enemies, the capturing of slaves, the stealing of horses from other tribes, and the taking of scalps as trophies of war.

These deeds were often the measure of achievement by which the male advanced in position and wealth within the tribe. They were extolled as virtues by war societies, by rituals of personal endurance such as the torturous sun dance, and by feast-dances that celebrated exploits of warriorship. The concept of war for the Plains Indian was interrelated with religion. A warrior might prepare himself for combat by fasting and weeping to appease the wrath of the "Evil Spirit." Sometimes he would sing or pray to obtain the aid of mythical forces.[24] Charles MacKenzie witnessed such a plea by a Mandan:

Hooee! great bull of the meadow, be thou there with thy white cow;—sagacious wolf, be thou there;—ye bears and cats, be ye there,—ye eagles and ravens be ye there—ye monsters of the hill, be ye there, with your claps of thunder and fire. Thou, great serpent of the bitter sting, be though there and do not come alone,—but bring all thy slaves to thy aid.[25]

Tribal medicine men performed rituals designed to solicit such divine help. The warrior's personal medicine bag, interpretations of dreams or acts of nature and animal life, fasting, and spiritual communion were important components of tribal warriorship. The Cheyenne war chief Roman Nose wore a beautiful warbonnet that he believed gave him special fighting prowess.

Medicine men often worked spells or issued signs to influence the Indians' entry into battle. When the Cheyennes prepared to contest the force of Col. Edwin V. Sumner in the spring of 1857, they were readied for battle by their great medicine man. He told the Cheyenne warriors that by dipping their hands into a small lake along the Smoky Hill River of western Kansas, they could stop the soldiers' bullets with their bare hands. When Sumner made a charge using sabers rather than guns, the surprised warriors broke and fled in confusion.[26]

In any consideration of Indian warfare, a distinction should be made between actions taken by the tribe or war society and those by individuals. Warriors and war captains were generally free to act on their own so long as they did not violate the general will of the tribe. Revenge, in the Old Testament sense of an eye for an eye, was not an uncommon motivation. Fathers, brothers, and uncles of slain warriors often felt compelled, as a matter of honor for the dead, to seek vengeance.

With the advent of the horse and hit-and-run attacks by small war parties, the old concept of an organized warrior mass was no longer needed or employed. Occasionally against white armies, however, a tribe would feel compelled to put on a display of massed might. Such was the case when Generals W. S. Hancock and Custer approached a Cheyenne-Sioux encampment on the Pawnee Fork of western Kansas in 1867 with a fourteen-hundred-man cavalry, infantry, and artillery force.

As the soldiers approached the village, their march was intercepted by a line of some three hundred or more mounted and well-armed warriors headed by the Cheyenne war leader Roman Nose. In a scene that would challenge movie makers, the Indians stood their ground, their ponies prancing nervously as the Seventh Cavalry, sabers flashing, formed in line to face them. A compromise was eventually reached, but it was apparent that the Indians were willing to fight the far superior force rather than let it advance on their camp.[27]

The Cheyennes put on another impressive display of military organization later that year at the Treaty of Medicine Lodge. Having let the peace commission dawdle in discomfort and uncertainty for a long, wearying period while they conducted their Medicine Arrow renewal rites, the Cheyennes made a sudden and dramatic appearance.[28]

On a quiet Sunday morning, some four to five hundred well-armed warriors rode down on the camp. Both they and their horses were belled and painted for war. Hooting and chanting, they brandished lances and fired their rifles in the air as they splashed across the narrow stream in well-formed lines to the call of a bugle. It was an experience that the commissioners and their small military escort would not soon forget.

Few people who cross the great American plains today remember that this land was once a warring ground, that here for centuries Indian tribes fought one another for their own survival and then stood bravely against the irrepressible forces of white civilization. Even for those who are aware of its history, the Plains Indian conflict has largely been seen in terms of American conquest. Seldom has it been seen as the struggle of a native people to retain their homeland and way of life.

This is that story, as best we know it.

The Comanche warrior, who seemed to be almost one with his war pony, was considered to be among the world's best military horseman. (Homer Thrall, *A Pictorial History of Texas* [St. Louis, 1879])

CHAPTER 2

Warfare on
the Plains

IT was a chance meeting. Neither the Comanches nor the Apaches were out to attack the other. But a long, deadly enmity existed between the two nations, and it was natural that they do combat. The warrior code of each tribe demanded it. For either party to have gone its way without a contest of arms would have violated the tribe's honor as warriors. In many ways, it was not unlike two ancient armies of Europe or Asia clashing on a bloody battlefield for name and glory.

The Apaches had been cooking meat near a spring somewhere deep in the trackless prairie of western Texas when the advance of the Comanche hunting caravan happened onto them. Immediately the Comanche scouts headed back to their main party to sound the warning. The cry of "Apaches! Apaches!" was echoed along the scattered caravan.

The Comanche fighting force, some 250 men, surged forward to a long, high ridge, yelping their war calls and stringing their bows as they formed in a line along the crest of the hill. Already the Apaches were coming at them, a mass of mounted warriors. The shrieking sound of war whoops mingled with the pounding charge of horses.

As the distance narrowed between the two tribal battalions, the air was darkened with swarms of arrows from both sides. Briefly the two groups of warriors clashed with one another, melding together in a violent storm of flashing war axes, lances, and knives. Texas Ranger Nelson Lee, then being held captive by the Comanche party, was a witness to the fight.

From the position I occupied I had a fair, unobstructed view of the battle. It was fierce and terrible. The horses reared, and plunged, and fell upon each other, their riders dealing blow for blow, and thrust for thrust, some falling from their saddles to the ground, and others trampling madly over them.

The Comanches outnumbered the enemy; nevertheless, they were forced to retreat, falling back down the hill almost to my position; but still they were not pursued, the Apaches appearing to be content to hold possession of the ground. Soon, the tribe of the Spotted Leopard [Lee's captors] again rallied and dashed once more to the attack. If possible, this contest was severer, as it was longer than the first. Again the fierce blow was given and returned; again horses and men intermingled in the melee—stumbled, fell, and rolled upon the ground, while the wide heavens resounded with their hideous shrieks and cries.[1]

The Apaches were finally driven from the field, but the Comanches did not pursue. They gathered their seventeen dead and retreated into the hills. Later the Apaches came back and claimed their own victims. The battle was essentially a draw, neither side having seriously damaged the other but both being satisfied that they had proven their warriorship.

Lee observed that "thousands of such sanguinary struggles take place on the lonely prairies, of which the world knows not."[2] Without question, he was correct. This chance eruption was typical in the endless contests between the warring tribes on the southern plains of North America. Although we know of many Indian battles on the southern plains during the more than four centuries of recorded history, multitudes of others of which we know nothing undoubtedly occurred.

Indirectly, we have ample evidence of prehistoric conflicts. Artifacts in the form of human bones, stone implements and weapon heads, dwelling outlines, robe pictographs, and Indian rock art provide us with a general concept of how the first tribal life on the southern plains evolved.[3]

Embedded in this lore are unmistakable signs of ancient warfare: burned villages, arrow points found inside skeletal remains, fractured skulls, indications of maiming and scalping, defensive fortifications, and other clues to prehistoric conflict and violence. One such case is the Wright Site in Nebraska where some fifty mutilated skeletons were found on the floor of a burned structure.[4]

These relics of the past tell us of a time when the forerunners of the tribal Indians roamed this land in groups as small, independent hunter-families, each fearful of and hostile to the others. Hunting and warfare went hand in hand, establishing traditions that were inherited by the larger tribal systems that eventually developed. The being of the Plains warrior was deeply rooted in his long ancestral struggle for survival in a perilous world.

It is known that humankind has existed on the southern plains for at least twelve thousand years and probably much, much longer. There exist written records for less than five hundred years. Thus, most of human history here is clouded with mystery. Very little is known about specific events in the centuries before the arrival of Europeans in America or, for that matter, about events in the two centuries following.

The adventures of Cabeza de Vaca provide the earliest, though vague, glimpse into life on the southern plains. After being shipwrecked along the Texas Gulf Coast, the Spaniard and three companions wandered across the arid country of southern Texas for six years before reaching a Spanish settlement in northern Mexico in 1536. During that time, the men met numerous Indian tribes and saw the great buffalo herds of the region. Evidently referring to the tribes in general, Cabeza de Vaca noted that the Indians' technique of warfare was so well developed that they appeared to have been trained in continuous wars.[5]

In 1541 the Spanish expedition of Gen. Francisco Vásquez de Coronado marched from present-day New Mexico across the Texas Panhandle and into Kansas. Reports of the expedition give us our first concrete look at Plains Indian life in its pre-European form. In the Texas Panhandle, Coronado encountered an Indian village that followed and lived close to the buffalo, depending on the animal for virtually all of its needs.[6]

The Spaniards later met another group of Indians who were enemies to the first as well as to a third tribe called the "Teyas." These natives, whom Coronado found on the Arkansas River of present Kansas, existed much differently. Though they hunted, these people did not move with the buffalo. Instead they resided in permanent, grass-hut villages surrounded by planted fields of maize, beans, and melons. They also baked bread beneath their lodge fires.[7]

Though Coronado and his men observed no actual warfare, they noted that the bands of this group lived in hostility to one another and spoke different languages. It was still a world without either horses or firearms. The bow and arrow, buffalo-skin shield, stone-headed spear, and club were the weapons of war common to these first Indians met by the Spaniards and would continue to be the weapons used throughout the seventeenth century.

During the ensuing years, stray or stolen Spanish horses adapted to the environment of the American Southwest and multiplied rapidly. When the Pueblo Indians revolted against the Spanish in New Mexico, they turned Spanish horses loose on the prairie, permitting them to propagate freely. By the end of the eighteenth century, most tribes of the prairie possessed horses and had incorporated them as an essential element of tribal society and warfare.

Frank A. Secoy, writing on Plains Indian warfare, divided the central plains into three regions: the southern subarea south of the Platte River, the northwestern region

located north and west of the Platte and west of the Rockies, and the northeastern sector lying north and east of the
Platte. He defined the military techniques of each of these
regions as falling into time segments identified as the pre-
horse/pre-gun, the post-horse/pre-gun, and the post-horse/
post-gun periods.[8]

In the earliest of these periods, tribal warriors fought
on foot and in large numbers, often in well-organized
squadrons. When unmounted warring parties such as
these clashed, they often drew up in long parallel lines
facing one another, with war captains in command of their
sections. The first weapon used was generally the bow and
arrow, with which an enemy could be felled at a distance.
In battle, showers of arrows would be launched, followed
by thrown spears at closer range. The battle axe and leather
shield were then employed in hand-to-hand combat.

Generally, sheer numbers decided the battle. This meant
that smaller tribes such as the Cheyennes were much at
the mercy of the more numerous Assiniboines and Crees,
who at times wiped out entire villages with mass assaults.
It was only when the victimized tribes acquired horses
that they were able to evade or resist such onslaughts and
to strike back.

The Apaches, having procured horses from the Spanish,
also adopted Spanish warring techniques. They began
making protective armor of tough, overlapping leather for
both themselves and their horses, imitative of the Spanish
mail. They also took the Spaniards' cutlasses, tied them
on ends of poles to make lances, and manufactured metal
darts called "chuzas." Their saddles, high-pommeled and
high-cantled in the style of the Spanish cavalryman, were
designed for support in fighting from horseback.[9]

The Apaches fought mainly with the bow when on foot
and with the lance when mounted. Whenever charged
by Spanish dragoons, the Apache cavalry would retreat
behind the infantry—and the Spanish soon learned not to
charge into a shower of arrows released by a band of
Apache footmen.[10]

It was the horse that most profoundly affected the Indians' style of fighting. In writing about the use of the horse in battle, Frank Gilbert Roe has stated, "Apparently the function of the horse in Indian warfare was seldom more than that of conveying the warrior to the area (not the *scene*) of operation, where he dismounted, dragoonwise, to fight, or preferably to surprise the enemy."[11]

The extent to which this statement is valid is questionable. Certainly there were many Indian battles known to have been fought in large part on horseback. A singular instance involved a Pawnee warrior who was attached to a U.S. cavalry unit during an engagement with the Sioux. When ordered by an officer to dismount and fight on foot, he refused. Instead he stripped himself completely naked, tied a red, white, and blue ribbon in his hair, and calmly sat his horse ready to fight, with a Spencer rifle and his reins in one hand and a Colt revolver in the other.[12]

It is certain that the horse had two major effects on tribal warfare. It was a potent weapon in extending the mobility and range of the warrior; and because of its emense value among all tribes, it was also the cause of much warfare. Without question, the incessant horse stealing among the tribes created more conflict than any other issue, even that of intertribal slave taking.

It was a general truth that among the Plains tribes, a warrior's most valuable possession was his horse. Further, as the horse became prevalent on the plains, it also became requisite to trivial survival. The challenge presented by dominant tribes and the ever increasing competition for the diminishing buffalo made the horse vital to tribal existence and independence. Any tribe without horses was destined soon to be conquered by another tribe or by whites.

The Apaches were the first Plains tribe to acquire horses from the Spanish. Horses gave them the ability to range north and east into present Colorado, Kansas, and Oklahoma. At first the Apaches dominated those areas, but during the eighteenth century, the horse spread northward to competing tribes. A part of the reason for the demise of the Apache empire was that they were not good stockmen.

Étienne Véniard de Bourgmond, who met them in Kansas in 1724, observed that they never raised colts. The mares always had miscarriages because the Apaches rode them in hunting and warring.[13] The Pawnees, on the other hand, were excellent stock raisers.

The Plains Indian warriors are reputed to have been among the most effective fighters on horseback in the world. And the Comanches were generally considered to be the best horsemen. Their riding ability and coordination with their mounts, their effectiveness with bows and arrows even at a hard gallop, their ability to drop to one side of their horses and continue firing, and their capacity to subsist on the sparse offering of the prairie during extended excursions all gave them a superior quality as fighters.[14]

The artist George Catlin, who observed the Comanches in 1835, wrote at length about their amazing capacity as horsemen:

> . . . a stratagem of war practiced by every young man in the tribe; by which he is able to drop his body upon the side of his horse at the instant he is passing, effectually screened from his enemies' weapons as he lays in a horizontal position behind the body of his horse, with his heels hanging over the horse's back; by which he has the power of throwing himself up again, and changing to the other side of the horse if necessary.[15]

Thus, with his horse galloping at full speed, the Comanche warrior could effectively fire his arrows or use his fourteen-foot lance. Eventually Catlin discovered that this feat was made possible by a short, hair halter that was braided into the horse's mane and looped down under its neck, providing a sling for the elbow of the rider. The technique was also common among other Plains tribes. Victor Tixier noted the use of this same method by Osage warriors in 1840. Tixier added: "The horseman seems to be one with his mount. On his back swing the shield, either in its case of painted skin or showing its paintings and its long crane feathers, and the kit of cougar skin adorned with the tail of an animal. At his belt hang the dreadful scalping knife and the tomahawk."[16]

Warfare from horseback caused a reduction in the size of the shield and the bow, the larger ones being too cumbersome for mounted combatants.[17] The Plains Indians' short, stout bow made from the tough bois d'arc tree, native to the southern plains, was a formidable weapon at close range. A warrior could shoot and reshoot it with great rapidity. Its force was tremendous, as indicated by numerous eyewitness accounts of Indian hunters who drove their arrows completely through a buffalo during a chase.

The Comanches, horsemen par excellence, were effective on foot as well. But it was the Osage warriors who were most noted for their speed as runners. Known to the Spanish as *Ligeros,* or "Swift Ones," they could run so fast that their foes often tied up a horse's tail so that it could not be grabbed by a dashing Osage.[18]

The Osage's principal aim in war was to take scalps. But his greatest enemy, the Pawnee Maha, was much more interested in stealing horses. The Pawnees conducted raids in groups of six to fifteen men; setting out on raiding expeditions across the prairie, they were armed with knives, arrows, and axes but carried no provisions whatever. Hunger, thirst, hardships, heat, or cold did not discourage a Pawnee—sometimes young warriors died during their first expedition without even seeing the enemy. They traveled during the day, hid in the woods at night, erased their tracks or mingled them with others, prowled enemy camps wrapped in animal skins, and by preference made their attacks at night.[19]

Tribes such as the Cheyennes, who fought mostly on horseback, were cautious about entering the rough, mountainous terrain of enemies such as the Utes of Colorado, who fought on foot. On the other hand, when the Arkansas Cherokees attacked Osage chief Clermont's village on the Verdigris River in 1817, they did so under the opinion that the Osages knew how to fight only in pitched battles

A Pawnee warrior uses his horse as an elevation from which to scout for game or enemies on the open plains. (*Illustrated London News*, April 3, 1858, p. 336)

on the open prairie and would be at a great disadvantage fighting on foot in broken country.[20]

The firearm reached the plains through English traders in Canada and French traders along the Mississippi River during the eighteenth century. It spread among the tribes through capture and trade and abetted the horse in creating a new balance of power among the Plains Indians, contributing greatly to upheavals in tribal dominance on the plains.

The gun's influence in warfare, however, was limited at first. At close range, an Indian warrior could easily fire arrows much more quickly than an enemy could fire and reprime a muzzle-loading rifle or reload a single-shot revolver. The ability to shoot arrows in rapid succession was often developed by contests in which tribal participants competed to see who could put the most arrows into the air at one time.[21] Whites were often amazed at the rapidity with which the Indian could shoot his arrows.

Col. Richard I. Dodge told of seeing an Indian using an old smooth-bore Tower musket. The warrior carried his powder in a buffalo horn and his bullet in his mouth. After firing the single-shot weapon, he would pour a random amount of powder into the barrel of the gun. Then he would spit in an undersized ball and fire away again— though not effectively.[22]

As the technology of the gun improved, the balance of weapon power changed. The Colt repeating revolver drastically reduced the effectiveness of the bow and arrow in fighting from horseback. Also, the improvement in rifle fire dramatically affected battle strategy. The role that the rifle played in the fight between buffalo hunters and Indians at the second Battle of Adobe Walls in 1874 clearly illustrates the change in warring technique that the buffalo gun and the rifle had caused. Fights were now often conducted at long range. Warrior hordes could no longer overrun a defended area with ease.

The Comanches secured guns from the Pawnees of the Loup River in Nebraska, who traveled as far south as the Brazos to trade. The Comanches, who were rich in horses well before the eighteenth century, swapped mules and horses for English-made weapons.[23] Later, guns and ammunition became prime trade items for Mexican and American traders on the plains.

The nature of a tribe's economy had much to do with a tribe's ability to conduct offensive or defensive warfare. Tribes such as the Cheyennes, who turned from a planter–small game economy to that of hunters, could move their lodges and families about at will on the prairie, making them difficult to find. However, tribes that lived in fixed villages were easily found and attacked by surprise. This contributed greatly to the Comanches' defeat of the Apaches, who lived in permanent rancherias, and to the Osages' vanquishment of the Wichitas, who resided in thatched huts.

Protection of the home camp was primary. When his village was attacked, the warrior immediately threw himself between it and the attacking force, often fighting desperately until the women, children, and old ones could flee to safety. This was the automatic reaction of the Comanches at the Battle of Little Robe Creek in 1858, of the Cheyennes when attacked by Col. John M. Chivington at Sand Creek in 1864, and of the Sioux at the Little Big Horn against Gen. George A. Custer in 1876.

Seldom did mounted Indians of western America form into large, consolidated units to stand and fight against an enemy force, as the Cheyennes did against Sumner, if their home was not threatened. It was not the Plains Indians' nature to contest ground in the fashion of the whites.[24] The Plains Indian would remain as long as he could effectively overwhelm the enemy; otherwise he would withdraw to fight on another day more to his advantage.

Still, there were times when he had no choice, when he was forced to do combat with an opposing army. Though without the formal training in military tactics and battlefield maneuvers that his sometimes West Point–educated opponent had, the Indian war leader was often a shrewd strategist who could successfully deploy his fighting men, feint skillfully, utilize existing terrain, and exploit his enemy's weaknesses. No better examples exist than the generalship exercised by Chief Joseph and his Nez Percé war chiefs in their masterful retreat through Yellowstone in 1877 and by the Northern Cheyennes during their 1878 retreat from Indian Territory to the north.

One standard ruse of tribal warfare was to feign an attack with a small party of warriors to draw the enemy out into a trap set by a larger force. Such a strategy, for example, was effectively used by the Cheyenne Dog Soldiers at present-day Julesburg, Colorado, on January 6, 1865,[25] and by the Sioux, the Northern Cheyennes, and the Arapahos at the Fetterman massacre in present Wyoming on December 21, 1866.[26]

The Indian was a great tactical innovator. Dodge told of a fight in 1867 between some Pawnee scouts and the Cheyennes at Plum Creek on the Platte Trail. Seeing that the Cheyennes were laying a trap for them, the Pawnees donned cavalry hats and overcoats. They advanced toward the Cheyennes, who thought that a sudden charge would stampede the poorly trained cavalry horses. But when the Cheyennes were within fifty yards, the Pawnees threw off their hats and overcoats and made their own war-whooping charge. The surprised Cheyennes broke in confusion, and the Pawnees were able to take sixteen scalps and two prisoners, plus a number of horses.[27]

A frontier cavalryman, writing a letter home, reported one of the most daring and innovative instances of a trap. He and a portion of his troop had been on the trail of a small band of Sioux for several days. He wrote, "They had dodged us, bothered us, and beat us, until we determined to have them, come what might."[28]

Finally, unexpectedly, the troopers came face to face with the Sioux, each man of whom wore a fiery red blanket about his shoulders, held a revolver in his hand, and sat his pony squarely facing the troopers. The warriors appeared to be completely indifferent as the cavalrymen spurred their horses forward in a mad gallop. The cavalry officer suspected a trap, but it was too late to halt the charge.

The Sioux did not move a muscle until the troops, who had given their horses free rein, were within twelve feet. Then suddenly, to a man, the warriors ripped off the red blankets and began waving them vigorously. The result was pandemonium among the cavalry horses, which reared and shied in panic, stampeding in all directions. "Troopers were sprawling on the ground, and others were clinging to horses' manes, with both feet not only out of the stirrups but pointing up in the air."[29] The Sioux, highly pleased that their maneuver had worked so well, did not press their advantage. They simply disappeared as if the earth had suddenly swallowed them.

A force of some one thousand Cheyennes, Sioux, Arapahos, and Kiowas was bested during the summer of 1853 when the Indians attacked a hunting party of Potawatomis, Shawnees, and others on the upper Republican River of western Kansas. The eastern Indians, having learned dragoon tactics, had trained their horses to stand steady under fire. Further, their warriors had learned the technique of dismounting in two ranks and firing alternately from a prone position, using forked sticks for rifle supports.

At the start of the fight, the Potawatomis were apart from their allies, who holed up in a ravine when attacked and held off the enemy until the Potawatomi warriors arrived. The forty Potawatomis, who were well armed with rifles, galloped to the rescue in military formation much like a troop of cavalry. One group rode forward, fired a volley, and then fell back to be replaced by a second platoon. The long-range, accurate, and disciplined fire of the Potawatomis overwhelmed the Cheyenne-led force, who had only bows, spears, and clubs.[30]

A Cheyenne-Osage force of fifteen hundred warriors was defeated in a similar fashion by a group of Potawatomis, Sauks, and Fox the following year near the Pawnee Fork of the Arkansas River. It was reported that the Cheyennes and Osages suffered twenty-six men killed and many more wounded. These defeats caused the Cheyennes and other prairie tribes to secure better weapons and improve their warring tactics.

On occasion, an Indian force would besiege an isolated group, as happened in 1868 to the fifty-man party under Maj. George A. Forsyth at Beecher's Island in present-day Colorado. After having a dream while fasting, the Cheyenne war chief Roman Nose wore his special medicine warbonnet, which had only one buffalo horn, into battle. He led charge after charge, failing to dislodge the small group of scouts, who were armed with repeating rifles and pistols. Eventually he was killed, and the Cheyennes withdrew.

It was not the tribal warrior's nature to allow himself to be pinned down and forced to defend a fortification. When meeting a head-on attack, the Indian force would usually blunt the charge with skirmishes, then melt slowly away while its mounted warriors charged or harassed the flanks and rear of the attackers.[31] This tactic was used by the Indians in numerous conflicts with whites. During the late 1860s the Kickapoos, originally of the Great Lakes area, used the ploy against a posse of whites after a horse-stealing raid in southern Texas.

The Kickapoos were tough, smart fighters. A war party stole some horses from a Texas ranch where a social get-together was in progress. A makeshift posse was quickly in the saddle in hot pursuit and soon began to close in on the Indians, some of whom were riding double. The Texans began firing, confident that they would soon run down the overloaded horses.

But the Kickapoos had other ideas. As their pursuers drew near, the warriors on the back of the stolen mounts slid off into the grass and began a blistering fire that stunted the Texans' charge. The mounted Kickapoos then looped on both flanks and encircled the whites, who were forced to dismount and fight on foot. The Texans lost several men as well as the horses.[32]

Without question, the favorite warfare practice of the Plains Indians was to strike a poorly defended, remote settlement, military post, or wagon train by surprise, and then quickly disappear back into their prairie stronghold. For many years, the undulating short-grass country of western Oklahoma and the Texas Panhandle was a haven from which the Comanches, Kiowas, and Plains Apaches could launch attacks south into Texas or north into Kansas.

"Counting coup" by simply touching an enemy with a long coup stick decorated with feathers and scalps was an accepted act of bravery among most Plains tribes. Some engagements between opposing Indian tribal forces consisted more of fanfare than bloodletting. At times, when two equal hostile forces met on the prairie, the fighting was done at long range with much dashing about of horses, feinting moves at the enemy, yelling with intense fury, and occasional firing.

Not unlikely, some young brave would dash his mount forward with great bravado to within two or three hundred yards of the enemy line, then circle back to his own party. Usually the casualties from such encounters were very light. This was the case in an 1868 Cheyenne raid—it was more of an outing—against the Kaws of central Kansas.[33] The francas involved little more than a great deal of riding about, whooping, shouting of insults, and firing from long range. A Kaw suffered a scratched hand, and one Cheyenne was shot in the foot. In the main, however, intertribal clashes were serious, deadly affairs.

Another unique aspect of Cheyenne warfare was the women who followed along behind when their warriors went out to battle an enemy. Their purpose was to provide support and to reap the spoils of victory after the fight. They would watch the battle from a distant rise, ready to disappear into the gulleys and bushes if the fight went badly for their side. Though this practice has gone unmentioned in Western warfare books, records are found in such instances as the Cheyenne attack on the Pawnees in 1830, the Battle of Wolf Creek in 1838, the Beecher's Island fight in 1868, and the attack on Adobe Walls in 1874.

Attempts to bluff the enemy with an extravagant show of force and hostility were not uncommon. The Indian's practices of wearing fierce garments such as the heads of wildcats or the horns of animals and painting himself and his mount were aimed at working a psychological influence on the foe. When facing an enemy in the field, the warrior would fire his gun in the air, jab his lance against the sky, sound his war whoop, rear his pony, throw dirt in the air, or make other menacing gestures. The Comanche warrior, who often went into battle wearing a helmet of buffalo horns complete with the long tuft of hair between, would sometimes dismount and paw the ground with his hands and feet while bellowing like a buffalo bull at the enemy.[34]

This psychological warfare was common to many tribes. It was witnessed by the Canadian trader Alexander Henry in 1806 when he accompanied a Mandan–Gros Ventre trading caravan to a Cheyenne camp. As they approached the Cheyenne village, they were met by a party of young men whose horses "were masked in a very singular manner, to imitate the head of a buffalo, red deer, or cabbrie, with horns, the mouth and nostrils—even the eyes—were trimmed with red cloth. This ornamentation gave them a very fierce appearance."[35] The practice was not unlike the horse masking by the Mongol cavalry of Asia under Genghis Khan.

A reporter at the Treaty of Fort Laramie in 1851 witnessed the arrival of a group of Cheyenne warriors. The manes and tails of their horses were painted various colors, and the animals were adorned with symbols of the scalps each warrior had taken and the horses he had stolen. The Cheyennes staged a mock battle for the benefit of onlookers.

All the Indians were painted in their war costume, and dressed in the best possible manner, armed, some with guns, some with lances, and others with bows and arrows. Their horsemen and footmen apparently mingled in a confused mass, but it could be seen that there was order in all their movements. They would fire their guns, shoot their arrows, give a shout, make a charge, and then the horsemen from the centre would rush out around and through the footmen, indicating the manner of protecting their men when too closely pressed. These exhibitions of the wild and savage mode of warfare are exciting beyond description, and when the Indian enters into it—when there are a number of them together—the whoops and yells seem to stir up every element of his wild nature. There is nothing in the trappings and excitement of war among civilized men that is more enlivening than the peculiar whoop and yells of savage warfare.[36]

The war whoop was, of course, a psychological tactic most effectively used by the Indian warrior to frighten the enemy or his mount. Texas Ranger Nelson Lee indicated another use of the whoop by the Comanches. He said that as he and his companions were being carried off onto the prairie, his captors raised the war whoop. An answering whoop from afar was heard. This interchange continued, with the answer becoming more and more distinct, and finally the two Comanche parties met.[37]

When the U.S. Indian-fighting army was formed after the Civil War, the slow, much-encumbered military expedition was soon discovered to be ineffective. Often it involved pack mules or wagon trains loaded with food, tents, ammunition, feed for the stock, and other impedimenta. The wagons were more often than not hampered by ravines, creeks, and sandy or muddy ground. Sometimes herds of extra horses and beef cattle were driven behind.

Even without such encumbrance, the invading military expedition was at a disadvantage simply because the heavier, grain-fed army horses were slower and had far less stamina than the prairie-raised, grass-fed Indian ponies. When Custer and the Seventh Cavalry met Pawnee Killer's band in western Kansas during the summer of 1867, they quickly realized that the cavalry mounts were incapable of catching the fleet Sioux horses. The same happened to Gen. Alfred Sully when he invaded Indian Territory the following spring.

Further, the Indians knew well in advance every move the soldiers made. The warriors used spies and listened for the inevitable bugle calls that the army sounded for everything from wake up to evening taps. During Kit Car-

Maj. Gen. Winfield S. Hancock's expedition to western Kansas in 1867 was typical of the clumsy, over-encumbered tactics of the Indian-fighting army just after the Civil War. Reproduced here is a sketch of Hancock's encampment at Fort Harker. (Western History Collections, University of Oklahoma)

son's battle with the Kiowas and Comanches at Adobe Walls in 1864, a bugler for the Indians confused the troops by answering each bugle call for advance or retreat with an opposite call.[38]

One old Kansas plainsman expressed his utter disgust. "Talk about regulars hunting Indians," he snorted. "They go out, and when night comes they blow the bugle to let the Indians know they are going to sleep. In the morning they blow the bugle to let the Indians know they are going to get up. Damn it, between their bugles and great trains, they manage to keep the redskins out of sight."[39]

The Cheyenne chief Whirlwind made a similar observation about the army of Gen. Nelson A. Miles: "Sundown, shoot 'um big gun—BOOM—tell every Indian for fifty miles where he [Miles] camp. Every morning shoot 'um big gun—BOOM—tell every Indian fifty miles he still there."[40]

Inevitably, the army strategists became wiser and improved their campaigning techniques. By using Indian guides and by attacking the Indian in his home camp, the U.S. Army was eventually able to conquer the Plains Indian. As Utley has pointed out, if the United States had developed a well-organized, well-equipped Indian auxiliary force, the American westward movement might well have been far less perilous.[41]

One can only wonder how the history of early Colorado and Kansas might have differed if at Denver in 1864 John Evans, the governor of Colorado Territory, and Col. John M. Chivington had accepted the offer of Bull Bear, the Cheyenne Dog Soldier chief. Bull Bear had said: "I am with you and the troops to fight all those who have no ears to listen to what you say. Who are they? Show them to me. I have given my word to fight with the whites."[42]

In truth, possibly the most effective weapon utilized by the U.S. Indian-fighting army was the Indian warrior himself. Army officers sometimes used Indians principally as scouts and trackers and at other times relied on them for battle. One of the more successful Indian units was the company of Pawnee scouts under Maj. Frank North.

Even with this help, victory over the tribes did not come easily.

CHAPTER 3

The Tattooed People of Kansas

OUR earliest account of tribal conflict on the central plains of North America was recorded by the Spanish expedition under Gov.-Gen. Don Juan de Oñate. Oñate and his seventy men, numerous servants, eight carts, four cannons, and seven hundred horses and mules arrived in the area of present-day southern Kansas in the year 1601. The Spaniards soon found themselves caught in a vicious contest between two warring tribes—the Escanjaques and the Rayados.

The Escanjaques, whom the conquistadores had met first, had followed the Spaniards to the Rayado village, just beyond a broad river thought to have been the Arkansas. Immediately it became clear that these two primitive peoples were bitter enemies and that the Rayados considered themselves direly threatened. Some three to four hundred of their foot warriors held the hilltop facing the small force of seventy-plus Spaniards. The warriors hooted and twanged their bow strings in fierce defiance.

Breechclouted war captains, their faces painted with stripes from ear to ear, came forward to toss dirt into the air, showing their readiness to fight. Behind the Spaniards the mass of largely naked Escanjaques, armed with stone-headed war clubs, bows and arrows, and huge leather shields, shouted insults and counterchallenges at the Rayados, whom they hated intensely. A battle appeared imminent, and the soldiers of New Spain realized the precariousness of their situation: alone and greatly outnumbered, they were caught between two unpredictable enemy tribes deep in a distant land.[1] All of them were aware that Fr. Juan de Padilla, who had been with Gen. Francisco Coronado in 1541 and had revisited this area the next year as a missionary, had never returned—and that in 1594 the expedition of Francisco Leyva de Bonilla and Antonio Gutiérrez de Humaña had been surrounded and massacred by natives of the region.

Wishing to avoid a fight, General Oñate sent a party to meet with the Rayados and invite them to come to his camp in peace. The Indians accepted, arriving to present their strange visitors with beads that they took from about their necks. The Spaniards returned the favor by giving them some knives and other items. Later, when Oñate had gone into camp across a river from their thatched-hut village, the Rayados brought their visitors ears of corn and round loaves of bread. The governor responded with gifts of tobacco and goods. By signs, the Rayados asked that their enemies, the Escanjaques, be sent away, and they invited the Spaniards to come to their village, where the visitors would be fed.

But the Escanjaques refused to leave and warned the Spaniards against the Rayados. They insisted that the Rayados had murdered two captive Spaniards of the Bonilla-Humaña expedition by burning them in a hut. They also claimed that another Spaniard who had escaped the fire but had badly burned feet was being held prisoner. Oñate consulted with his officers. The Rayados seemed to be an orderly and peaceful people; but to verify the Escanjaques' story, the Spaniards decided to take some Rayados as prisoners.

On the following day they did so, capturing a visiting Rayado chief and a few of his followers. Though the chief insisted that there was no Spaniard being held by his people, one hostage was released to carry Oñate's demand that the Spanish prisoner be brought to him. However, to the Spaniards' dismay, the Rayado tribespeople simply abandoned their village and disappeared.

On learning this, Oñate crossed the river and entered the deserted town. The Rayado huts were well stocked with corn, and all around were fields planted with corn, beans, and melons. The Escanjaques, who had followed behind, began looting and burning the village. Oñate ordered his soldiers to put a stop to it and drive the plunderers away. It was not something the Escanjaques took lightly, as the Spaniards would soon discover.

After exploring for a short distance beyond the Rayado village and finding more such settlements, Oñate's officers convinced him that it would be unwise to continue with such a small force. Turning about, the Spaniards headed for the first Rayado village. An officer and a dozen men who were scouting ahead found that the village had been reoccupied by the Escanjaques.

The Indians attacked the scouting party with bows and arrows. The Spaniards managed to retreat back to the main unit with only a wounded horse or two. Still, it was necessary to pass through the Escanjaque country in returning to New Mexico. Oñate ordered the men to armor their horses, as they themselves already were, and prepare their harquebuses with powder and ball. As the small Spanish army marched resolutely forward, it was confronted by a swarming semicircle of Escanjaque warriors, estimated from fifteen hundred to almost three thousand in number.

The Indians refused to answer signs of peace. Instead they showered the mailed soldiers with arrows. The Spaniards replied with gunfire, their bullets smashing through the buffalo-skin shields and driving the Indians into nearby rocks. From there the Escanjaque warriors dashed out to let more arrows fly. The intensity of their attack subsided only when the Spaniards released four or five Escanjaque women who had been taken prisoner. Several Indian boys were kept captive, however, at the request of the two Franciscan friars, who wished to teach them the Catholic faith.

During this engagement, which lasted from three to four hours, some thirty of the Spaniards were wounded, though none seriously. Oñate withdrew to his camp, and on the following morning the Spaniards began the long march home, happily without encountering further hostility from the Escanjaques.[2]

The buffalo-dependent tribe of the Escanjaques, whose numbers were estimated at six thousand by the Spaniards, lived in transportable leather huts. A tall, well-proportioned people, they went about virtually unclothed in the summertime, though the women wore small pieces of soft skin over their pubic areas. The faces, bare breasts, and arms of the women were painted profusely with stripes.

The Spaniards took the name Escanjaques from the word the natives shouted when they made their gesture of peace: an Indian would stretch a hand to the sun and then place it on his chest. Historians have yet to determine with certainty just which modern Indians are the descendants of the Escanjaques. They were clearly not Apaches, since they did not speak that tongue.[3]

It is generally accepted that the Rayados were the Wichita Indians, very likely the same people as those identified as "Quiviras" by Coronado.[4] The sparse information provided by European intrusions into the region indicates that the Wichitas resided in what is now southern Kansas until the middle of the eighteenth century. During that time they were forced to defend their permanent-home villages from attacks by the Apaches of New Mexico and Texas, from the Comanches, who were pushing southward from the upper Rockies, and from Missouri River tribes, in particular the Osages of Missouri.

The Wichitas proper were the largest, central body of a Wichita confederacy that also included the Taovayas, Tawakonis (or Taracaras), Yscanis, Kichais (or Keechis), and Wacos, most of whom were originally located in present-day Texas. Smaller groups of Wichita kinship have become lost through absorption into other bands over the years.

Authorities believe that both the Wichitas and their kinspeople, the Pawnees of Nebraska, had earlier migrated northward from the lower Red River, leaving behind other Caddoan tribes, who populated western Louisiana and eastern Texas into modern times. The Spiro Mounds of eastern Oklahoma are evidence of a thriving Caddoan mound-building culture that once existed there.

It is thought that perhaps some Caddoan bands moved north and west to find a better food source on the buffalo plains or to escape from some tribal enemy. The Wichitas settled on the Arkansas River of present Kansas while the Pawnees continued on to northern Kansas and the Platte River of Nebraska. The Caddos never organized into a formal tribal unit; various Caddoan village groups functioned independently and adopted their own names and identities while remaining connected to other groups by language and general welfare.

The Wichitas' permanent home and their planting and hunting mode of existence set them apart from most other Plains Indians. These practices also made them vulnerable to marauding enemies, who attacked them for the maize, melons, beans, and other produce of their fields as well as for children and women slaves. There is little record of the Wichitas as an aggressor, unlike many other Plains tribes. Their men were often described as good-natured and their women as cheerful.

Because of their distinctive style of tattooing for both men and women, the Wichitas were generally known to the French as the Pawnee Picts (Panipiquets or Pani Piques). This band was often confused with the Pawnees (Pawnee Mahas), their kindred who lived to the north. Further confusion existed between the Pawnee Picts, who were sometimes called the Taovayas, and the Wichitas proper. Historical record indicates that these names were applied variously to one body of people who were divided between a war and a peace segment.[5]

The Taovayas were the more militant branch of the

Wichitas and coexisted with the main band for some periods of history. It is likely that their warrior units included young men of both bands. During the first half of the nineteenth century, they became a dominant and much-feared force west of the Cross Timbers, which cut north-south across present-day northern Texas and Oklahoma. Since the Wichitas were a sedentary people, it can be speculated that their militancy evolved from the continuous need to defend themselves and their homes from the pressure of aggressive tribes such as the Escanjaques of Oñate's time and later the Apaches, Osages, and Comanches.

Five years after the Oñate expedition, in 1606, a Wichita chief and six hundred warriors arrived at Santa Fe.[6] They came to request help against their enemies, the Ayjaos (Ahijados)—the Rayados, perhaps. The chief promised friendship and land in return for Spanish help and protection. Just what came of this proposal is not known, for during virtually the entire century to follow, the records fall silent on Spanish contact with the Wichitas.

It is known, however, that during these years the Wichitas were beset by raids from the Apache Indians, who ranged as far north as the Loup River in Nebraska. The first of the Plains tribes to possess the horse as well as metal weapons—lances, knives, and hatchets—the Apaches preyed on the Wichita villages, taking women and children captives. The Apaches developed a large slave trade with the Spanish of Mexico.

It is known that in 1692 the Apaches made a major assault on the Wichitas, killing many men, burning their villages, and taking a number of prisoners to New Mexico to trade to the Spanish for horses and weapons. Two years later, when the Apaches brought in another large group of captive children, the Spanish refused to purchase them. The Apaches were enraged and proceeded to behead the Wichita children as the horrified Spaniards watched.[7]

The Wichitas clung desperately to their homeland along the Arkansas River of present Kansas. During the late 1600s, French traders began supplying them with firearms, and it was probably possession of the gun that enabled them to severely defeat the attacking Apaches in 1697. However, the following year the Apaches retaliated by destroying three Wichita villages.

A fortified Apache settlement called El Quartelejo in western Kansas (ten miles north of present Scott City) was visited in 1706 by a Spanish expedition under Juan de Ulibarri. While there, he learned that Apaches were warring with the French and Pawnees to the northeast. When Antonio de Valverde made a visit to El Quartelejo in 1719, he talked with an Apache chief who had suffered a gunshot wound. The man claimed that he and his people had been ambushed by a party of French, Pawnees, and Wichitas while planting corn.[8]

During 1719, the year that Valverde was at El Quartelejo, two separate French explorations were made to the central plains. Benard de La Harpe marched from Louisiana into present-day eastern Oklahoma, where he visited a Caddo-Wichita encampment on the Arkansas River. Also, the Missouri trader Claude Charles du Tisné ventured beyond the Osages of southwestern Missouri to Wichita camps located either in present Kansas or northern Oklahoma.[9]

A significant fact revealed by these two visits was that the Wichitas now possessed the horse. Their warriors had been purely infantry at the time of Oñate's visit in 1601. But sometime during the ensuing obscure century they had made the all-important transition to mounted fighters. The tribe now possessed large numbers of ponies, which had been stolen from the Spanish or captured from the wild herds that roamed the prairie.

Some of the Wichita mounts that La Harpe saw during his visit were handsomely equipped with Spanish-style saddles and bridles, revealing either trade or war with the Spanish dominions to the south. Other evidence indicates that the Wichita bands did as much warring as trading, for they bragged much to La Harpe of their fighting power and pridefully displayed many scalps that had been taken in battle.[10]

They also presented the Frenchman with numerous

gifts, among them a Lipan Apache slave boy. This captive from the tribe of southern Texas was missing both of his little fingers, which his captors claimed to have eaten to signify that he would one day serve as food for the cannibalistic practice of his captors. If La Harpe had only arrived a few days earlier, one chief said, he would have been given the seventeen captives that had been eaten in a public feast!

In his account of the approximately six thousand Indians he found here, La Harpe listed nine different Wichita bands, including the Ousitas (Wichitas proper), Touacaros (Taracaras), Toayas (Taovayas), and Ascanis (Yscanis). Other bands listed by La Harpe were identified as the Caurunches, Aderos, Quataquois, Ouicaspueris, and Honechas, all soon to lose their identities.

These Indians constantly made hunting excursions to the prairies. In doing so, they risked the danger of encountering Comanche war parties. Osage warriors too made regular hunting and warring forays onto the plains and were a serious threat to the Wichitas. Still another danger were the Lipan Apaches, who often passed through the region to war with the Comanches and to procure salt along the Cimarron River.

While La Harpe was being given a royal reception in eastern Oklahoma, Tisné was making a daring venture westward after trading with the Osages in present-day southwestern Missouri.[11] He had found this tribe rich in horses also and willing to trade them. However, the Osages were much opposed to his continuing on to contact the "Tattooed Pawnees," as the Osages called the Wichitas.

The trader mollified the Osages by agreeing to leave most of his trade goods behind. He then plunged southwestward some forty leagues until he located two Pawnee Pict villages. These bands too owned numerous horses— Tisné counted some three hundred—but the animals were so highly prized that the Indians were extremely unwilling to trade them. The Frenchman finally managed to trade three guns, gunpowder, a pickax, and a knife for two horses and a mule that carried a Spanish brand.

In October 1724, Étienne Véniard de Bourgmond, the conqueror of Detroit, and his party visited a large village of Indians in present-day western Kansas.[12] The Frenchman identified the band as "Padoucas." Scholars have speculated that these Indians were Comanches or Apaches. However, both of these tribes were nomads in Kansas, whereas Bourgmond's Indians lived in permanent villages, one comprising 140 huts. This permanency would point to their being Wichitas.[13]

The one village contained some eight hundred warriors, fifteen hundred women, and over two thousand children. On being presented gifts and a French flag, their grand chief told Bourgmond that his nation conducted extensive trade with the Spaniards, who were only twelve days' journey from the village. The Indians bartered buffalo mantles and smaller furs for horses in great numbers—so many, in fact, that unlike the Indians met by Tisné, these were eager to trade horses to the French. Seven mounts were presented to Bourgmond as a gift.[14]

The Indians complained that the Spanish goods were inferior. The hatchets were of soft iron, and knives broke easily. They welcomed trade with the French, they said. However, when they learned that Bourgmond had not brought guns for trade, the Frenchmen found themselves dangerously unwelcome. It is evident that this tribe was not receiving guns and ammunition from the Spanish.

One of the chief defensive measures of these Indians was apparent when they set fire to the prairie as the French approached. Their warring propensity was indicated by the grand chief's claim that he commanded some two thousand warriors. The chief welcomed the protection offered by the French, however, and expressed his desire for peace with neighboring tribes, including the Pawnee Mahas, the Kaws, and the Osages. During their council, the Padoucas sang songs and danced a pantomime of the pleasures of peace.

Throughout the eighteenth century, the Wichitas came under attack from the Comanches, who were pushing southward. They also suffered a long period of warfare with the Osages of present Missouri. The tall, powerful warriors of this formidable Indian nation often made long marches and attacked their enemy on foot. The Osages were probably the most responsible for finally driving the Wichitas from Kansas into Oklahoma.

In 1741 the Frenchman André Fabry de La Bruyère, guided by Pierre and Paul Mallet, headed westward up the Canadian River to Santa Fe. When the river became too shallow for their pirogues, in present McIntosh County, Oklahoma, the Mallets continued by foot. La Bruyère, who turned back to procure horses, later went to the Red River, where he met the same Indians that La Harpe had visited— an indication that the Wichitas had already moved south.[15]

Some of the bands had consolidated into one large village on the Arkansas River. Six years after La Bruyère's tour, three deserters from Arkansas Post, located at the juncture of the Arkansas River with the Mississippi, set out for Santa Fe. Somewhere, probably in northern Oklahoma, they came onto a Wichita village.[16] Then, in 1749, Felipe de Sandoval and a small party of Frenchmen left Arkansas Post and canoed up the Arkansas River, with Taos, New Mexico, as their destination. After fifty days they arrived at two adjoining Wichita villages, which may also have been in northern Oklahoma.[17]

Surprisingly, they found two grass-hut settlements defended by loopholed stockades and a moat. A French flag flew over the place, revealing the presence of French traders. Outside of the fort were plots of corn, beans, and pumpkins. Sandoval reported that though these Indians worked and tilled their fields, they were also fierce cannibals. He indicated that he had, in fact, seen them eat two captives. The tribe had only a few horses, stolen from the Comanches to the west.

Although the location of these villages seen by Tisné, the three deserters, and Sandoval may never be known for certain, there is good reason to believe that one or all may have been the Pawnee Pict–French settlement on the Arkansas River known as Ferdinandina. This Wichita trading center, located on the west bank of the Arkansas

River just south of the present Kansas-Oklahoma border, is believed to have existed from the mid-1740s into the 1750s. Hundreds of relics of French-Indian trade have been found at the site in Kay County, Oklahoma: parts of flintlock guns, lead bullets, flints, gun trim, adzes, axes, knives, porcelain beads, scissors, copper bells, copper and brass ornaments, glass, potsherds, flint hide-scrapers, skinning knives, arrowheads, Indian pipe bowls, hatchets, and many other items that reveal an active trading operation.[18]

Little is known about Ferdinandina directly, but it is a matter of record that many of the traders on the Arkansas River were renegade deserters from the French army or from ships docking at Louisiana ports. Men who had committed robberies, rapes, or murders now engaged in the kidnapping and slave trading of Indian children and women on a grand scale. Not unlikely, some of these men found their way up the Arkansas to Ferdinandina to help construct the blockhouse, log cabins, stockade, and surrounding ditch fortifications that archaeological studies indicate once existed there.

It was the Osages who brought an end to the Wichita stronghold. Equipped with guns from trade with the British, the Osages had begun establishing themselves on the plains even more extensively. They attacked the Pawnee Picts and other Wichita bands with such ferocity as to force the abandonment of Ferdinandina and a retreat of the Wichitas to the south. In 1751 the Osages reportedly destroyed a Pawnee Pict village that was already decimated by the measles and smallpox brought by whites.[19] This could well have been Ferdinandina, which the Osages are also said to have burned.

Osage war parties continued to be active in eastern Oklahoma and Texas. Undoubtedly it was their pressure that caused the bands met by La Harpe to retreat southward. Other Caddoan tribes such as the Caddos, Kichais, and Yscanis, who frequented the land flanking the Red River, suffered so much from robberies and murders at the hands of the Osages that they fled deep into the piney woods of East Texas.[20]

It is probably erroneous to think that the Wichita bands all departed Kansas at the same time. In 1883, the Tawakoni chief Ni-as-tor recounted how his great-grandfather had told of living on the Arkansas River near the present town of Wichita, where there was good flint for arrows and clay for pottery. Indians from the north and east forced them to move south to a bend of the North Canadian River and settle among some red sand hills. It was here, Ni-as-tor claimed, that they got the name *Tawakonis*. After some years on the North Canadian, Boy Chief (To-de-kits-a-die) took them farther south to the Wichita Mountains.[21]

By the mid-1700s, the Wichitas had reestablished themselves on the Red River, where, though still oppressed by the Osages and other enemies, they joined the Comanches in aggressively warring against the Apaches and the Spanish.

KANSAS

Arkansas River

Little Ark.

Little Arkansas
Treaty - 1865

Medicine Lodge
Treaty - 1867

MISSOURI

Grand (Neosho)

Cimarron River

COLORADO

Salt Plains

Wolf Creek

North Canadian River

Verdigris

White River

Canadian River

Fort Holmes Treaty -
1835

Arkansas River

Red River

Washita

River

OKLAHOMA

ARKANSAS

NEW MEXICO

Cross Timbers

Red River

TEXAS

Comanche Peak
Treaty - 1846

Council Springs
Treaty - 1844

Sabine River

Trinity River

LOUISIANA

San Saba
Treaty - 1850

San Saba River

Brazos River

Colorado River

Rio Grande

MEXICO

*MAJOR INDIAN BATTLES
ON THE SOUTHERN PLAINS*

S. Hoig

Major Indian Battles on the Southern Plains: A Selected List

1 Oñate fights Escanjaques, 1601
2 Ferdinandina destroyed by Osages, circa 1751
3 Norteños attack San Saba Mission, 1758
4 Comanches and Wichitas attack Osage villages, 1758
5 Parrilla attacks French fort, 1759
6 Spanish attack Comanches at Taos, 1761
7 Comanches attack El Valle, 1773
8 Spanish attack Comanches east of Santa Fe, circa 1774
9 Spanish attack Comanche village, 1779
10 Spanish kill Comanche chief Cuerno Verde, 1779
11 Spanish attack Apaches on San Gabriel, 1723
12 Spanish-Apache battle near San Antonio, 1731
13 Spanish-Apache battle on San Saba, 1732
14 Spanish incursion into Apache country, 1739
15 Apaches ambush Spanish expedition, 1743
16 Spanish destroy Apache settlement on Colorado, 1745
17 Comanches and Wichitas attack Osages, 1789
18 Spanish-Comanche-Wichita force defeats Apaches, 1790
19 Choctaws fight Caddos at Caddo Hill, 1797
20 Choctaws attack Bogy at mouth of Verdigris River, 1807
21 Cherokees massacre Clermont's village, 1817
22 Comanches massacre Skidi Pawnees, 1819
23 Cherokees attack Chouteau's Post, 1821
24 Cherokees attack Osage caravan, 1821
25 Comanches and allies battle Osages, 1824
26 Cherokees attack Tawakonis on Brazos, 1829
27 Osages massacre Pawnees, 1830
28 Cherokees attack Tawakonis near Mexia, 1830
29 Cheyennes attack Pawnees on Loup River, 1830
30 Osages attack Kiowa village, 1833
31 Comanches attack Parker's Fort, 1836
32 Battle of Wolf Creek, 1838
33 Texans attack Cherokees, 1839
34 San Antonio courthouse massacre of Comanche chiefs, 1840
35 Comanches raid Texas coastal towns, 1840
36 Texas Rangers ambush Comanches at Plum Creek, 1840
37 Sumner attacks Cheyennes, 1856
38 Rangers attack Comanches on Little Robe Creek, 1858
39 Van Dorn attacks Comanches at Wichita village, 1858
40 Van Dorn attacks Comanches on Crooked Creek, 1859
41 Wichita Agency–Tonkawa massacre, 1862
42 Eayre attacks Cheyennes, kills Lean Bear, 1864
43 Kiowa-Comanche massacre on Elm Creek, 1864
44 Kit Carson's battle at Fort Adobe, 1864
45 Sand Creek massacre, 1864
46 Cheyenne attack on Julesburg and Fort Rankin, 1865
47 Cheyennes attack Smoky Hill route, 1866
48 Battle of Beecher's Island, 1867
49 Custer massacres Cheyennes at Washita, 1868
50 Carr battles Tall Bull's Cheyennes, 1869
51 Kiowas raid wagon train, May 17, 1871
52 White Horse raids wagon train at Howard Wells, 1872
53 Mackenzie destroys Comanche village, 1872
54 Fort Clark troops battle Kiowa-Comanche war party, 1873
55 Cheyennes and Comanches attack Adobe Walls, 1874
56 Kiowas attack Loving ranch, 1874
57 Baldwin attacks Cheyennes on McClellan's Creek, 1874
58 Kiowas besiege wagon train on Sweetwater, 1874
59 Mackenzie attacks tribes in Tule Canyon, 1874
60 Battle of Sand Hills, 1875

CHAPTER 4

The Norteños
of Texas

BY 1757 the Wichitas and the Taovayas had established two new villages on the north bank of the Red River fifteen miles east of present Ryan, Oklahoma. French traders, possibly those who had been with them at Ferdinandina, joined them and helped construct a palisade and bastions against enemy attack. The traders flew the French flag over the fortified towns.

Here the Indians planted new crops. They also developed a brisk trade in furs, robes, horses, and Mexican mules, as well as slave women and children captured from other tribes. In return they received guns and ammunition, cloth, clothing, cooking utensils, blankets, knives, axes, and other manufactured items brought up the Red River from Louisiana. They also became much wealthier in horses, a fact soon enough discovered by the marauding Osages.

When they had first arrived on the plains, the Comanches had been the enemies of the Wichitas. However, in 1746 the two tribes agreed on an alliance, not only as a counter to the Osages but also for help in horse-stealing and slave-taking raids against the Apaches and the Spanish to the south. Possibly the most notable of these strikes was made in 1758, when they learned that the Spaniards had established a new mission on the San Saba River of South Texas.

The Apaches, besieged by the northern tribes, had asked for the establishment of the Catholic church, far less for religious purposes than for Spanish military protection. Fray Alonso Giraldo de Terreros, with the support of a wealthy brother in Mexico, built the Franciscan mission of Santa Cruz and embellished it with gold religious ornaments. The military presidio of San Luis de las Amarillas, commanded by Don Diego Ortiz Parrilla, was also constructed, as protection for the mission, just across the San Saba River near present Menard, Texas.

The Spanish had still other reasons for creating the presidio and mission. The establishments would benefit commerce between San Antonio and New Mexico, permit the Spanish to exploit the silver-mining potential of the area, and spread the teachings of Christianity among the Apaches and other Indians.

Some three thousand Lipan Apaches assembled at the mission that summer, but not to accept Christianity. They were headed north to hunt buffalo and attack their enemy tribes, the Norteños. After doing so they were afraid to settle at the mission, fearing reprisal attacks. Their fears proved justly founded when the Comanches, Wichitas, Taovayas, Tonkawas, Tawakonis, and others committed a bloody massacre of the mission in the spring of 1758.

The Apaches had made the mistake of bragging to other tribes about the protection they now enjoyed and the riches the mission held. The northern tribes were infuriated; and it may well have been, as the Spanish believed, that the French on the Red River helped incite the Indians to make their attack. By whatever cause, in March 1758 a combined force of two thousand Comanches, Wichitas, Taovayas, and other northern tribes descended on the San Saba settlement.

Parrilla, forewarned by reports of Indians in the vicinity, had requested that the three Catholic priests at the mission come in to the safety of the fort. Only a guard of five soldiers protected the priests and their Indian servants at the stockaded church. But the fathers said they did not fear the Indians and refused to leave.

Just after sunrise on the morning of March 16, the cry of "Indians! Indians!" was sounded. Immediately the gate of the mission stockade was closed, and the soldiers took up their positions. The sight presented when soldiers peered through the cracks in the stockade was spine-chilling. Swarming the grounds outside were a multitude of mounted warriors. Their faces were painted black and crimson, and the tails of wild beasts hung down about their heads, producing horrific effects. They were all armed with spears, sabers, and guns. At their lead was the large, commanding figure of a Comanche chief who wore a French military uniform.

Though they had already captured, stripped, and beaten some early risers from the mission, the Indians did not make an assault. Instead, they professed friendship to secure entry. Once inside, they made demands of horses and food, at the same time helping themselves to whatever they desired.

The priests attempted to pacify the Indians, but it was useless. The invaders fully intended to see bloodshed. Before the day was done, two of the priests, along with others, had been killed and stripped, their bodies mutilated. The mission buildings were sacked, the storerooms plundered, the holy images of saints destroyed, the mission cattle shot, and the church set afire.

Parrilla, who was forced to hold his badly outmanned garrison inside the presidio walls to protect the 237 women and children there, could offer little help to the mission. When he sent a squad of nine men in relief, they were severely mauled by the Indians. The two cannons at the presidio were useless against the swarming Norteños. It was four days before the presidio command could venture forth to view the destruction. Virtually all of the mission had been gutted by fire. The bodies of ten dead people and numerous dead animals lay strewn about,

among them the corpses of Frays Terreros and Jose San-
tiesteban. The latter's corpse had been decapitated.[1]

Parrilla, an able soldier who had fought Apaches on the
Gila River, was determined to discourage future attacks.
He decided on a punitive strike of his own against the
Norteños and began making plans for an expedition to the
north. During the ensuing year, he managed to assemble
a 500-man army consisting of 130 presidio garrison and
241 mounted militia men—mostly cowherds, tailors, laborers, and peons from Spanish mines—plus 120 untu-
tored and militarily untrained Tlascalteco Indians and a
few Apaches. When Parrilla finally marched north from
San Saba, his long cavalcade included over sixteen hundred head of horses, mules, and cattle.

North of the Brazos River, Parrilla's men won an easy
victory over a Tonkawa village. Taking the Tonkawas by
surprise, the Spaniards and their Indian allies, who were
armed with swords, muskets, blunderbusses, and knives,
killed fifty-five villagers and took forty-nine prisoners
without losing a man. The Spanish force then marched on
for the Norteño village on the Red River.

When word came on October 7, 1759, that a large Spanish army was advancing from the south, the Wichita village stirred with the ferocity of a disturbed wasp's nest.
Warriors rushed to daub themselves with paint and take
up their war gear—their plumed leather helmets, buffalo-
hide shields, and weapons. Women, children, and old
ones scurried from their grass huts, taking refuge in the
mud-covered, split-log fortifications that had been readied
for such an occasion at the center of the town. Horse herds
were rushed to the safety of corrals behind the log palisade
that fronted the river. The news quickly reached the large
Comanche encampment, whose conical lodges dotted the
riverbank nearby, and it too prepared for war.[2]

With the help of the fourteen French traders who resided in the village, the Taovaya war captains had already
made their battle plans. As soon as the war ponies were
equipped with bridles, saddles, and leather breastplates,

squads of mounted warriors well supplied with French muskets and supported by reloading crews on foot were formed. Armed defenders were stationed along the long stockade where a deep, moatlike ditch and a winding entrance gave added protection against an assault.

But the militant Taovayas had no intention of remaining behind the walls and waiting for an attack. A party of sixty or more warriors charged across the swift-flowing, ocher channel of the river and through the forest of trees on a road that had been hewed there. They swooped down on the Spanish vanguard in a war-whooping attack.

As the Taovayas sallied forth from their Red River fortress, Parrilla formed a portion of his men into a dismounted battle line and halted the charge. He followed this with a determined attack by the presidial soldiers, who drove the Taovaya attackers back into the trees, with three Indians left dead on the field. The Spanish cavalry plunged headlong in pursuit of the raiders. Charging pell-mell through the trees, the Spaniards suddenly emerged onto a level plain alongside the south bank. They were just in time to see the Taovayas disappear into the walled, zigzag entrance to the gate at the very edge of the far side of the channel.

Only a portion of the village was protected by the palisade. Upstream from the town were fields of maize, pumpkins, watermelons, and beans. A ford just below the settlement was guarded by a large body of warriors, evidently representing several tribes. It was later estimated that the Indian force possibly numbered as many as six thousand.

The Spaniards were astounded by the well-fortified, heavily armed Indian village they now faced. Beyond the walls that bristled with men and guns, they could see the rounded tops of the tall grass huts as well as the French flag, which waved at them with impudence. Behind them the crisscross tops of buffalo-skin lodges revealed the Comanche presence. It quickly became apparent to Parrilla that this time he would have no easy victory.

The Spaniard went into camp to ponder his problem. But even as he and his officers debated their next move, they were kept on the defensive by repeated sallies of Wichita and Taovaya raiders. One Taovaya chief, who carried a shield of white buckskin and wore a helmet of white buckskin plumed with red horsehair, was especially valiant in the skirmishing before he was finally knocked from his stallion by Spanish musketry.

The Spaniards now unlimbered the two brass cannons that they had brought with them from the San Saba presidio. But the artillery fire proved ineffective, and each shot was greeted by laughter and jeering from inside the fort. As a result, the men of Parrilla's army became badly demoralized. Their Indian allies also became disgusted and began a wholesale desertion, taking some of the Spaniards' horses with them.

Inside the fort, the Indians and their delighted French allies contemptuously staged a war dance at night by the light of a huge bonfire. Finally, at the insistence of his officers and two Franciscan friars, Parrilla gave the order to return home. The retreat became so frantic that the Spanish dead and wounded, along with the army's baggage, many muskets and saddles, and both cannons, were left behind. Eleven Spaniards, one Tlascalteco, and one Apache were killed; about the same number were wounded. The Taovayas and their allies suffered no additional losses.[3]

The Spanish lieutenant Antonio Trevino, who was captured by the Taovayas during a 1763 engagement and eventually released because of the bravery he had shown in battle, provided a detailed description of the Red River villages and the Taovayas.[4] In his testimony, Trevino described the fortifications of the villages, including four large underground houses that provided safety to those inside during a siege. He said too that the French had shown the Indians how to fire the two captured cannons, which they had mounted at the entrance to the fort. In 1760, when they met with Friar Joseph de Calahorra y Saenz at the Tawakoni villages on the Sabine River, the Taovayas offered to return the cannon in order to restore good relations.

When the European Seven Years War ended with the defeat of the French by the British, virtually all of the territories west of the Mississippi came under Spanish control. In 1769 the Spanish appointed the Frenchman Athanase de Mézières as the principal agent at Natchitoches, Louisiana, in charge of Indian affairs in north Texas. He immediately set out to improve relations with the Norteños. In 1770 he signed peace treaties with chiefs of the Taovaya, Tawakoni, Yscani, and Kichai bands at a council held near present Texarkana, Texas.[5]

After the murder of five French traders who had ventured into the Washita River country of present-day western Oklahoma, another trader, J. Gaignard, was sent up the Red River from Louisiana to make treaties with the Comanches.[6] When Gaignard arrived at the Taovaya settlement, he found that the Indians were angry that the Spanish had cut off their horse and slave trade. They refused to permit Gaignard to continue on to the Comanche camps and treated him roughly, even taking away his trade goods and denying him his sleeping blankets during cold winter weather.

It is not surprising that the trader had little good to say about the Taovayas. In his journals he tells of captured tribal enemies who were horribly tortured, broiled, and feasted on—much to the displeasure of the Comanches. He found both the men and the women to be savage and cruel-natured. While he was there, two parties of unlicensed French traders arrived to trade for horses, mules, and slaves.

De Mézières himself led a peacemaking expedition to the Wichita villages in 1778. He was more generous than Gaignard in his appraisal of the Taovayas, seeing them as "cheerful, affable, and docile in their manner, compassionate toward the sick, orphans, and widows, respectful to their elders, generous toward strangers, kind to guests." At the same time he admitted, "[They] are more revengeful for injury than grateful for benefits, as is proved by the atrocities which their prisoners experience at their hands, which are so great that even to relate them would cause horror."[7]

Whereas Parrilla and Trevino reported villages on only the north side of the river (Gaignard listed four villages but was not clear on their location), de Mézières found one on each side. The one on the north bank contained 37 thatched huts, and the one on the south bank numbered 123 houses. He named the two villages San Theodoro and San Bernardo. Each house was well stocked with maize, beans, and calabashes, which the Indians raised along with watermelons and tobacco. A nearby quarry conveniently supplied them with metates for grinding corn, white stones for lances, and flint rock for arrowheads.

The men were solely hunters and warriors who gained their wealth through horse stealing and their prestige through battle. Their dependence on the buffalo was clear from the leather that was used in their shirts, leggings, moccasins, shields, horse equipment, and heavy caps that they wore as battle helmets.

Though apparently well established in their walled towns, the Wichitas still lived in constant fear of marauding Osage war parties. They maintained their tentative peace with the Comanches, who visited them under the guise of friendship to steal their horses and corn. The Wichitas pretended not to notice this pilfering, well aware they could little afford to make enemies of such a large and powerful nation.[8]

Wichita and Comanche raids against Spanish settlements did not cease. It was often difficult to tell what tribe or tribes committed the depredations However, when an attack was made on San Antonio on July 16, 1784, a young captive of the Indians escaped. He revealed that the raiders on this occasion were Taovayas under Chief Grand Sol.[9]

Grand Sol later relented his hostility toward the Spaniards. On his deathbed in 1785, the chief appointed his successor with the stipulation that the new chief, Guersec, remain friendly with the Spanish crown. Not long afterward, Guersec made a trip to San Antonio to secure powder, bullets, and horses. He said that the Osages had recently surprised them, taken most of their horses, and killed two of their people. The Osages had also threatened to return later and kill them all.

The Osage threat continued to hang over the Wichita villages. In 1789, a combined force of Wichita and Comanche warriors again attempted an assault against the Osages, once more with tragic consequences. The Osages' home villages were in the forest to the northeast beyond the prairie's edge. Like other prairie Indians, the Wichitas did not like to enter the woods, where they were at a fighting disadvantage. Still, they reluctantly joined with the Comanches in a consolidated attack against the Osage towns in present-day Missouri. Again, they fared badly.

During the fall of 1807, a group of Wichita and Taovaya leaders led a Comanche delegation to Natchitoches to talk with American officials about securing more guns for use against the Osages. The Indians indicated to the agent Dr. John Sibley that if American traders would come to the camps, they would find all the horses and hides they desired and even silver ore.[10]

In response Sibley dispatched a trader, Anthony Glass, to the Wichitas, along with an interpreter, nine other men, and sixteen packhorses loaded with trade goods.[11] The American party arrived at the villages, to which the Wichitas had returned, on August 11, 1808, and was given a generous reception by Chief Awakahea.

Glass was to learn that the chief, who was about fifty years of age, had been born on the Arkansas River, where his tribe had then resided. The chief verified that it was because of the Osages that the Wichitas had moved south, first to the Brazos and then back northward to their present site. Some of the Tawakonis still resided on the Brazos

The Wichita war leader Chickiskinik had recently visited the governor of the Texas province at San Antonio and had been advised against being friends with the Americans. But the Osages were still the Wichitas' main problem. Even while Glass was at the Wichita camps, the

Osages came on one occasion with enough warriors to brazenly plant a pair of flags between the villages while driving off five hundred horses. The Wichitas dared not venture out to stop them.

In another instance, however, an Osage was killed while his war party attempted to steal some Wichita horses. According to Wichita custom, the Osage's body was cut into pieces and given to the villagers to be hung up and danced about for several days.

Glass also described the treatment of prisoners, which de Mézières and others had only hinted at. He told how live enemy captives were stripped naked and tied to a post. The people of the village then came and beat them to death with sticks. Young prisoners were usually kept as slaves or adopted into families

Because of the unrelenting Osage threat, sometime early in the nineteenth century the Wichitas abandoned their fortified villages and moved westward along the Red River. As could be expected, the Osages came and destroyed the deserted fortress. In November 1809, Spanish authorities sent a military unit to the area to search for Americans who they had heard were operating in the Spanish province of Texas. When they visited the site now known (erroneously) as "Spanish fort," they discovered the Wichita stronghold abandoned and in ruins.

An American sent to contact the Pawnee Picts in 1819 reported them gone from the Red River. After a long search, he found them on the upper Brazos, where they had fled to escape "the ravages of the Osages."[12] However, the main band of the Wichitas soon took up residence along the Red River west of the Wichita Mountains.

Four years later, in 1823, Thomas James and his party, who were trading on the North Canadian River in present northwestern Oklahoma, met a Wichita chief named Alasarea. The chief stated that his people lived on the headwaters of the Red River, and he claimed that his tribe owned sixteen thousand horses. He presented his own mount, a beautiful black war-horse, to James as a gift.[13]

This period marked a watershed in Wichita wealth and military power. There would still be intertribal battles, raids into Texas, and new conflicts with both the displaced Indians of the American South and the advancing whites. But the deterioration and ultimate subjugation of the Wichita Nation had begun.

CHAPTER 5

Comanche Conquest
in New Mexico

IN the month of June 1806 a show of military pageantry took place near the Canadian River in either present-day western Oklahoma or the Texas Panhandle. The event was a meeting of two military forces, one a Spanish army and the other a huge force of Comanche warriors at the prime of their empire. The two groups met in a dusty but dazzling display of mounted pomp and ceremony. The Spanish had come to exhibit their martial prowess and desire for friendship with the Indians of the plains. The Comanches, as lords of the vast prairie domain they roamed, flaunted their numbers, their wealth of horses (many wearing Spanish brands), and the riding and fighting skills of their warriors.

The Spaniards, under the wealthy aristocrat Lt. Facundo Melgares, had marched from Santa Fe, New Mexico, down the Canadian River—one hundred mounted dragoon regulars, five hundred mounted Mexican militiamen who had been pressed into service, and over two thousand horses and mules. When contact was made with the Comanches, Melgares ordered his troops to ride only white horses. He and two of his aides rode at their head on jet-black steeds.

The Spanish dragoon regulars wore short blue coats

with red capes and cuffs, blue velvet waistcoats and trousers, broad-brimmed high-crowned hats banded with brightly colored ribbons that had been adopted in gallantry for their ladies, and jackboots with glistening spurs. Many of them sported long moustaches and side whiskers that covered most of their faces. As they rode, the dragoons' lances gleamed aslant above them. An Indian observer thought they looked much like "a flock of bluebirds on the prairie."[1]

The dragoons carried their fusils slung in leather cases at the right of their high-pommeled saddles, and behind their saddles were tied a small bag and two pistols. Each man was equipped with a rounded shield of three-doubled sole leather bent to deflect arrows. Gilded in gold on each were the Spanish coat of arms and the name of Don Carlos IV, king of Spain. The saddles were ornately trimmed in silver and gold; the stirrups were of wood carved to the shape of the head of a lion or some other animal. The Spaniards smartly performed their military maneuvers to the rolling command of a drummer corps.

The Comanches were not to be outdone. Exhibiting their own flair of color and showmanship, fifteen hundred riders on their war-painted ponies galloped forward en masse, their battle whoops filling the air. Some wore brightly colored robes, some mere breechclouts with their bronze skins daubed and streaked with fanciful designs; all were armed with bows, arrows, lances, and war shields. Their young men, perhaps the most skilled riders on the plains, performed impressive feats of horsemanship. Behind the warriors came the young boys driving the immense herds of Comanche horses. After them the women, with their dog travois, quickly erected a city of lodges teeming with life on the edge of the meadow. When the Comanches were settled into their encampment, Melgares met with their chiefs and smoked the calumet.

The Spaniard presented the Indians with medals and commissions from the king of Spain, a Spanish flag, and four mules for each chief. He reiterated his government's desire for friendship with the Comanches. He also expressed the wish that the Comanches would refrain from raids such as the one they had made recently on the village of Agua Caliente, where some two thousand head of horses had been driven off.[2]

Melgares' visit to the Comanches was in response to reports that Pres. Thomas Jefferson had sent an expedition under Thomas Freeman and Peter Custis to explore the Red River region of the Louisiana Purchase. Despite the agreement between the United States and France concerning the purchase, the Spanish still felt they held a proprietary right to much of the region, and they were angered by American intrusion.

The conspiracy of Aaron Burr to invade Mexico, the connivance by the general of the U.S. Army, James Wilkinson—who still accepted a pension from Spain and was doing much to foster suspicion in both American and Spanish leaders against one another—and the natural competition between the Old World throne of Spain and the upstart American democracy had created much talk of war between the two nations.

Thus when the Spanish officials learned that the Freeman-Custis expedition was headed up the Red River from Louisiana, a military force was quickly assembled in New Mexico for the purpose of intercepting the Americans.[3] Melgares also hoped to establish better relations with the Comanches, Pawnees, Kaws, and other tribes of the area west of the Missouri River, as a buffer against the Americans. On discovering from the Comanches that he was on the Canadian rather than the Red River, the Spaniard headed his army off northward to meet with the Pawnees on the Loup River. The American Capt. Zebulon M. Pike, he had learned, was on his way to that region.[4]

Melgares' visit to the Comanches marked a century of warfare between that tribe and the Spanish in New Mexico. The Comanche Nation in 1806 was at the apex of its power, and for years its warriors had terrorized Spanish-held New Mexico. The Comanche invasion of the southern plains had begun in the early 1700s. This large body of Shoshonean people, who were essentially scattered bands of wanderers, had once resided in the Great Basin country west of the Rocky Mountains. Through time they migrated across the Rockies and along the Snake and Green rivers into Wyoming, fighting wars with the Sioux and others as they went. A short-statured, dark-skinned people, during their stone-weapon history they had lived mostly on roots, berries, birds, snakes, turtles, and small animals. Arriving on the prairie, they learned to catch and kill larger game.

The Comanches came south for several reasons. Among them were pressures from better-armed northern enemies and the desire for Spanish trade goods. And there can be no doubt that they were lured southward in large part by their discovery of the horse.[5] The Spanish mustang, which had been brought to America by the conquistadores, had multiplied into wild herds that roved freely across the grassy southwestern plains. It was inevitable that some of these captured animals would appear in the northern country and be introduced to the Indian tribes there. It was also just as inevitable that those tribes would be drawn southward to obtain more horses, either on temporary excursions or in permanent migrations.

Few people better adapted to the horse than did the short-legged Comanches, for whom the beast provided a new mobility and increased prowess as hunters and warriors. Now they were able to fight on equal terms with the other tribes east of the mountains. Soon they learned that great numbers of horses were to be found running wild on the southern prairies as well as in the corrals of the Spanish or the camps of the Apaches.

The Comanche bands began moving southward, allying themselves with their kindred the Utes of the mountains of present Colorado as they pushed aggressively against the frontier of northern New Mexico. At first they attempted to trade with the Spanish for horses. When their efforts were rebuffed, the Comanches found an even easier way of obtaining the animals. They simply raided Spanish and Apache settlements alike, killing, burning, carrying away captives, and driving off large numbers of horses and mules.[6]

A Spanish officer testified to the Comanche warring power when he reported to his superiors that the Jicarilla Apaches were "commonly harried by the nation of the Comanches." He added, "They [the Comanches] dominate with the power of arms all the nations who live in that region, because they terrorize them with the ferocious war which they make."[7]

Spanish records show that the Comanches appeared in New Mexico as early as 1705 and that during the following year they were making threats against the Spanish settlement of Taos. The New Mexico settlements were easy prey for the Comanche raiders, and the Spanish authorities could do little to protect the villages.

Finally, after a Comanche raid on Taos in 1716, the Spaniards pursued the perpetrators with a sizable force. They overcame a Comanche camp and took captives, which were later released to spread the word that the Spanish now wished to conduct trade with the tribe in peace. A similar offer was made after another successful Spanish strike in 1719.

Spanish authorities considered building and operating a presidio at El Quartelejo, but the cost and difficulty of maintaining such a far-flung outpost was too much. Instead they decided to locate their military forces at Taos, New Mexico. As a result, the Comanches encountered little resistance as they migrated across present-day eastern Colorado and western Kansas to the horse- and buffalo-rich country beyond the Arkansas River.[8]

Absence of the Spanish in Kansas also permitted the French to gain access to the region. Thirty-three French traders were reported to have been at El Quartelejo in 1748.[9] However, the Spanish still considered the territory to be under their jurisdiction. In 1750 Bernardo de Bustamente y Tagle pursued a Comanche war party down the Arkansas River until he reached some Wichita villages.

During the following summer, some three hundred Comanches returned to Taos and conducted a peaceful trade. Afterward, however, they attacked Galisteo. Spanish forces overtook some of the Comanches and cornered them in a small grove of brush and trees. Setting fire to the concealment, the Spaniards managed to kill over a hundred Indians and capture the remainder.[10]

In 1761, when the Comanches came to Taos and offered to trade back some prisoners they had captured at the settlement earlier, the governor of New Mexico became outraged. He ordered the chiefs of the band imprisoned and the Comanche camp attacked. The Spaniards claimed that they killed some three hundred Indians and captured over four hundred more. Afterward, the Spaniards executed the captured chiefs.[11]

In an effort to halt the raiding, the Spanish signed peace agreements with the Comanches in 1762 and again in 1772. But each time, the pacts were broken by Comanche raids such as the one against El Valle, only fifteen leagues from Santa Fe, in July 1773. Some five hundred Indians swooped down to drive off most of the presidial horse herd. Two hundred of the animals were recovered when the scouts of a Spanish pursuing force surprised the raiders. The Comanche forays continued unabated, with five occurring during the summer and fall of 1774.

Another successful counterstrike was made under the seasoned Indian-fighter Don Carlos Fernandez. His force of six hundred troops, settlers, and Indian allies followed the trail of a Comanche war party and fell on their encampment east of Santa Fe. The Spaniards drove many of the villagers into a pond, killing approximately four hundred and capturing large herds of animals and other spoils. Comanche raids continued, however, and the Spanish were hard-pressed to effectively strike back while at the same time attempting to control the troublesome Apaches to the south.[12]

In 1779, during the period of the American Revolution, New Mexico Gov. Don Juan Bautista de Anza took advantage of a hostility that had developed between the Comanches and the Utes. He put together an army of lancers and civilian militiamen, supported by 259 Utes and Apaches, for a punitive expedition against the Comanches.

Marching northward from Santa Fe into Colorado, Anza

scoured the mountainous country beyond the Arkansas River as far as Pike's Peak before swinging back southward along Fountain Creek. There he found and attacked a lightly manned Comanche village. A number of the villagers were killed in the melee, and others were taken prisoner. Some five hundred horses were captured, along with all of the camp's goods and baggage.

From captives, Anza learned that the chief of this band and four of his principal captains had taken their warriors on a raid against Taos. This chief was the famous Cuerno Verde, or Green Horn, whose father, a chief before him, had been killed by the Spanish. In revenge for his father's death, Cuerno Verde had exacted an especially cruel toll on the New Mexico settlements, destroying many pueblos, killing hundreds of people, and executing his prisoners in cold blood.

Anza also learned that Cuerno Verde had arranged for his people to meet him at a site near present Colorado City, Colorado. Recrossing the Arkansas, Anza pushed southward to the Huerfano River near present Greenhorn Mountain of southern Colorado, where he set a trap for Cuerno Verde and his warriors. Hiding his horse herd and train, the Spaniard waylaid the advance of the Comanche party in a valley, driving them back after killing eight and wounding many more. Against the advice of his Indian guides, Anza held to the field through a rainy and severely cold night, waiting "for the honor of our arms"[13] to meet Cuerno Verde there.

When the Comanches did not arrive on the following morning, Anza began moving forward. Soon a party of some fifty Comanches appeared and daringly charged the Spanish force of six hundred, dashing close enough even to fire their muskets. Cuerno Verde was at their lead. The chief, decked in insignia that clearly indicated his rank, was mounted on a charger that curvetted spiritedly. Having been convinced by his medicine man that he was indestructible, the Comanche rode with an air of invincibility and haughty superiority.

Anza was determined to destroy the chief even if it

meant killing fewer of the Indians. He ordered his cavalry vanguard and Indian allies to cut off the main body of Comanches from the chief's party. He then drove Cuerno Verde and his men into a gully, forcing them to dismount and take up positions behind their horses. There the Comanches put up a "defense as brave as it was glorious."[14]

During the battle and even while he was in great danger, the disdainful Cuerno Verde scorned even to load his own musket, having others do it for him three times before his illusion of immortality was finally ended. Also killed were his four captains, his first-born son, and others, including the medicine man.[15]

Despite Anza's success, the Spanish were restrained from further campaigns against the Indians while funds were diverted to support Spain's war against England. After the war's end in 1783, however, the Spanish picked up their action in New Mexico as well as Texas, putting new pressures on the Comanches. The new offensive saw success when, on July 12, 1785, four hundred Comanches arrived at Taos to ask for amnesty and an end to hostilities.

Anza responded by demanding that the Comanches show that they were united in their desire for peace. According to information supplied to Anza by an emissary who went among the Comanches, the tribe at this time was said to be composed of three major groups spread out among more than six hundred separate camps or "rancheros." They were the Yupes, the Yamparikas, and the Cuchanecs (Cuchanticas). The Yupes still ranged north of the Arkansas River as far as present southern Wyoming; the Yamparikas, who ate a sweet root called the *yampa*, held the country of present Colorado south to the Arkansas River; and the Cuchanecs hunted the buffalo plains between the Pecos and Red rivers, an area that included much of present-day western Texas.[16]

The celebrated chief Ecueracapa—or Leather Jacket (he was known in Texas as Cota de Malla, or Coat of Mail)—was selected to represent the Comanches in peace negotiations with the Spanish. Because of his skill and valor in war, Ecueracapa also held the surname of Contatanacapara, or One without Equal in Military Achievements. Anza would be further impressed with the Comanche's intelligence and adroitness in political matters. Ecueracapa also demonstrated his political ruthlessness by having Chief Toro Blanco (White Bull), the principal opponent of his peace efforts, assassinated.[17]

Taking advantage of the opportunity presented when an Indian ally of the Spanish was taken prisoner while buffalo hunting, Ecueracapa dispatched three emissaries to Santa Fe to recommend that a peace council be held. Anza responded by sending the chief a horse and a headdress of fine scarlet, suggesting a date for the council. Immediately, the happy news of a possible peace with the Comanches spread through the pueblos, and the New Mexicans celebrated. The Utes, however, were very disturbed that the Spaniards and their dreaded enemy would become allies. They sent two chiefs to issue their complaint to Anza.

When Ecueracapa and three of his men arrived at Santa Fe on February 25, 1786, Anza ordered a cavalry troop out to escort them into the settlement, where a large festive crowd awaited. The chief embraced the governor and made a speech saying that he had the full support of the Comanche Nation in seeking peace and trade with the New Mexicans. Ecueracapa also met with the two Ute chiefs, the longtime foes embracing one another and smoking together in reconciliation.

On the twenty-eighth, Anza and his guests traveled to the pueblo of Pecos, located in a valley southeast of Santa Fe, where 593 lodges of Comanches eagerly awaited them. Councils were held with the most esteemed leaders of various branches of the nation. In making their speeches, the Comanche chiefs bared their breasts and declared their desire for peace and trade with the Spanish.

The governor responded by presenting Ecueracapa with a staff carrying the image of the Spanish king as a symbol of his authority. Anza then outlined his stipulations for peace. The Comanche chiefs responded with their approval, agreeing not only to desist in their raids against New Mexico but also to help the Spanish in their war against the Apaches. In return they would be permitted to trade freely in New Mexico. Further, New Mexican traders, known as Comancheros, were now safe to enter the Comanche camps and trade and to take the Comanches the goods they much wanted, including arms and ammunition. An agreement of peace was also worked out between the Comanches and the Utes.

The Indians were anxious to hold a trade fair with the New Mexicans. Anza set the rules of exchange and marked off two lines for each group, with space between to exhibit items of trade, and the bartering began. During the fair, the Comanches exchanged more than six hundred hides, fifteen horses, three guns, and many loads of buffalo meat and tallow. They departed Pecos extremely pleased with their trades and looking forward to more. Their peace with the Utes would not last, but the agreements with Anza marked the end of their warfare against New Mexico.

CHAPTER 6

Comanche Conquest in Texas

THE Spanish of Texas had also come to dread the Comanche raiders, who during the eighteenth century drove south to replace the Apaches in terrorizing the Spanish missions and rancheros. From the time that the presidio of San Antonio de Béxar had been founded in 1718, there had been trouble off and on with the Apaches, Mostly it was the Lipan, Natagés, and Mescalero bands living south of the Colorado River in present western Texas who came to kill the Spaniards and to steal their stock

The Spanish missionaries worked hard to Christianize the Indians. But even they were eventually forced to call for armed punishment of the Apache perpetrators after a Franciscan lay brother was murdered near the San Gabriel River in 1723. The friars offered the services of thirty mission Indians to accompany a force of thirty presidials under Capt. Nicolas Flores in a daring invasion of the Apache country.

Marching north and west, the small party located an Apache village. They killed thirty-four villagers, captured twenty women and children, and reclaimed 120 stolen horses and mules.[1] This reduced the Apache assaults for a time and even brought about some peace agreements and friendly trading visits to San Antonio.

But a reduction in the San Antonio garrison force, despite the protests of the missionaries, brought renewed Apache raiding. In 1731 a hard-fought battle took place between the presidials and the Indians close to San Antonio. During the next year, a punitive campaign was launched by the new governor, Bustillo y Zevallos. With 157 Spaniards, 60 mission Indians, and 900 horses and mules, Zevallos rode westward to the San Saba River.

There he was met by an Apache army of several hundred warriors who wore leather breastplates for protection. A bloody, five-hour conflict ensued. Two hundred Indians were killed, thirty women and children captured, and seven hundred horses and mules taken. Over a hundred mule-loads of peltry and other booty were additional rewards for the victorious Spanish force.[2]

Another successful incursion into the Apache country was made in 1739, again with many Indian captives taken. In 1743, however, a Spanish expedition of two hundred men was ambushed and severely defeated. Two years later, this defeat was avenged when a small force of fifty Spaniards destroyed an Apache settlement north of the Colorado River. Again Apache women and children were taken captive. By now, in fact, the capture of "horses, hides, and Indian men and women to serve them" had become a primary purpose of men who put up the money to finance the expeditions.[3]

These punitive strikes contributed to an improvement in Apache-Spanish relations. But there was another reason that the tribe became more friendly with the Spaniards. The Comanches had now begun to push deeper and deeper into Texas. They raided Apache and Spanish settlements alike—killing, burning, and looting—and took women and children captives. After much abuse by the Comanches, the captives would be taken to New Mexico, where they were traded for horses, guns and ammunition, tobacco, and other goods. Often the women had been raped and made pregnant by their Comanche masters; the children were poorly kept and were often treated badly.

The Comanche entry into the area between the Arkansas and Red rivers in present-day southern Kansas and western Oklahoma had been opposed for a time by the Wichitas. With the end of hostilities between the two tribes in 1747 and their joint victory at San Saba, the Comanches ruled virtually all of western Texas and northern New Mexico with a reign of terror. Bypassing the Spanish garrisons, war parties hit isolated rancheros, destroyed villages, and waylaid travelers, safely escaping back into their sanctuary without fear of pursuit.

Parrilla's defeat at the Wichita villages on the Red River and his resulting disgrace had a severe effect on the Spanish military. For many years afterward, no Spanish officer had any desire to lead an expedition into the vast and dangerous stronghold of the Comanches. The threat of another Comanche attack kept the San Saba presidio under siege. Even at San Antonio de Valero, which the Spanish had established in 1718, soldiers dared not venture west or north from the post.

It would have been pure folly for the presidio soldiers to pursue the Comanches. The Spaniards' horses were too slow, and their march was too encumbered with equipment and supplies. An Indian could fire several arrows while the Spaniard was reloading his musket, which was virtually useless from horseback.

The Comanches continued their southward invasion down into the arid prairies of the Texas Panhandle, western Oklahoma, and north Texas, meeting little resistance. Soon their bands were populating a vast horse- and buffalo-rich area from the Arkansas River to deep within Texas—a region that would become known to the Spanish as the Comanchería. The vast numbers and intense militancy of the Comanches dominated the smaller tribes already in residence there.

The Comanche threat spread not only southward but also well into eastern Texas. In 1774 a Spanish settlement and mission was established on the lower Trinity River in the vicinity of present Crockett, Texas. It was believed that the Tonkawas and Tawakonis offered a barrier against Comanche intrusion. But in May 1778 a party of thirty Comanche warriors appeared in the area. The alarmed Spaniards sent out a presidial force that pursued the Comanches to the Brazos, where three of the intruders were killed. There were conflicting reports as to whether the Comanches were friendly or hostile.[4]

There was no doubt about their visit to Bucareli the following October. A much larger Comanche party made a raid on the Spanish horse herds, taking 176 animals. When the Spaniards discovered that the retreating Comanches had set a trap for them, they did not pursue. The Comanches left the horses under a seven-man guard near a Taovaya village. A group of Quitseis and Texas Indians friendly to the Spanish raided the herd, killing three Comanches in the process. The main Comanche party followed, killed three of the Texas Indians, and recaptured the horses.[5]

Having now expanded into five major bands, the Comanche tribe ruled the rolling buffalo grounds from the Arkansas River southward to the Rio Grande. These bands were the Kotsotekas (or Buffalo Eaters) of western Oklahoma along the Canadian River, the Kwahadis (or Antelopes) to the west on the Llano Estacado, the Yamparikas situated north to the Arkansas River country, the Nokonis (or the Wanderers or People in a Circle) along the upper Brazos and Colorado rivers, and the Penatekas (or Honey Eaters) in south Texas.[6]

Each of these bands could put in the field some five hundred warriors, all well mounted, all ready to fight at a moment's notice, all capable of moving great distances across the harsh terrain to strike an unsuspecting victim or enemy. When the trader J. Gaignard visited the Wichita villages on the Red River in 1774, he met with some Comanches who came there. He found them to be fine men, their warriors great fighters; although they killed their adult captives, he felt they were not a cruel people in other

The Comanche and Lipan Apache Indians often came to San Antonio to trade and to hold councils with the Mexican or Texas military. (Western History Collections, University of Oklahoma)

ways. Their commerce consisted of slaves and buffalo hides, which they exchanged for tobacco, knives, axes, and glass beads. Gaignard presented the Comanche headman with a French flag and signed an agreement of peace with him in the name of France.[7]

These Comanches were Yamparikas from north of the Red River. The southern Kotsoteka and Penateka bands continued their harassment of settlements in lower Texas to the point that the Texas governor, Domingo Cabello, complained in 1780, "There is no instance day or night when reports of barbarities and disorders do not arrive from the ranches."[8]

It was not until 1785—at about the same time that the northern Comanches were at Taos seeking a peace arrangement—that Cabello reached an accord with three Comanche chiefs representing the southern Comanches in a council at San Antonio. By the pact, both sides agreed to treat each other as brothers. The Spaniards promised to send presents and traders, and the Comanches were to bring in their Spanish captives.[9] In 1790 Juan de Ugalde, the governor of Spain's province of Coahuila, secured help from the Comanches and Wichitas in severely defeating the Apaches in a battle west of San Antonio.[10]

Despite the difficulty in restraining their young men from stealing horses and conducting raids, the Comanche leaders were able to work with the Spaniards in establishing an era of trade and friendship in Texas. Hunting parties could safely roam the vast reaches controlled by the Indians while the Comanches could go freely to San Antonio to trade and to meet with Indian friends. Treaty presents were annually distributed among the Comanche leaders.[11]

The peace was almost broken during the fall of 1801 when five Comanches were killed by unknown persons. One of the murdered Indians was the son of Chief Toro Blanco. When Blanco's followers threatened a war of vengeance, other Comanche leaders declared that they would fight with the Spaniards. Still another serious threat to the peace came when the Lipan Apaches killed twenty-five Comanches of Chief Yzazat's band. It was rumored that Spanish troops were also involved, but the provincial governor was able to mollify the angry chief.

It was not easy for the chiefs to restrain the war faction of their tribe from seeking revenge, but they were able to do so for the most part. On another occasion, Yzazat was leading a party of 225 warriors on a search for Apaches when he encountered a Spanish packtrain on the Frio River. The frightened driver of the packtrain fled to San Antonio and claimed that the Comanches had robbed him. But a few days later, Yzazat and his men arrived at the presidio with the animals and goods, minus only some sugar that the Comanche chief had allowed his men.

In the spring of 1803 the Comanches came to San Antonio to reaffirm their desire for peace. The following summer, a Tejano party was given royal escort by the Comanches on a hunting trip to the west. The Comanches continued to flock to San Antonio and trade at its weekly fairs even as they pressed a relentless war against their Apache enemies.

In the following years, the Spanish authorities kept their promises of presents, sending large amounts of tobacco, cloth, wearing apparel, and trinkets to the Indians. In 1805 a Comanche chief named Chihauhua visited the Spanish governor at Béxar to request that thirty of his braves be given Spanish uniforms. In return these men would serve in policing those Comanches who would break the tribe's treaty obligations. The governor complied with the request at a cost of 172 pesos each.[12] However, the Comanches still conducted incessant warfare with the Apaches residing in far south Texas and the Rio Grande country as well as with the Spanish of that region.

In 1807 a group of Comanches led by Chief Cordero accompanied a delegation of Taovayas and Wichitas on a visit to Natchitoches, Louisiana, to council with the U.S. agent Dr. John Sibley. It was not a happy experience for them. Sibley provided only a few of the guns they had hoped for. They were victimized by horse thieves, and a number of the Comanches became diseased in Louisiana and died on the way home.[13]

Comanche trade with the Americans began in 1808 when Sibley sent the trader Anthony Glass up the Red River to the Wichita settlements with a supply of goods. Despite the Spanish disapproval of this contact with the Americans, the Comanche-Spanish peace held. However, while Cordero and his warriors were away on a raid into New Mexico in 1810, Comanche horse thievery very nearly ignited a war. Learning of this, Cordero hurried back to Texas and called a council of Comanche chiefs. The horse thieves were found, and the stolen stock was returned.

During the following year, however, the harmony between the Comanches and the Spanish nearly fell apart. The governor of Texas made the mistake of arresting and deporting the Comanche chief El Sordo. Though he was a known troublemaker, El Sordo had come to San Antonio unarmed and in good faith. When other chiefs cried for vengeance, Cordero sought a peaceful solution. Leading a huge body of Comanche warriors to San Antonio, he was met on the village outskirts by Gov. Manuel de Salcedo and a force of 675 men. Once again, the peace was reaffirmed. The imprisonment of El Sordo in Mexico remained a sore spot with the Comanches, but in the ensuing years the tentative friendship held.

When the Frenchman Jean Louis Berlandier visited San Antonio de Béxar in 1828, he found that a Comanche group regularly attended the presidio to trade buffalo hides, deer skins, meat, and bear grease for guns and ammunition. Some five hundred tribespeople were in the party, including women and children. All were mounted on good horses and mules. Normally the garrison troops would go out with bugles sounding and sabers flashing to escort the Indians to the main square, where they would camp.[14]

The Lipan Apaches also came to San Antonio to trade. By agreement, the two tribes would not fight in the vicinity of the presidio. However, the Apaches came one night while the Comanches were there. The Comanches immediately packed up and left, but the Lipans pursued them all the way to the Colorado River, where the Apaches stole more than two hundred of the Comanches' mounts.

Shortly after Mexico won independence from Spain in 1821, a Mexican officer estimated that there were more than twelve thousand Indians in Texas, nearly half of them implacable enemies of the Mexican citizens. He referred in particular to the Comanches and the Apaches, who were almost constantly at war with the people of San Antonio.[15]

The American Stephen F. Austin founded his colony on the lower Colorado River during the early 1820s, even as the small band of Caranchua Indians of Galveston Island were being overwhelmed by other Texas Anglo-Americans.[16] At the time of Texas independence in 1836, the Comanche warriors still ruled most of central, west, and north Texas, as well as western Oklahoma. For now, the Comanche Nation was threatened not so much from the south as from the north.

CHAPTER 7

Challengers from
the North

AT the start of the nineteenth century, the Comanchería extended from the Arkansas River southward to the Rio Grande, from central Texas to eastern New Mexico—a vast area of rolling prairie grassland slashed by ravines and canyons, dotted with buttes, and marked by snaking, tree-lined watercourses. The Comanches freely moved their villages of buffalo-hide lodges about the prairie seeking water, grazing pastures for their huge horse herds, and safety for their families.

They killed the buffalo by chase from the backs of their well-trained ponies, sometimes with the lance but more often with the bow and arrow. They also hunted the river bottoms, procuring the meat and skins needed for their daily tribal life. Often, when the men were not hunting, they joined war parties to steal horses or attack an enemy. They did so at the risk of leaving their own villages undefended with their women, children, and horse herds prey to predators from other tribes.

They were especially vulnerable in this respect from northern war parties that habitually came south of the Arkansas River to prey on the Comanche horse herds as well as those of the Wichitas and other tribes of the Comancheria. Principal among these intruders were the Kiowas, Osages, Pawnees, and affiliated Cheyenne and Arapaho tribes.

The Kiowas had been the first to contest Comanche dominance of the region. They had moved down from the high country of present Wyoming and Montana, where they roved about between the Black Hills of South Dakota and the headwaters of the Yellowstone River. A Pueblo tribe of the Southwest who for some unknown reason had migrated to the north, the Kiowas spoke the Tanoan dialect of the Uto-Aztecan family. Because the tongue was not understood by any of the other Siouan or Algonquian tribes of the upper plains, the Kiowas were entirely dependent on sign language in communication. Undoubtedly, this contributed to the alienation of this small but determined group of people.

Evidence indicates that they had few friends and many enemies in the north. According to Kiowa tradition, in about 1775 they were defeated by the Dakotas (or Sioux), who exterminated the entire Kuato band of Kiowas.[1] At the Treaty of Fort Laramie in 1851, an Oglala Sioux chief named Black Hawk spoke on the matter to the peace commissioners:

> You have split the country, and I don't like it. What we live upon, we hunt for, and we hunt from the Platte to the Arkansas, and from here up to the Red Butte and the Sweet Water. The Cheyennes and Arapahos agree to live together and be one people; that is very well, but they want to hunt on this side of the river [north of the Platte]. These lands once belonged to the Kiowas and the Crows, but we whipped these nations out of them, and in this we did what the white men do when they want the lands of the Indians. We met the Kiowas and Crows and whipped them, at the Kiowa Creek, just below where we now are. We met them and whipped them again, and the last time at Crow Creek. This last battle was fought by the Cheyennes, Arrapahoes and Ogallahlaha combined, and the Ogallahlaha claim their share of the country.[2]

Though overwhelmed by the allied northern tribes, the Kiowas were extremely fierce, capable fighters. Lt. T. H. Wheelock, who saw his first Kiowas while with the Leavenworth expedition in 1835, was impressed with them. "They are bold, warlike-looking Indians; some of their horses are very fine; they ride well, and were admirably equipped, today, for fight or flight; their bows strung and quivers filled with arrows."[3]

The artist George Catlin, who was also with the expedition, commented similarly:

> The Kioways are not so numerous as the Camanches, but they are a more fearless and warlike people. They dress and equip themselves in a style surpassing in richness and elegance all the other Indians of the "far west," and they are large, athletic, and fine-looking men. They formerly occupied the regions of the Rocky Mountains, and have been only a few years the near neighbors and allies of the Towayahs [Taovayas] and Camanches.[4]

When the Kiowas and some of the Comanches were still north of the Arkansas, the two tribes were at war. The Kiowas were able to inflict injury often enough to drive the Comanches south, eventually following them on into New Mexico and the Texas Panhandle. In about 1790 a peace was finally worked out between the two tribes. The agreement was arranged by a New Mexican who was friendly with both tribes. Gui-k'ati, or Wolf-Lying-Down, the second-ranked Kiowa chief, accepted an invitation from the Comanche headman Paréiya, or Afraid-of-Water, to visit his camp on the Double Mountain Fork of the Brazos River in Texas.

Wolf-Lying-Down remained with the Comanches through the summer and was treated well. Afterward, the two tribes held a council and agreed to live together in peace.[5] The alliance, which was strengthened in 1806 when the Kiowa chief Roncon married the daughter of the chief of the Comanche Yamparika band, has never been

Plains Indians could drive an arrow completely through a buffalo with a bois d'arc bow such as the one held by this Kiowa
warrior. Note his battle breastplate. (Western History Collections, University of Oklahoma)

broken.[6] When the Kiowas moved on south, they also became friendly with the various Wichita bands. The Wichitas liked them more than the Comanches. The Kiowas did not steal and treated the Wichitas with more respect.

The Kiowas were still present along the South Platte River of present Colorado in 1806 when American explorers under Capt. Zebulon M. Pike visited the area. In his report on the expedition, Pike noted the Kiowas' presence there, estimating their warrior force to be a thousand strong, all well armed with bows, arrows, and lances. They also owned immense herds of horses. Despite the earlier peace agreement between the two tribes, Pike claimed that the Kiowas were still at war with the Comanches as well as the Sioux and the Pawnees. While marching up the Arkansas River on his way to the mountains, he had met a party of sixty Pawnees on their way to attack the Kiowas.[7]

When the Stephen H. Long expedition of 1820 visited the region, the Kiowas were still camping along the upper Arkansas River. Arriving at the Arkansas after marching south along the Colorado Rockies, Long and his small party met a Kaskaia (Plains Apache)[8] Indian man and woman who told them of a large group of six nations camped several days' travel down the river. These included the Kiowas, who had recently taken part in a successful war expedition against the Spaniards on the Red River.[9]

For exploration purposes, Long decided to split his party. One group, under Capt. J. R. Bell, continued down the Arkansas while Long led the other on south to return east by another route. Soon after dividing, Bell's twelve-man group encountered the large congregation of Indians mentioned by the Kaskaias. The camp was composed of Kiowas, Kaskaias, Cheyennes, and Arapahos. The Indians received the explorers warmly, providing food. They were also helpful to Bell in his effort to record words of the various tribal languages. An interview with an aged Kiowa chief was fruitless, however, since not even the guides could understand a word that the amused old man spoke.[10]

Long's group, meanwhile, headed on south, eventually
turning back to the east at the Canadian River, which,
like Melgares, they mistook for the Red River. As they
struggled across the arid, midsummer prairie of the Texas
Panhandle, Long and his nine companions met a migra-
tory village of about 250 Kaskaias—a long, scattered string
of warriors, women, and children, all mounted and driving their horse herds with them. Some of their horses
pulled travois loaded with packs of meat, the results of a
hunting excursion on the headwaters of the Brazos and
Colorado rivers in Texas. They were returning to their
home range at the head of the Arkansas and South Platte
rivers.[11]

Uniquely, among this Rocky Mountain tribe the symbol
of the alligator was a religious fetish, prominently displayed as an ornament throughout the band. The Kaskaias
valued it highly as a cure for disease and protection from
misfortune. Whether the symbol reflected a visit to the
gulf coast regions or a migration from there is not known.

When the American explorers prepared to depart, they
discovered that some of their horses, camp kettles, and
other items were missing. Major Long ordered his interpreter to issue a complaint to the chief and demand a
return of the stolen property. No sooner had this been
done than a large number of warriors, bows strung and
arrows in hand, surrounded the Americans. The Indians
appeared ready to use their weapons, and Long's badly
outnumbered party faced them with cocked guns.

For a desperate moment, it appeared that a serious clash
was about to take place. But then the chief appeared,
ordered his men back, and had the missing goods brought
forward, much to the relief of the explorers. The parting
was a friendly one, and Long's segment met no more Indians on their journey down the Canadian River to the Territory of Arkansas.

During 1821–22, the Glenn-Fowler expedition, led by
Hugh Glenn, visited the upper Arkansas River on a hunt-
ing-trapping venture, remaining through the winter before
going on to Santa Fe. They were befriended by a large

encampment of Indians, among them a Kiowa band. The Kiowa chief said that recently the Comanches had tried to persuade them to join in a war against the Osages and whites but that the Kiowas had refused.[12] Jacob Fowler, a Kentuckian who served as guide and who chronicled the sojourn, told of a Spanish prisoner who had been captured at San Antonio. The man indicated that the Kiowas were then at war with the Spanish of Texas but at peace with New Mexico.[13]

Though they shared encampments and often hunted with the Comanches, the Kiowas continued to live apart in their own villages. Also, they usually made war separately. They raided deep into south Texas, west into New Mexico, north into Colorado. They fought and eventually made a tremulous peace with the Mescalero Apaches. They also waged war at times with the Cheyennes, Osages, Dakotas, Pawnees, Caddos, Tonkawas, Utes, Navahos, and Jicarilla Apaches.[14]

The Osages would prove to be the Kiowas' most dangerous enemy. For many years the Osages in the present state of Missouri and those on the Verdigris and Grand rivers of present-day eastern Kansas and Oklahoma persisted as a major threat to the security of the Comanches, Kiowas, Wichitas, and other southern tribes. The much-dreaded Osage warriors, their heads shaved to leave a crest of hair down the center, ranged as far west as Colorado and New Mexico and south to the Red River. The Osage trademark in battle, in addition to scalping, was the decapitation of their victims. An intense enmity between the Comanches and the Osages developed, and their intertribal warfare continued for many years.

For a time the Osages were wealthy in arms but poor in horses. They had been able to procure guns, powder, and balls from the French traders on the Mississippi and Arkansas rivers but horses were available to them only on the great prairies.[15] There was still another reason for their intrusion. The traders incited the Osages to steal women and children from the Plains tribes.[16] As a result, Osage war parties regularly raided the camps and villages of the Comanches, Wichitas, and other tribes, taking horses, mules, and captives.

Pike had visited the Osage villages in present southwestern Missouri while on his way to the Rocky Mountains during the summer of 1806. At that time he had returned to the tribe a number of their people who had been captured in a raid by the Potawatomis the year before. Pike and his party of 25 were met by 180 mounted Osage warriors, each painted and decorated in gala fashion. Entering the village, the Americans were greeted by a salvo from four swivel cannons, which the Osages said they had taken from an old Spanish fort.[17]

After a brief visit, the Americans continued northwestward to the villages of another inveterate raider of the Comanchería, the Pawnees, who were then situated on the Republican River of northern Kansas. In going there, Pike's Osage guides had cautiously skirted the country of the fierce Kaw tribe of present northeastern Kansas, who were then at war with both the Osages and the Pawnees.

Pike and his men arrived at the Pawnee village only a short time after a visit by the Spanish lieutenant Facindo Melgares. Three hundred mounted, whooping Pawnee warriors, naked except for breechclouts and dabs of yellow, blue, and black clay, charged out to meet them. A Spanish flag left only recently by Melgares still waved above the village of round, grass-and-mud huts.

Pike soon made friends with the Pawnee chief Characterish (Cher-a-ta-reesh), presenting him with a double-barreled gun and a gorget necklace. While at the village, Pike learned that the Pawnees were wealthy in horses, being good breeders who protected their breeding mares. Despite this, the Pawnees habitually went to war on foot, often in groups of two to three hundred. They possessed some firearms secured in trade with the French and English, whereas their enemies fought mostly with bows, arrows, lances, and slings.

Despite his admiration for Pike's bravery, Characterish attempted to prevent Pike from continuing on to the Spanish country, as Melgares had asked of him. "You are a brave young warrior," the Pawnee chief said on the night before Pike was to depart. "I respect you . . . I love brave men. Do not oblige me to hurt you. You have only twenty-five men, while I can command a thousand. You must not pass."[18]

At sunrise the next morning, the Americans found themselves surrounded by some five hundred warriors, their bows strung and their spears, tomahawks, and guns ready. Despite a final appeal by the chief to desist, Pike led his men through the Pawnee throng. The chief waved his men back. "Were I now to stop you by destroying you," he said to Pike, "I should forever after feel myself a coward."[19]

In 1811, five years after Pike's expedition, the Indian agent George Sibley joined a Missouri-based Osage hunting caravan, which included women and children, on a journey into present-day central Kansas. During the excursion, Sibley requested that the Osages escort him to a much-rumored mountain of salt located on the Cimarron River north of present Woodward, Oklahoma. They consented to do so only with a one-hundred-man force for protection against the other tribes that often came to that region to gather salt. The Osages were especially concerned about the threat of Comanches.[20]

This concern, however, did not restrain Osage war parties from venturing farther south, well into Comanche country along the Red River. In August 1812, a band of Osage warriors attacked a group of American traders under Alexander McFarland, who had come to trade for horses and mules with the Wichitas. The Osages killed McFarland and made off with all of the trade goods.[21]

By the time the British botanist Thomas Nuttall traveled up the Arkansas River to its juncture with the Verdigris and Grand in 1819, an American presence had been established there by three trading houses. Also permanently located in the area was the large band of Osages under Chief Clermont, who had been encouraged to settle in present northeastern Oklahoma by the trader Auguste P. Chouteau. Nuttall was told that during the past two summers the Verdigris Osages under Clermont had hosted a general council of Indian tribes, including the Comanches, at the salt plains in an attempt to form an alliance against their enemy, the Western Cherokees of Arkansas.[22] There is no evidence that these efforts at conciliation with the Comanches were successful.

The Comanche-Osage conflict had been witnessed by Bell and his men after leaving the Indian encampment on the Arkansas in 1820. As they were marching down the river, a war party suddenly appeared from over a hill near the site of present Hutchinson, Kansas. It was a band of Comanches returning from a foray against the Osages. An attack on an Osage village had left three Comanches killed and six wounded. The attackers had also lost fifty-six horses and most of their robes. One of the Comanches, in his sorrow over the loss of a brother in the fight, had slashed himself with over a hundred parallel cuts, three to four inches long, across his arms and thighs.[23]

The Frenchman Jean Louis Berlandier, who went on a hunting excursion with a band of Comanches in southern Texas in 1828, described the Comanche-Osage war as having a seasonal character, its rhythm being related to the movement of the buffalo. The Comanches were more aggressive during the period from May to August, when the buffalo were moving north. The Osages did much of their raiding during November, December, and January, when the herds were moving south.[24] Although large, massed battles between the tribes were rare, raiding, horse stealing, and minor engagements between warrior groups were constant.

A daring trade adventure was conducted through the Comanche stronghold of present western Oklahoma and the Texas Panhandle in 1821 by the traders Thomas James and John McKnight, who were headed for Santa Fe. Composed of eleven men and twenty-three horses loaded with goods, the trading party left Clermont's village on the Verdigris and headed up the Arkansas to the Cimarron, then turned west along that river past Sibley's salt mountain. Not far from present Fort Supply, Oklahoma, they met a band of nearly one hundred Comanches.

The Indians were led by two chiefs, one friendly, one belligerent. The latter, a mean-looking older man with only one eye, was especially incensed because the Americans were riding Osage horses. However, the other chief protected the visitors and sent them on their way, warning them that the one-eyed chief planned to ambush and kill them. The party turned southward to the Canadian River, striking it near the site of present Borger, Texas. They were near the New Mexico border when they encountered another body of Comanches, a large village of nearly a thousand lodges.

The chief of this band was also hostile to the Americans. He stopped them, demanding their trade goods and letting his men steal the traders' horses. A circle of determined warriors was closing about the embattled traders when they were saved by the opportune arrival of a Mexican military force of fifty men. Also making an appearance was a force of three hundred Comanches under Chief Cordero.

A tall erect man of seventy years, Cordero wore the full regimentals of an American colonel, complete with blue coat, red sash, white pantaloons, epaulets, and sword. These had been given to him by the American Indian agent at Natchitoches, along with a note validating him as a true friend of the United States. The chief lent his protection to James and his party as they continued on to Santa Fe.[25]

James and McKnight again entered the Comanche stronghold in 1823, leading a trading party up the North Canadian River. They began building a fort near present Geary, Oklahoma, but later the men moved on upstream to construct another fort near the mouth of Wolf Creek in northwestern Oklahoma. In the meantime, McKnight and two other men had separated from the main party to go out and bring in the Indians to trade. McKnight was murdered by the Comanches, though his companions were released.

Despite this incident, an extensive trade was conducted with both the Comanches and the Wichitas through the winter. James's former antagonist, the one-eyed Comanche chief, brought his band in to trade, now giving the traders the benefit of his protection. The traders saw many Mexican captives among the various bands.

One day word came that the Osages were nearby on the Cimarron, the news greatly exciting the Indians. After a council, the Comanche chiefs sent their women, children, and old people away to the west while a warrior force rode out to block any Osage attack that might come. No fight is known to have resulted, but as the traders were returning east along the North Canadian the next spring, they met a group of Wichita and Caddo warriors who were returning from a battle with the Osages to the north. James and his men dressed the wounds of seven warriors who had been injured.[26]

No official or known private explorations were made into the northern region of the Comanchería for several years, and our records of tribal warfare for the remainder of the 1820s are limited. But there can be no doubt that the raiding back and forth among the tribes continued or that many conflicts occurred. Col. José Francisco Ruiz told Berlandier that in 1824 he was present at a gathering of Comanches, Arapahos, and others that organized a force of some two thousand well-armed warriors for an expedition against the Osages. An advance party of fifty Comanches was sent forward, only to run into an Osage ambush. The main Comanche force galloped forth to do battle. They found the Osages drawn up in a strong defensive position on the opposite bank of a river, thought to be a branch of the Arkansas. The Osages were supported by fourteen white men. With no possibility of surprising the enemy and with clear evidence that a hard fight would ensue, the Comanche force abandoned the field, after losing two men, and returned home.[27]

The Kiowas too were persistently victimized by the Osages. One of the most significant and bloodiest incidents took place in 1833. On this occasion a large body of Osages rode westward from Clermont's village on the Verdigris River near present Claremore to the salt plains of north-central Oklahoma. En route they discovered a Kiowa party's trail leading to the northeast.

Concluding that the Kiowas were not headed for the Verdigris, the Osages tracked their trail back southwestward to the Kiowa camp at Rainy Mountain Creek near the Wichita Mountains. According to Kiowa accounts given many years later, some of their young men learned of the Osages' presence when they found a buffalo with an Osage arrow in it. Others claimed that there was an exchange of gunfire before the virtually defenseless Kiowa camp fled in alarm, splitting into four divisions. One Kiowa group, thinking it was safe, went into camp on Otter Creek.

The pursuing Osages found the camp and surrounded it. They waited through the night and at daybreak began creeping up to attack. A Kiowa youngster who had risen early to look for his ponies saw the Osages and hurried to warn his chief. The chief immediately ran from his lodge, calling to his people, "To the rocks! To the rocks!"

The Kiowas fled in all directions with the gun-and-tomahawk-wielding Osages in pursuit. Panic-stricken mothers, carrying babies or dragging tots, scurried frantically for safety; old men and women stumbled helplessly along; terrified young girls screamed as they dashed to escape; adolescent boys, already trained in the defense of their village, heroically fought to hold back the enemy long enough to permit others to escape.

Few made it to the rocks. Virtually all were caught by the merciless Osages and killed on the spot. Only two prisoners, a ten-year-old boy and his twelve-year-old sister, were taken. Five men and a large number of women and children were killed in the massacre. But the Osages were not done. They began applying their victory trademark, hacking off heads from the bodies of their victims. This done, the heads were then placed in brass buckets around the camp. The bodies were left strewn around the smoldering remains of the village, which the Osages burned to the last tipi.

Among those killed was the wife of the Kiowa keeper of the tribal spiritual medicine bag, the taíme, as she tried to untie it from the tipi pole. The Osages carried off the precious taíme. This was a severe blow to the entire Kiowa tribe; the Kiowas did not hold their annual sun dance for two years.

The Osages also discovered a large amount of Mexican bullion in the camp. This had been captured by the Kiowas in the Texas Panhandle the year before when they had attacked a group of American traders returning to Missouri from Santa Fe. The Osages took the money—along with over a hundred Kiowa scalps, the captive children, and some four hundred horses—with them back to the Verdigris settlement. The jubilant Osages celebrated the victory with several nights of dancing and feasting. In the Kiowa calendar, the event became known as "the summer that they cut off their heads."[28]

The Osages were deeply involved during this period in warring with the Cherokees, who had been moved from the South into Arkansas. However, this did not stop their predatory raids against the tribes along the Red River. The Pawnees were also of particular menace to all of the tribes who lived between the Arkansas and Red rivers or hunted there. They were known on the early frontier as the Pawnee Mahas, as distinguished from the Wichita band often identified as the Pawnee Picts.[29] Members of the Skidi branch of the Pawnees were particularly active marauders.

Pike, who had visited the Pawnees on the Loup River in 1806, found them to be better than the Osages as horse raisers. Even though they were wealthy in ponies, Pawnee war parties came south regularly to hunt, steal horses, and take scalps.[30] The Pawnee raiders were not only bitter foes of the Cheyennes and Arapahos but also enemies of the Comanches, Osages, Creeks, Delawares, Wichitas, Kickapoos, and Caddos. Parties from these tribes ventured westward to hunt buffalo or chase wild horses knowing that they might well run afoul of the Pawnees. Even worse, their home camps were constantly preyed on by Pawnee horse thieves.

The Osages of Clermont's village on the Verdigris River were particularly hard-pressed by the Pawnees, who were a constant threat to Osage hunting sojourns westward to the buffalo prairie. In the spring of 1818, somewhere in the general vicinity of present Enid, Oklahoma, a large party of Pawnees, numbering around four hundred, spotted a group of forty-eight Osages on their way toward the salt plains. Sending a small force of warriors out to engage the Osages in a running fight, the Pawnees drew the Verdigris River Indians into an ambush laid by their main force. The Osage war party was annihilated except for one man who managed to escape.[31]

The Pawnees themselves suffered a similar massacre the following winter when ninety-three Skidi warriors went south on foot to steal horses from the Comanches. When they were close to the Comanche camp, the Skidis paused to braid rawhide lariats for leading back the horses they would steal. But as they were doing this, they were surprised by mounted Comanches attacking from several directions. Cut off from a nearby timbered creek, the Skidis were forced to make a stand in the open. Throwing off their clothes for battle, they fought desperately. The mounted and much better armed Comanches circled their prey, war whooping and shooting until finally they attacked for hand-to-hand combat with war axes, knives, and clubs. Forty of the Skidis managed to escape; all but seven of these were wounded. Those who could walk made pole drags for the others and pulled their freezing comrades back to the Loup River. Several died along the way.[32]

A Pawnee defeat of the Osages was recounted to Thomas James by a Pawnee chief during James's trip back to Missouri from Santa Fe in 1822. The Pawnee, a handsome man with a muscular six-foot frame, was at the lead of several hundred Pawnee warriors whom James and his party encountered on the Arkansas River in present Kansas. The chief said that during the previous fall of 1821, he and a war party had approached a large Osage village. The Pawnee force, however, was too small to assault the Osage town. Instead, he sent eight warriors mounted on fast horses to ride in close to the village while the rest of his force hid behind a large mound some distance away on the prairie. The Osages spotted the eight Pawnees and immediately gave chase. Four of the fleeing Pawnees went on one side of the mound and four on the other. The Osages plunged after them, blind with desire to catch and kill them. The Pawnee chief sounded the war whoop, and his warriors on their fresh horses fell on the Osages, whose horses were badly jaded from their dash after the decoys. A hundred of the Osages were killed as they attempted to escape on their weary ponies.[33]

The Osages were determined to avenge themselves. During the spring of 1830 their chance finally came. An expedition of over three hundred Osage warriors well armed with guns and war hatchets, advanced up the Arkansas River, turning due west along the Cimarron. Beyond the salt plains—probably in the vicinity of the rumored salt mountain in present Woodward County, Oklahoma—the Osages discovered a Pawnee camp, which included families, near a lake.

Catching the camp by surprise, the Osages surrounded it and attacked with brutal force, pinning the Pawnees against the lake. After their gunfire had driven many of their enemies into the lake, the Osages tossed aside their rifles and used their tomahawks against the floundering victims. Not one of the Pawnees escaped. The Osages returned to the agency post with more than sixty scalps, five captive women, and eighty-four Pawnee horses. Though they had not lost a man, they said that they had never had a fight with the Pawnees in which so much blood had been spilled. The Osages were so elated with the victory that another war party was organized to go against some immigrant Choctaws on the Red River, with whom they had been at odds.[34]

Still another fight between the Osages and the Pawnees took place late the same year, less than thirty miles from the previous battleground. The Pawnees had come south seeking revenge and attacked an Osage hunting party. The Osages were armed with guns, whereas the Pawnees had only spears and battle axes. The Osages killed eighteen of the enemy, losing only two killed and eight wounded.[35]

Tixier, the Frenchman who accompanied an Osage war party to this area in 1840, was told of the conflicts. During one of the fights, the great Osage warrior Bahabeh had been killed. It was said that after a fight in 1831, many warriors of both nations had been left unburied on the ground. Tixier wanted to visit the site and gather up skulls, but his Osage hosts were anxious to move on.[36]

For most of the first half of the nineteenth century and beyond, the Pawnees, Osages, Kaws, and occasionally other tribes from the Missouri River country continued their raiding of the Red River tribes. Numerous clashes, small and large, many never recorded, made a warring ground of most of what is now Oklahoma—while the Comanches and Kiowas were doing the same in Texas.

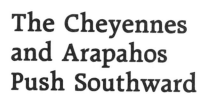

CHAPTER 8

The Cheyennes
and Arapahos
Push Southward

EVEN while the Osages and Pawnees were regularly invading the Comanche-Kiowa-Wichita domain, the latter tribes were being pressed hard by still other Indians from the north. Among them were the allied Cheyenne and Arapaho tribes of the upper Arkansas River country of present Colorado. Following the Comanches and Kiowas, these two smaller but war-effective Algonquian tribes had migrated from the Black Hills and the surrounding area.

The Cheyennes, who were first witnessed by the French in present Minnesota in 1680, are known to have moved westward to the Sheyenne River of present North Dakota around 1700. There, in their pre-horse period, they lived in permanent-type villages and were subjected to decimating raids by the larger Cree and Assiniboine tribes. Eventually the Cheyennes had been forced across the Missouri River, where they met the Arapahos, who joined them in wars against the Gros Ventres and Mandans.

During the late eighteenth century, these two tribes became acquainted with the horse. Like the Comanches and Kiowas, the Cheyennes and Arapahos quickly adapted the horse to vital use in both their everyday livelihood and their warfare. Now they not only could more effectively hunt the buffalo, which provided them with most of their necessities of life, but also could range far and wide to hunt and make war on their enemies.

Some Arapaho bands eventually pushed south well beyond the Arkansas River. Berlandier claimed that Arapahos had been in Texas since early in the nineteenth century, camping along the Colorado and Brazos rivers among the Comanches and Plains Apaches. By his account, the Arapahos, who numbered twelve hundred or more, often made war on the Osages and then fell back to the Comanche country. Though they possessed some guns, they fought mainly with the lance and the bow.[1]

A sizable Arapaho and Cheyenne group was seen by Bell on the Arkansas River in 1820. The Arapaho chief Bear Tooth appeared to hold dominant power among the bands. The Americans were impressed with an unnamed Cheyenne leader, a man "born to command," whose demeanor was endowed with unconquerable ferocity. The Cheyennes had just recently fought a big battle with the Pawnees. Though the Cheyennes were at war with all the Missouri River tribes, the Pawnees and the Utes of the Rocky Mountains were their principal tribal enemies.

When the Cheyennes departed the Arkansas River encampment, their young warriors made a display of their warriorship. They rode up and down alongside their caravan brandishing their bows, arrows, lances, war shields, war clubs, knives, and tomahawks.[2]

As Bell and his men marched eastward down the Arkansas River, they encountered a Cheyenne war party that was returning from a raid against the Pawnees. The Cheyenne warriors carried lances decorated with strips of red and white cloth, beads, and eagle tail plumes. From the lance of one dangled the scalp of a Pawnee woman; in celebration of this deed, the party's leader had blackened his entire body with charcoal.[3]

The Cheyennes were located east of South Dakota's Black Hills in 1825 when they were met by an American exploring party under Gen. Henry Atkinson. But already some Cheyenne and Arapaho bands, encouraged by the promise of the Bent brothers and St. Vrain to establish a trading post on the Arkansas, had begun to take up permanent residence to the south. Eventually this created a split in the two tribes, between northern and southern divisions.

Cheyenne raiding of the abundant Wichita, Comanche, and Kiowa horse herds became a regular practice. Often the Cheyenne raiders were pursued by the Comanches. In 1829 the Comanche chief Bull Hump caught up with a group of Cheyenne horse thieves north of the Arkansas and retook the herd they had made away with. However, the Cheyennes pursued the Comanches and recaptured the herd. The Comanches then gave chase, but the Cheyennes were armed with guns, whereas the Comanches had only bows and arrows. The Cheyennes drove back the Comanches, and finally escaped with the thrice-stolen horses plus some Comanche scalps.[4] Cheyenne war parties returning from the Red River country and driving large herds of stolen horses across the Arkansas River would become a common sight to the residents of Bent's Fort.

Even as the Cheyennes were pressing against the Comanches, they continued their long-standing war with the Pawnees. Of the many battles, small and large, between the two tribes, the most disastrous for the Cheyennes took place in 1830. Supported by their two great medicines, their Medicine Arrows and their Sacred Buffalo Hat, the Cheyennes set out en masse to attack the Skidi Pawnees on the headwaters of the Loup River.

At the time, the Skidis were gathered for their ceremonial killing of a captive sacrificed to the Morning Star. A party of Skidi buffalo hunters was first attacked by the Cheyennes, but the main force of Skidis soon came galloping forward on their war ponies. The two Indian armies faced one another in a long battle line. Before the fight started, an old Pawnee who was ill and wished to die went out between the lines and sat down. He began singing his death song.

Somehow the old man survived the first Cheyenne

charge. Bull, then the Cheyenne keeper of the Sacred Arrows, had the Medicine Arrow bundle tied to his lance. He charged and attempted to impale the Pawnee. But the old man avoided the thrust, grabbed the lance, and jerked it from the grasp of Bull. Other Pawnee warriors rushed up and made off with the Sacred Arrow bundle. The loss demoralized the Cheyennes, who gave up the fight.[5]

The Cheyenne-Arapaho invasion of the Comanchería continued, their presence south of the Arkansas becoming more and more intrusive until eventually it reached the point of serious conflict. On one occasion in 1836, Chief Yellow Wolf's Hairy Rope band of Cheyennes invaded the North Fork of the Red River and drove off a large number of animals from the Comanche herd. The Cheyennes were pursued beyond the Arkansas River by the Comanche chief Bull Hump with a large party of warriors, but to no avail. It was inevitable that such incursions would lead to serious conflict.

The matter came to a head in 1837 when a party of forty-eight Cheyenne Bow String Society warriors ventured deep into the Comanchería to raid the horse herds of the Comanches and Kiowas. Leaving their camps along the Arkansas River, the Bow String soldiers set out on foot to the south.[6] They found little game on the arid prairie and used many of their arrows and ammunition in killing what they found.

After many days' travel they reached the Washita River country. There two scouts, who had been sent ahead, discovered a large encampment of Comanches, Kiowas, and Plains Apaches. While the scouts were spying on the camp from atop a nearby bluff, their heads were spotted by a Kiowa hunter. The scouts attempted to kill the hunter, but the man escaped to warn his village.

Mounted warriors from the Kiowa village rushed out in defense. The Cheyenne spies had fled their roost, but eventually the Kiowas located the group of Cheyennes, who had taken refuge in a stone breastwork at the head of a ravine. The surrounded, foot-bound Bow Strings fought bravely, killing a few of the Kiowas. But their supply of ammunition soon ran out. They were charged and overrun by the mounted Kiowas, killed to the last man, and scalped.

Since there were no Cheyenne survivors, accounts of this attack did not reach the Arkansas camps for some time. The Cheyennes finally learned of it when a party of Arapahos were visiting the Kiowas at the abandoned Bent trading post, known as Fort Adobe, on the Canadian River of the Texas Panhandle. The Arapahos had observed a war dance celebration and recognized the ornamented braids of two Bow String scalps.

The Cheyennes were infuriated. Runners carried the news of the Bow String defeat to Cheyenne camps spread from the Arkansas to the Platte. Warriors gathered for a war of revenge against the Kiowas and Comanches. Little Wolf, head of the Bow Strings, incited the assembled force into a great passion for vengeance.

Through the winter of 1837–38, dances were held, death songs were sung, and vows were made that no mercy would be shown in striking back. The Cheyennes' friends the Arapahos joined the planned expedition. During the early summer of 1838, the combined Cheyenne-Arapaho warrior force took its entire village, including women and children, from the Arkansas River of present-day western Kansas southward into northwestern Oklahoma.

When they reached Crooked Creek, their spies had still seen no sign of the enemy. But one day, from a ridge overlooking Wolf Creek, the scouts spotted a few Kiowa warriors, with lances and shields, leading their horses eastward down the stream. The main body of Cheyennes now moved farther south to Beaver Creek and camped. From there they sent out search parties. Finally, a Kiowa-Comanche buffalo hunt was spotted on the high ground between Beaver and Wolf creeks.

Determined to have the advantage of surprise, the Cheyenne and Arapaho force marched all night. Just after sunrise they came onto an unsuspecting Kiowa hunting party, which they charged and destroyed almost to the man. This was followed by a massive attack on the Kiowa and

Comanche camps scattered along the north bank of Wolf Creek.

The onslaught that followed, what has become known as the Battle of Wolf Creek, was described shortly afterward by a U.S. dragoon officer. His command, which included a group of Osage guides, happened to be on its way from Camp Holmes up the North Canadian on a prearranged visit to the Comanches and Kiowas. Lt. L. B. Northup, arriving at the battle scene just two days after the fight, reported:

> As the Cheyennes advanced to attack their enemies, they were met by the latter about a mile from the encampment. The latter were slowly beaten back into their encampment, though disputing desperately every inch of ground. The whole scene was in an open prairie. The women dug holes in the earth, in which to hide themselves and their children. The Cheyennes continued to make dreadful havoc of their wretched enemies, and would have soon reduced the whole to a heap of corpses, when a messenger from camp mounted a horse, and set off to meet the detachment of dragoons to solicit assistance. As he was leaving, a Cheyenne, who understood the language of the Comanches, was informed by one of the latter that the messenger had gone to hasten the white men and Osages, whom they every moment expected to come to their assistance. The Cheyennes instantly retired, leaving fourteen [of their] dead on the ground. Fifty-eight of the Kiowas and Comanches were killed. More than one hundred horses lay dead on the ground, chiefly within the encampment.[7]

The Osages wanted to follow the retreating Cheyennes and Arapahos and continue the fighting. But the Comanches and Kiowas had been badly mauled, and they were content to let the matter end. Though they were by no means destroyed as an effective fighting force, the two tribes had their families to consider. The chiefs did not want their villages under the constant threat of attack from the north.

As a result, the Comanches and Kiowas sent emissaries

to the Cheyennes on the Arkansas and indicated that they wished to hold a peace council. They promised not only to return the scalps of the dead Bow String soldiers but also to make gifts of many horses. The offer pleased the Cheyenne chiefs, and during the summer of 1840 a great peace council was conducted near Bent's Fort on the Arkansas River.[8]

There was much feasting, dancing, and gift giving. As they had promised, the Comanches and Kiowas returned the Bow String scalps and brought many fine horses and gifts. In return the Cheyennes offered guns, blankets, cloth, and beads, as well as coffee and sugar, which were new to the southern bands. The agreement of peace made during the celebration promised greater security for the Comanches and Kiowas on the north. Its most significant result was to allow the Cheyennes and Arapahos to hunt and camp as far south as the Washita and beyond.

The Southern Cheyennes and Southern Arapahos continued to reside in the region between the Platte and Arkansas rivers, east of the Rocky Mountains. They were held there by the abundance of game and by the advantages of trade at Fort William (Bent's Fort) on the Arkansas and at Forts Lupton and St. Vrain on the South Platte. In 1846 the United States established an Indian agency of the upper Platte and Arkansas rivers and assigned the mountain man Thomas Fitzpatrick as agent. Then, by the Treaty of Fort Laramie in 1851, the region was legally designated as the homeland of the Cheyennes and Arapahos jointly.

From their camps east of the mountains, the Cheyennes continued their persistent wars with the Pawnees, partly to establish hunting rights to the buffalo range of present western Kansas and partly to satisfy the tribal warrior function. War parties regularly raided the horse herds of the Loup River villages, and the Pawnees regularly retaliated in kind. When Fitzpatrick attempted to persuade the Cheyennes to end the war, they replied (as worded by the agent): "What, do you wish us to remain here inactive while our brethren are being murdered and plundered by our enemies? No, we will [go] forward and seek revenge."[9]

The Pawnees were not the only warring foes of the Cheyennes. Raiding enmities continued with the Utes and Shoshonis of present-day western Colorado and Wyoming, and hostile excursions were conducted into New Mexico. In 1847 when Fitzpatrick complained about Indian depredations against transportation on the Santa Fe Trail, the Cheyenne chief Yellow Wolf offered assistance in punishing the Comanches, on whom they placed the blame.[10]

Even the alliance with the Arapahos was tentative. Though the Cheyenne tribe was smaller—Fitzpatrick estimated the Cheyennes at 300 lodges, compared with 350 for the Arapahos—occasional conflicts broke out between the allies. But these troubles were soon settled in recognition of the two tribes' strong need for the warring assistance of one another.

Even in the face of such warring inclination, the Cheyennes still maintained their peace element. Chiefs such as Yellow Wolf, Old Tobacco, and Lean Face saw the potential demise of the buffalo on the plains. They suggested to Fitzpatrick that their people would be willing to take up planting and raising corn, as they had during the old days in the north.

But there were too many factors working against the peacemakers. The Cheyenne way of life was now firmly tied to a buffalo-hunting existence, and there were still plenty of buffalo to be found. Warriorship, now an integral part of the once oppressed tribe, was abetted by a steady flow of whiskey, which excited the fighting passions of their young men. It was hardly possible for the Cheyenne peace chiefs to exercise much influence over the destiny of their people.

The Cheyenne propensity toward war was also stimulated by the ever increasing flow of whites across their strategically located homeland. Ox-drawn wagon trains lumbered back and forth over the road between Missouri and Santa Fe, and covered-wagon caravans of white immigrants plied the trails to Utah, California, and Oregon. The poorly protected travelers were prime targets for attack by independent war parties, and it was often unclear which tribe was responsible.

Almost inevitably, the Cheyennes became involved. One nearly serious conflict occurred at Fort Atkinson on the Santa Fe Trail in 1851. An army officer, accusing a Cheyenne warrior of unseemly conduct toward the officer's wife, flogged the Indian with a carriage whip. The entire Cheyenne camp was aroused over the matter, nearly causing a confrontation with a detachment of dragoons under Col. Edwin V. Sumner.[11]

The Fort Laramie treaty defused the Cheyenne-white conflict for a time. There were minor conflicts but no major encounter until August 1856, when trouble erupted along the Platte Trail. Some saucy young Cheyenne and Arapaho warriors stopped a mail wagon and demanded some tobacco. When the driver made a run for it, he was wounded. Older Cheyenne warriors whipped the young men for their act, but army troops organized a retaliatory strike, killing ten Cheyennes and wounding several more. The Cheyennes struck back in revenge, killing a number of immigrants along the Platte Trail.[12]

This outbreak prompted Sumner to conduct a major military expedition against the Cheyennes. Sending one column up the Arkansas under Maj. John Sedgwick and leading another up the Platte, Sumner consolidated his army on Cherry Creek near present Denver, Colorado. With Fall Leaf, a noted Delaware Indian, as his guide, Sumner drove eastward into present-day western Kansas.

As they approached the Cheyenne camps on the Solomon River, Sumner pushed ahead with his cavalry. A Cheyenne warrior army met them in a long, well-formed line. It was here that the medicine man had told the Cheyennes that by dipping their hands in a nearby lake they could stop the soldiers' bullets. However, the flashing sabers ordered by Sumner surprised and demoralized the Cheyennes. A war chief in a flowing bonnet attempted to rally his young men, but he could not stop a precipitous flight. The Cheyenne battle loss was believed to be less than ten; Sumner lost two troopers killed and several wounded. Among the wounded was Lt. "Jeb" Stuart, later to become famous as a Confederate general during the Civil War.[13]

This clash took place on the eve of an event that affected the Cheyennes and Arapahos on a much larger scale. In 1858, the discovery of gold at Cherry Creek led to the Colorado gold rush and the inundation of the land by whites. This invasion amounted to no less than an illegal takeover of the Cheyenne homeland. In 1860 the U.S. government made the intrusion "legal" by initiating the Treaty of Fort Wise.

By this pact, the Cheyennes were to give up all of the land assigned to them under the Treaty of Fort Laramie except for a small, gameless reserve in southeastern Colorado. By any reckoning, it was a "steal" by officials who had taken advantage of the worldly naïveté of chiefs such as Black Kettle and Lean Bear, men who had had little, if any, previous contact with whites and knew nothing of land or mineral values.

The greed of whites and the warring propensity of the Cheyennes were a certain mix for future conflict.

CHAPTER 9

Wars of the
Immigrant Nations

AS Dr. John Sibley, the U.S. Indian agent at Natchitoches, Louisiana, revealed in his extensive report on the Indian tribes of his area in 1805, the forest Indians of the South had begun making excursions to the prairie beyond the Mississippi River to explore and to hunt long before they were removed there by the U.S. government. Sibley told of Cherokees from the Tennessee River who came west to hunt and of Choctaws who often warred with the Caddos.[1] Conflict between these intruding tribes and those already in residence was predictable.

Choctaw tradition speaks of one engagement that took place. A Choctaw hunting party, on an expedition from its home area of Alabama, was returning from the Red River, its horses loaded with robes, buffalo tallow, and jerked meat, when it was attacked by a large band of Caddos. The Choctaws, being better armed, repulsed the attack and drove the Caddos back to their village—located at Caddo Hill near present Caddo, Oklahoma—killed many of them, and destroyed their village.[2]

This may well have been the incident reported by U.S. Commissioner Andrew Ellicott, who said that while he was in Natchez in 1797 a large Choctaw war party arrived.

He wrote: "A short time after our arrival at Natchez, a body of those Indians [Choctaws], crossed the Mississippi, to make war on the Caddos. In this expedition they were very successful, and returned with a number of poles filled with scalps."[3]

The Choctaws were still making excursions westward a decade later when, on January 7, 1807, a band led by the famous Chief Pushmataha came on a French trader, Joseph Bogy, unloading a cargo of trade goods near the mouth of the Verdigris River. Bogy had extended his operation at Arkansas Post up the Arkansas River to barter for furs and pelts from the Osages, enemies of the Choctaws. Pushmataha attacked Bogy and his men, drove them back, and plundered the goods.[4]

Later that year the Choctaws destroyed an Anadarko village on the Sabine River, killing two women and escaping back to American soil, where the Spanish authorities could not punish them. It was reported that the Choctaws had been indulging in such raids for well over a decade.[5]

In the spring of 1807 a small party of Cherokees, whose home territory was along the Tennessee River in Tennessee and Alabama, arrived at Natchitoches. They had been on a hunt up the Red River and were returning in two pirogues loaded with deerskins.[6] They too told of hostile relations with the Caddos over an incident in which a Cherokee had accidentally been killed seven or eight years earlier.[7]

But it was the Osages of present Missouri and eastern Oklahoma with whom the Cherokees maintained a long and bloody war. There is indication that the feud began as early as the Revolutionary War, when westward-ranging Cherokee hunters were attacked by Osages. This friction increased during the early 1790s when a dissident Cherokee band migrated to the St. Francis River of Missouri and became engaged in an exchange of killings with the Osages.

However, it was when a sizable group of Cherokees under Chief Tahlonteskee migrated westward—first to the St. Francis in 1810 and then, after the great earthquake in that region in 1811, on to the Arkansas River of present Arkansas—that brutal warfare with the Osage Nation began. Although clashes were often brought about by horse-stealing raids and murders, there was a particular point of contention above all others.

This conflict involved the band of Osages under Chief Clermont on the Verdigris River of what is now northeastern Oklahoma. When the Cherokees arrived in Arkansas, they found that Clermont's band presented them with a deadly barrier to the western prairies. The Cherokees, who felt the government had promised them a "clear opening to the setting sun," found this especially hard to accept, and their hostilities with the Osages continued unabated.

In July 1817 the Arkansas Cherokees wrote to Gov. William Clark of Missouri Territory, charging that the Osages had stolen their best horses and killed their people. "The rivers are red with the Blood of Cherokees," the letter claimed. The Cherokee chiefs vowed to take revenge.[8]

Soon afterward, a report reached New Orleans of a small army being assembled at the Cherokee villages for a grand assault on Clermont's village. This force, led by the silver-haired, hawk-faced war chief Takatoka, consisted not only of Arkansas Cherokee warriors but also of a large party of fighting men from the Old Nation villages in Alabama and Tennessee.

The latter group had brought with them six field artillery guns that they had learned how to use while serving with Gen. Andrew Jackson against the Creeks at the Battle of Horseshoe Bend in 1814. The Cherokees felt they were more experienced in the art of warfare than the Osages, who knew how to fight only in pitched battles on horseback on the open plains. The Cherokee force was further bolstered by other tribes who held grievances against the Osages and by a few whites who were associated with the Arkansas settlements, making a total of 565 combatants.[9]

Though the Cherokees later claimed the Osages were waiting for them and had built a fort at the Grand River saltworks, the facts appear otherwise. As the attackers marched westward up the Arkansas River (there is no

While at Fort Gibson, George Catlin drew the portrait of Osage chief Clermont, whose nearby village was attacked by the Cherokees in 1817. (Catlin, *North American Indians* 2, pl. 150)

indication they had the artillery guns), Clermont's village lay virtually undefended. Most of the Osage warriors, as the Cherokees likely knew, were away on their annual buffalo hunt.

The result was one of the deadliest massacres in the history of the region. Osages encountered in the path of the advancing legion were killed on the spot. The inhabitants of the Osage village on the Verdigris were caught totally by surprise.[10] The Cherokee force fell on the Osage town with savage fury, killing all before them. Mostly the victims were old people, women, and children, even infants. Many were driven into the river and slaughtered. Other women and children were taken captive.

A Shawnee chief reported that eighty-three Osages were killed and more than one hundred taken prisoner.[11] Accounts provided for Governor Clark broke down the casualty list to fourteen men and sixty-nine women, children, and boys. He set the captive list at just over a hundred.[12]

The vengeance-minded Cherokees burned the thatched-hut settlement to the ground and destroyed its crops and winter food stores. Claiming a loss of only one man killed (a Delaware) and a few wounded, the Cherokees returned home with their prisoners and plunder, which included many horses, to celebrate their victory.

The Cherokee-Osage war was far from over, however. Despite the loss of their people and village, the Verdigris River Osages still blocked the Cherokees' path westward. Even with the establishment of Fort Smith between the two tribes in 1817, Cherokee hunters who ventured into eastern Oklahoma did so at great risk. In February 1820 a Cherokee group was intercepted on the Poteau River by an Osage war party under Mad Buffalo, Chief Clermont's son. Three of the Cherokees were killed, and the party's furs were taken.[13]

Despite efforts by Arkansas Territory Gov. James Miller and other whites to settle the differences, the two tribes continued their hostilities unabated. In April 1821 Mad Buffalo led a large war party down the Arkansas River in a threatened invasion of the Cherokee village areas.

However, after failing in an assault on Fort Smith, the Osages were content to kill three Quapaws and three Delawares who resided nearby, and return home.[14]

In June 1821 a Cherokee war party headed by the half-blood chief Walter Webber struck the Chouteau trading post on Grand River, murdering and scalping its manager, Joseph Revoir.[15] The justification given was that Revoir had been selling guns and ammunition to the Osages. The Cherokee attackers took the scalp back to their villages, using it as the focus of a Fourth of July celebration. The Revoir murder was followed in September by another major Cherokee assault against Clermont's Osages.

The Osages had departed on their fall hunt to the west, taking their women and children with them. However, near the Cimarron River the caravan split, most of the warriors going ahead to drive off any enemy Pawnees they might encounter. The old men, women, children, and a few warriors took their camp equipment and continued on by another trail toward the buffalo grounds.

Led by the well-to-do Tom Graves—who was either a half-blood or an adopted white captive—a Cherokee invasion party of more than three hundred warriors picked up the two trails. The Cherokee group too divided. One contingent caught up with the Osage women and children and ravaged them without mercy, killing and scalping sixty-three. The Cherokees took thirty Osages captive and absconded with seventy horses. An Osage woman who refused to go with the Cherokees was shot and her body thrown into a campfire.[16]

The larger Cherokee division caught up with the Osage warrior force and attacked it. The Cherokees were repulsed and forced to retreat. They later arrived at Fort Smith carrying five Osage scalps plus two that they had taken from their own dead to prevent the scalps from falling into Osage hands.[17]

Ever since the 1817 massacre of Clermont's village, efforts had been made to secure the return of captive Osage women and children to their tribes. Tom Graves was accused of murdering a captive Osage woman, her child, and a girl and throwing their bodies to his hogs while he was in a drunken rage. Some Osage women, however, had become intermarried with Cherokee men and did not want to be returned to their former homes.[18]

The Osages obtained some revenge for Graves's alleged barbaric act when they came onto a Cherokee hunting camp on the North Fork of the Arkansas. The Cherokees were led by Graves's nephew, Red Hawk. The Osages killed and beheaded Red Hawk and chased the other Cherokees back to Arkansas.[19]

Despite a treaty between the two tribes, the aging Takatoka gathered some fifty or more warriors for a raid into the Osage country as far as the Verdigris River in August 1823. After stealing a large herd of Osage horses, they waited in ambush for pursuers. In the fight that ensued, one Osage was killed and several Cherokees were wounded.[20]

In 1825 the U.S. government and the Osages negotiated a treaty whereby the Indians gave up their claim to land in eastern Oklahoma. However, the Osages relinquished neither their land nor their enmity with the Cherokees. Conflicts between the two tribes continued. The bloody feud was again inflamed in 1826 when Dutch, a noted Cherokee war leader, recklessly dashed in among a group of Osages at Chouteau's trading house to kill and scalp an Osage warrior.[21]

Actual warfare had begun to slacken by 1828 when the Arkansas Cherokees and the United States signed a treaty in which the Indians traded their lands in Arkansas for a large tract in eastern Oklahoma. With the two blood enemies now living near one another, they exercised a cautious, unspoken truce while their attentions were focused on combating other foes.

The Osages still warred with the Comanches and the Pawnees, among others, while the Cherokees undertook a brief but gory war with the Tawakonis of central Texas. A dissident party of Cherokees, who had become unhappy with their situation in Arkansas, had moved southwestward into East Texas in about 1820. Led by the elderly, half-white Richard Fields, the Bowl (or Bowles), and Big Mush, they established themselves on the Neches and Trinity rivers west of the present city of Tyler. They were joined later by Dutch, who likewise left the main body of Western Cherokees and moved his band south of the Red River. An attempt by the Texas group to gain a land grant from Mexico was unsuccessful.

In 1826 Stephen F. Austin, on behalf of the Mexican government, asked the Texas Cherokees to join in a punitive attack on the Tawakonis, Wacos, and other tribes at war with Mexico. The Cherokees had agreed to send one hundred warriors, but the expedition was cancelled by Mexico.[22] This was not the end of the matter by any means. Though accounts are somewhat contradictory, it is clear that a major battle was fought between the Cherokees and the Tawakonis and Wacos on the Brazos River.[23]

The trouble began in 1827 when a group of five Cherokees and a Creek Indian were spied trying to steal horses from a Tawakoni village. Three of them were caught and scalped. The others escaped, but one watched from hiding as the Tawakonis lashed the bodies of the dead Cherokees to poles and celebrated their victory with a scalp dance.

The Texas Cherokees took great offense at this and sent a letter concerning the matter to the Arkansas Cherokees, who were now residing in present northeastern Oklahoma. A Cherokee half-blood war captain named John Smith was aroused and became determined to have revenge. In July 1829 a war dance and council were held at Bayou Menard, east of Fort Gibson. Smith encouraged the assembly of Cherokee and Creek warriors to join him in an expedition to assist their Texas brothers.

Sam Houston, who had recently joined the Western Cherokees after resigning as governor of Tennessee, attended the council in the stead of the ailing chief John Jolly and attempted to stop the "raising of the Tomahawk of War."[24] Houston failed, and Smith succeeded in persuading a large party of Cherokees and Creeks to follow him to Dutch's village south of the Red River.

From there the visitors were taken to the Cherokee set-

The noted Cherokee warrior Tah-chee, or Dutch, led an attack against a Tawakoni village near present Waco, Texas, in 1830. (Smithsonian Institution)

tlements of Chief Big Mush, where they were greeted ceremoniously with speeches, music, dancing, and singing. During the visit, an expedition to seek vengeance against the Tawakonis was organized. Dutch was chosen as the leader of the revenge raid. A powerful and well-proportioned man of about forty years, the Cherokee had a high reputation for bravery and cunning. In readiness for the raid, he shaved his head except for a small tuft at the top on which to attach some hawk feathers. He painted his head and the lower portion of the feathers red, leaving them white at the tips. The other warriors followed his lead in preparation.[25]

Mounted on his prize war-horse, Dutch led the Cherokee expedition of horsemen and footmen west, marching for two days to reach a saline where a white man named Marshall maintained a trading post with a large stock of goods and a sizable number of horses, cattle, and hogs. Here they were joined by Cherokees from the other villages.

Marshall and his people were very fearful when the war party rode in whooping and firing guns. Their consternation was only increased when the Cherokees murdered and scalped a Tawakoni chief who was visiting a village of Indians encamped near Marshall's place. The Cherokees threw the body into a cedar forest and left it unburied. This sordid act set the tone for the action that followed, as Smith himself later admitted to a Cherokee friend.[26]

Now sixty-three strong, the Cherokee force moved on westward. They crossed the Trinity River (probably in the vicinity of present Corsicana) and proceeded on with six spies in front and six to each side until the Tawakoni village was located on the Brazos. While their scouts reconnoitered the village and beyond, the Cherokee warriors stripped themselves of all but their shirts, which they kept to distinguish themselves from the enemy during battle, painted their bodies and heads, and adjusted their headdresses.

During the early hours of morning, the predators stealthily crept up to the sleeping village—so silently that the rattle of their powder horns was the only sound. Men were posted outside the entrances of lodges to begin the attack by slaughtering anyone who came out. The massacre that followed, as described by Smith, was ruthless to the extreme.

A woman and a man who emerged from separate lodges at virtually the same moment were shot and tomahawked to death. This signaled a charge on the village. War whoops and screams alike filled the air as Tawakonis fell prey to the tomahawk, rifle, and knife. Not even mothers with suckling babies were spared, nor the babies themselves, who were dashed to death against the hard ground or rocks. A briar patch sheltering a group of Tawakonis was surrounded and its inhabitants were killed despite the emergence of one man who slapped his breast in a gesture of peace and friendship. He was immediately struck down by a Cherokee bullet.

A large portion of the village, however, made it to the protection of their great lodge. Twelve by forty-five feet, half-buried, and supported mainly by a long ridge pole, the structure's cornstalk-and-dirt roof extended to the ground. The Cherokees attempted to burn the occupants out but were unsuccessful because of the arrows and gunfire that poured forth from the redoubt. When one of the Cherokees was shot through the head and killed, the attackers mercilessly knifed and axed to death all of the captives that had been taken.

Another battle ensued when a rescue force of Tawakoni warriors, mounted and well armed, appeared on the scene. Three Cherokees on horseback and several on foot took off in pursuit and ran into a deadly trap. Their scalped corpses were later found pierced by lances and feathered with barbed arrows. Still unable to burn out the refugees in their earth-protected lodge, the Cherokees made their retreat with their trophies of war, some fifty-five to sixty Tawakoni scalps. They left behind five dead of their own.

Though their hunger was almost intolerable as they returned home, the Cherokees took time to prepare themselves and their trophies for a grand entrance. Stripping a pine sapling of its bark, they strung up the dried Tawakoni scalps, combed them out, and painted the scalps, the poles, and themselves red with vermilion. Dutch led the way, singing his war song and giving as many whoops as they had scalps. His village welcomed the victorious war party with great feasting and much handshaking. A scalp-dance celebration was held all through that night.

Gen. Matthew Arbuckle later reported that the Cherokees returned to the Fort Gibson area with more than sixty scalps. He said too that during the summer of 1830, Smith organized a war party to go south and conduct still another raid against the Texas tribes. Evidently this took place, for other accounts tell of a second bloody fight in which 125 Cherokees fell on a Tawakoni village near present Mexia, Texas. When the Tawakonis took refuge in caves, the Cherokees built fires and smoked them out, killing them as they ran to escape.[27]

During that same summer, a posse of U.S. dragoons and about 180 Creek Indians pursued into Texas some Caddos who had killed a Creek man. The pursuers lost the Caddos' trail in country filled with tracks of buffalo and wild horses.[28]

In making separate treaties with the Creeks of Georgia in 1826 and the Western Cherokees in 1828, the federal government had made the blunder of assigning the two Indian populations to the same area near Fort Gibson. The Osages too were still present in the vicinity. In May 1831, a council was conducted at Gibson to find a compromise. It took two long weeks to work out an agreement.

For the first ten days, the Osages and the Cherokees remained apart in sullen hostility. But finally General Arbuckle, the Cherokee agent George Vashon, the Osage agent P. L. Chouteau, the subagents Nathaniel Pryor and A. McNair, and the Creek chief Chilly McIntosh were able to devise an acceptable peace pact. The Osages returned horses they had stolen from the Creeks, Delawares, and Shawnees. Then all of the tribesmen mingled together and shook hands, essentially ending the long, bloody conflict between the Osages and the Cherokees.[29]

Though the Cherokee-Osage conflict subsided, intertribal warfare in the area between the Arkansas and Red rivers had by no means ended. Defeat at the hands of the Osages did not deter the Pawnee invaders, who threatened revenge for their losses during the 1830 and 1831 fights.

In July some four thousand Osages moved their camps to within eight or ten miles of Fort Gibson in fear of a Pawnee attack. At the same time, they sent out a war party, reinforced with two hundred Creek warriors, to meet and combat the Pawnees.[30] There is no evidence that a conflict resulted.

In the fall of 1831 Rev. Isaac McCoy, who was surveying the boundaries of the Western Cherokee country in present northeastern Oklahoma, came onto a Delaware camp. Among the Indians was a Delaware woman who, with her child, had recently escaped from the Pawnees on the Canadian River some fifty miles above the mouth of the North Canadian (near present Holdenville, Oklahoma). Her small group of two men, two women, and a child had been attacked just before sunset by a large war party of Pawnees. The woman had been a short distance away from the camp and had seen the Pawnees approaching. Unable to warn the others, she hid behind a log with her child and watched the attackers massacre her companions with bows and arrows.[31]

In July 1832 the *Arkansas Advocate* carried the report of a man who said he had seen the scalps to prove a Shawnee claim that 25 of their warriors had attacked a party of 350 Comanches. According to the Shawnees, in a fight that lasted from dawn until dusk the Comanches had lost 77 dead, whereas the Shawnee's loss was 9 killed. As a result of this report, the Shawnees, Choctaws, Kickapoos, Cherokees, and Creeks made plans for a council preparatory to conducting war on the Comanches and Pawnees.[32]

Reports were reaching Fort Gibson that the Osages were still causing trouble, this time for whites along the Red River. It was said that they had run white families out of their homes, killed stock, and made off with clothing, quilts, knives, spoons, and other goods.[33]

In February 1833, after seventeen days of council at Fort Gibson, the commissioners S. C. Stambaugh, ex-governor Montford Stokes of North Carolina, Henry R. Ellsworth, and John F. Schermerhorn worked out an agreement between the Creeks and the Cherokees regarding their land, each tribe giving up part of its treaty rights. Also, talks were held with the Osages concerning their abuse of whites on the Red River.[34]

Pawnee incursions were still continuing in 1837 when Col. A. P. Chouteau reported that the northern Indians had been raiding along the Red River, attacking the Wichitas and Wacos and badly depleting horse and mule herds. Even worse, they had wiped out an entire season's crop of corn, pumpkins, beans, and melons belonging to the Wichitas. In some instances, he said, Pawnee foragers had nearly destroyed whole towns. The Caddos too told of Pawnee raids. Chouteau reported more of the same in 1838, with the Comanches, Kiowas, Delawares, and Osages all greatly excited against the Pawnees.[35]

There was still another tribe suffering much injury from the Pawnees. When the Creeks had been moved from Georgia to present Oklahoma during and after 1828, they were a badly impoverished people. They were also severely split after the murder of their half-blood chief William McIntosh and some others over the sale of Creek lands to the United States. Gradually the industrious Creeks improved their situation, building homes and farms westward along the Canadian River.

These isolated settlements were easy prey for the Pawnees, and the Creeks began to suffer badly in murders and stolen stock. Greatly alarmed, Chief Rolly McIntosh (a brother to Chilly) called together a general council of the Indian tribes in the region at North Fork Town on the Canadian in May 1842. Attending were the Seminoles, Choctaws, Chickasaws, Cherokees, Kickapoos, Shawnees, Wichitas, Delawares, Pinakeshaws, Osages, Senecas, Quapaws, Caddos, Kichais, and Tawakonis.[36] The prairies and woods at the meeting site were filled with horses, lodges, tents, and wagons. Gen. Zachary Taylor was there to hear the chiefs agree on making an effort at establishing friendly intercourse with the Pawnees.[37]

Still another council was held by the Creeks the following year, and eventually an agreement of peace was worked out with the northern tribe. This was soon broken, however, after an Osage massacre of a party of fifteen Pawnee Mahas who had come south to barter guns and ammunition to the Comanches in return for furs and pelts, which they planned to take back north to sell at a profit to white traders.[38]

After a successful trade, the Pawnees had made the mistake of stopping at a Wichita village. An Osage visitor who was also there quietly slipped away and rode to the camp of the Osage chief Black Dog. Knowing the trail that the Pawnees would likely take back to the north, Black Dog sent his warriors to set up an ambush at the trail's crossing of the Canadian River. After several days' wait, Osage spies reported the approach of the unsuspecting Pawnees, whose horses were abundantly laden with their trade goods. When the Pawnees had made camp and gone to sleep, the Osages fell on them, killing nine men and taking a woman captive.[39]

Returning home, the Osages generously sent some of the Pawnee scalps to other tribes as an invitation to conduct an excursion against the Pawnees. During the summer of 1843, a white hunting party traveling up the Platte Trail encountered a party of about seventy Osages. The Indians, who had been out against the Pawnees and held a number of scalps, were infuriated when they discovered three Pawnees who had been tagging along with the whites. Only the intervention of two priests saved the Pawnees from being murdered.[40]

Some of the Pawnee scalps were given to the Kickapoos, who were then residing in Creek country. The Kickapoos proceeded to hold a scalp dance celebrating the defeat of their enemy to the north. When the Creek chief Chilly McIntosh heard of this, he was alarmed that it would break the peace the Creeks had made with the Pawnees. He sent a runner to persuade the Kickapoos to stop their dance.

However, this did not prevent a new flare-up in hostilities. Early in 1845 a party of Pawnees attacked a Creek settlement at the Little River junction with the Canadian and stole some horses. They were overtaken by a Creek posse, which killed six of them. On another occasion, a Pawnee was slain by the Kickapoos, who reportedly ate an arm of the victim. They sent a severed hand to the Creeks as a present.[41]

In an effort to quiet the new outbreak of hostilities among the tribes, the alarmed Creeks called for another general council of the tribes to be held at the salt plains. They ran into new trouble, however, when the Comanches, upset with encroachments onto their hunting grounds, mistreated the Creek emissaries and sent back the Creek peace emblems—tobacco encircled with white beads—charging that the Creeks had "false tongues."[42]

In June the Wichitas killed six more Pawnees in a skirmish. Nonetheless, the Pawnees accepted the Creeks' emblems of peace and agreed to meet them at the salt plains in the fall.[43] But this peace council failed to come about; and in 1846, when the Creeks sent another invitation for a salt plains meeting, the Creek delegates had to fight the Pawnees to get back home.[44]

The Pawnee intrusion into the country south of the Arkansas River reached no formal resolution. Bill Connor, a Delaware half-blood, indicated in 1851 that the Pawnee raids continued off and on for several years. The frontiersman reported that in an effort to stop the excursions, some twenty thousand Comanches had congregated on the upper Red River. Some of them were talking of conducting a war of extermination against the Pawnee Mahas.[45]

The immigrant tribes became an increasing threat to the Comanche dominance of the prairie, particularly as more of them arrived. In 1832 the U.S. government removed the Choctaw Indians of Mississippi to a body of land that today would stretch from the Oklahoma border with Arkansas to the one-hundredth meridian, which marks the Oklahoma boundary with the Texas Panhandle.

Six years later the Chickasaws of Mississippi and Alabama were also moved west and assigned a portion of the new Choctaw country. The Comanches considered these sizable tribes to be a threat to their hunting grounds. Because of this, the newcomers became the targets of depredations by the Comanches and other prairie tribes along the Red River.

Another southern tribe, the Seminoles, who had been removed from Florida to the Canadian River country of present central Oklahoma, was an especially aggressive intruder on the prairie. Chief Wild Cat (Coacoochee), who had decided to form an Indian colony in Mexico, recruited a following of Seminoles, Creeks, Kickapoos, freed and escaped slaves, a few Cherokees, and a number of Seminole-black families. He hoped to form an alliance with the Comanches to secure a land grant in Mexico just south of the Rio Grande.

In December 1849, Wild Cat led his group to the Brazos River, where during the ensuing spring they planted crops. In the fall of 1850, he returned to the Canadian River to propose that the entire Seminole tribe, as well as blacks of the area, move with him. The Creeks, already disturbed over the loss of slaves, marshaled their warriors to resist Wild Cat. In the meantime, the Comanches attacked the Brazos settlement, captured the blacks, and ransomed them to a Creek war party. Many other blacks trying to escape across the plains to Mexico, where slavery was illegal, were captured by the Comanches and either killed or ransomed.[46]

Wild Cat took the remnants of his mixed band on to Mexico and settled across the Rio Grande from Eagle Pass. There he was joined by a party of some five hundred Kickapoos. From this base, the Seminoles, Kickapoos, and others raided the settlements in southern Texas. While scouting for Mexico against hostile Plains Indians in 1857, Wild Cat and many of his men died from an outbreak of smallpox. After his death, most of his remaining Indian followers returned to the Canadian River.[47]

The Delawares, Shawnees, and Kickapoos were among the Indian Territory tribes that regularly invaded the prairie, generally with better arms than those possessed by the Comanches and often ready to engage in hostilities. On one occasion, a mostly Delaware party of twelve or more met a Comanche war party that had returned north of the Red River after a raid into Texas. The raiders bragged of their exploits and exhibited a war shield that was adorned with the scalps of fifteen or twenty women. The Delawares camped near the Comanches and joined them that night for a gambling session. While the games were going on, other Delawares cut the strings on the Comanches bows so that they would break when used. Then, at dawn, the Delawares attacked the Plains warriors, killing all but one whom they let escape to tell his people of their deed.[48]

The challenge of tribes from the north and of emigrant nations contributed much to the erosion of Comanche dominance on the Comanchería. But there was still another player, one that would soon prove to be an even greater threat to the Comanches and the other tribes of the southern plains.

CHAPTER 10

The American Presence

AT the start of the 1830s the influence of the United States extended west of the Territory of Arkansas only as far as the famed Cross Timbers. This line of scrub oak and heavy brush reached from the Cimarron River of present Oklahoma southward to the Brazos River of Texas. It served as a recognized landmark of the region, indicating the division between the eastern wooded country and the western prairie. Fort Gibson, at the conflux of the Grand and Arkansas rivers, and Fort Towson, at the mouth of the Kiamichi on the Red River, constituted the forward extensions of U.S. military presence.

On the north of the Comanchería, the Americans had opened the trading route known as the Santa Fe Trail. American and Mexican caravans were bringing an ever increasing number of intruders across the empire of the Plains Indians. Now began the first incidents of conflict between the native tribes and the whites who called themselves Americans.

During the summer of 1831 the highly respected mountain man and western explorer Jedediah Smith was guiding a wagon train to Santa Fe. While searching for water in the arid Oklahoma Panhandle, Smith was waylaid and killed, probably by Comanches. In 1832 a party of twelve American traders headed by Judge W. C. Carr of St. Louis was returning from Santa Fe to Missouri. Near present Lathrop in the Texas Panhandle they were attacked by a combined force of Kiowas and Comanches.

For some thirty-six hours the traders were besieged by the Indians. Finally, under cover of darkness, they slipped out of their trap and escaped, leaving behind all of their goods and a considerable amount of Mexican specie—the same found by the Osages when they massacred the Kiowa village the following year. Five of the survivors later stumbled into Fort Gibson after a grueling trek across the prairie.[1]

Private parties of trappers, hunters, and traders also began to venture beyond the Cross Timbers into the mysterious domain of the Comanches and the Wichitas. On one such occasion Albert Pike—an Arkansas lawyer, poet, and, later, Confederate general—joined a small party in safely traversing the prairie via the Red River to Santa Fe and back to Arkansas in 1831–32.[2]

The first official American exploration to the Cross Timbers was made in the fall of 1832 by a unit of U.S. Rangers under Capt. Jesse Bean from Fort Gibson. Accompanied by a party that included the noted writer Washington Irving, the rangers explored up the Cimarron, then followed the Cross Timbers to the Canadian River before turning back to Gibson. They saw deer, black bear, buffalo, and wild horses; but the only Indians they encountered were a party of Osages returning from a hunt—not the much dreaded Pawnee Picts (Taovayas).[3]

In the spring of 1833, concerned about the threat that the Plains tribes posed to travelers, Gen. Matthew Arbuckle at Fort Gibson issued orders for two companies of Seventh Infantry (mounted) and three companies of mounted rangers under Col. James B. Many to reconnoiter west of the Cross Timbers. If the force should meet hostile Indians east of the Washita, they were to drive them westward.

However, if peaceful Indians were encountered on the upper Red River, Many was to present them gifts of medals and flags and invite them to Gibson for talks.[4]

It was during this expedition, while west of the Blue River, that one of the rangers, Lt. George B. Abbay of Missouri, went off from camp alone to hunt. A large band of Indians, no one knew which tribe, grabbed Abbay and carried him off. Colonel Many followed the Indians' trail as far as the Washita, which was in flood stage. After several days of fruitless scouring of the country, the command began to run out of provisions.

Colonel Many decided to push on into buffalo country, where meat could be procured. Though game was plentiful as they neared the Wichita Mountains, the troops were becoming ill and their horses badly jaded. The weary, discouraged command finally returned to Gibson after having lost the one man and making no contact with the Indians.[5]

The kidnapping of Abbay caused American officials serious concern, which intensified after another incident in May 1833. Judge Gabriel N. Martin, a planter who resided along the Red River in what was then Miller County, Arkansas (now eastern Oklahoma), had taken his son and some servants on a hunt to the Washita country. There they were attacked by Indians, the judge was killed, and his nine-year-old son, Matthew Wright Martin, was carried off along with one of the slaves. American authorities resolved to send a sizable military expedition into the Comanche country in an attempt to rescue both Abbay and the Martin captives and at the same time make a show of strength that would impress and intimidate the Indians.[6]

A large dragoon expedition, commanded by Gen. Henry Leavenworth and accompanied by George Catlin, the Indian artist, departed Fort Gibson in July 1834. The command marched southwestward to the mouth of the Washita, where Fort Washita was under construction. A severe malady that struck men and horses alike forced Leavenworth to turn his command over to Col. Henry Dodge, who

Catlin shows the Leavenworth expedition of 1834 being received by the warriors of a Comanche village near the Wichita Mountains. (Catlin, *North American Indians* 2, pl. 163)

pushed on west toward the Wichita Mountains with a made-up unit of healthy men. After an uneventful march, the dragoons found a large Comanche village of nearly two hundred lodges near the Wichita Mountains. The Indians welcomed them in peace and without any evidence of fear.

The Comanches, whose chief was absent, professed to know nothing of the missing dragoon officer or the captured boy and slave. They said that such a boy, however, had been seen among the Toyash (or Taovayas), who then resided to the west of the Wichita Mountains. Following a rugged course around the southern foothills of the mountains, Dodge located a Wichita village in the deep canyon of the North Fork of the Red River. There he held talks with the seventy-year-old We-ter-ra-sharro, the Wichita chief; with the Comanche chief Ta-we-que-nah (probably Taba-queena, or the Big Eagle), who arrived later; and with Titche-toche-cha (or the Black Bird) of the Kiowas. He also found and rescued young Matthew Wright Martin and his father's former slave from the Wichitas.

Dodge won the friendship of the Indians by returning two girls who had been captives of the Osages. One was a Wichita and one was the Kiowa girl captured in the 1833 massacre, her brother having been killed by a ram at Fort Gibson. By restoring the girls to their respective families, Dodge was able to persuade some twenty headmen and others to accompany him to Gibson for a peace council. These included Titche-toche-cha, We-ter-ra-sharro, We-ta-ra-yah of the Wacos, and His-oo-san-chez, a Comanche warrior of Mexican blood. The deadly sickness still prevailed among the dragoons as they made a punishing return march. En route it was learned from a courier that General Leavenworth had died while trying to catch up with Dodge's command.

On September 2, a meeting was conducted at Gibson by Dodge and Indian Bureau Superintendent F. W. Armstrong with the prairie Indians and eastern tribes—the Osages, Cherokees, Creeks, Choctaws, and Senecas. Armstrong opened the meeting by expressing the government's desire to bring about peace between the Osages and the prairie tribes. He promised the Kiowas that he would try to obtain and restore the taíme medicine bag taken by the Osages the previous year.

The Western Cherokees were represented by Chiefs John Rogers and Thomas Chisholm, who presented gifts of white beads and tobacco to the prairie Indians. They were emblems of "peace and purity." Chisholm noted, "When you smoke the tobacco of friendship, all evil will go off with the smoke."[7]

Titche-toche-cha of the Kiowas was eager to make peace with the Osages, who were such a threat to his people. He embraced and shook hands with the haughty and aloof Chief Clermont. However, the Kiowa was anxious to receive the presents that Dodge had promised and return home. His speech was short and to the point: "I have not much to say. I have shaken hands with you. I wish to continue at peace with you. I am not fond of words. The

Comanche chief Ta-wah-que-nah (or Mountain of Rocks) welcomed the U.S. dragoons to his village. (Catlin, *North American Indians* 2, pl. 109)

His-oo-san-ches (note the last two syllables) was a Mexican captive boy who became a Comanche warrior. (Catlin, *North American Indians* 2, pl. 172)

road is now open to all our Red Brethren. They shall come to us in safety and we will receive them with open hearts."[8]

The Wichita chief too was especially concerned about ending the Osage forays into his country. "Why are there not more Osages here?" he asked. "It is they we wish most to see. . . . They have one of my people, my sister's child. I want them to restore the girl."[9]

The Waco chief, We-ta-ra-yah, was pleased with his visit. "I see it is the white man who will be our friend. White men have all the things we want. We have been a long time at war with our Red Brethren here; we have warred much with the Osages. . . . We will hereafter throw aside our bad practices."[10]

Clermont replied by noting that the Osages now lived in peace with the whites and that the prairie tribes should

We-tara-sha-ro was the head chief
of the Wichita Indians at the time
of the visit by Col. Henry Dodge.
(Catlin, *North American Indians*
2, pl. 174)

do the same. "Tell your friends when you go home. They must listen to all that the white people say to them. You may see among the Osages many chiefs, many great men; but look upon me and behold the Great Chief of the Osages. When my people are informed that Clermos [Clermont] has shaken hands with you, it will be enough. They will all shake hands with you."[11]

Responding to this encouragement and that of the U.S. commissioners and Cherokee leaders, the prairie chiefs agreed to make peace with the Osages. Silver peace medals and U.S. flags were presented to the Indians. Vows of friendship were made by all, and it was agreed that a treaty-making council would be held in the buffalo country, where all the tribes could conveniently attend.[12]

The Treaty of Camp Holmes, held during the summer

of 1835 near present Lexington, Oklahoma, was the first pact made between the United States and the Comanche, Wichita, and Plains Apache tribes. The site was located in advance by Maj. Richard B. Mason, commanding a regiment of the First U.S. Dragoons, along with the Osage agent Col. Auguste P. Chouteau. The prairie bands began arriving in June to spread their camps along the Canadian River and its tributary, Chouteau Creek.[13]

The Indians, seven thousand of them, had come en masse with families and all of their possessions, leaving their hunting grounds in expectation of finding food and presents. However, the U.S. commission party dallied at Fort Gibson during most of the scorching hot month of July. With little buffalo in the area, the Indians soon grew very hungry and more and more discontent. The chiefs complained to Mason that the white man had agreed to come when the grass was in the blade, not in the leaf.[14]

An attempt was made by the battle-scarred Comanche chief Taba-queena (the Big Eagle) to get others to join him in an attack on the small party of dragoons and steal their mounts. His scheme was defeated when the Comanche head chief, Ichacoly (the Wolf), an impressive figure of a man, persuaded the tribes to remain peaceful and wait a while longer. During late July a party of Comanches, eight men and seven women, rode to Fort Gibson to find out what was causing the delay. They were given pipes, tobacco, handkerchiefs, shirts, and other presents and were promised more at the council.[15] However, by the time the commission arrived on August 19, the Kiowas, along with some of the Comanches and Wichitas, had packed their tents and goods onto their lodge-pole travois and disappeared onto the uncharted prairie.[16]

Arriving with the commission party were delegations from the Cherokees, Choctaws, Creeks, Senecas, Quapaws, and Osages who, along with the United States, hoped to work out peace arrangements with the prairie tribes. Finally, on the twenty-second, the council got under way with speeches by the commissioners and various chiefs. All indicated their desire for peace and harmony. Ichacoly, who claimed that he spoke for all the Comanches, expressed his wish for peace with the Osages, saying, "Half of my body belongs to the Osages and half to the Comanches."[17]

The treaty, completed on August 24, bore the names of 149 prairie and immigrant Indians. Ichacoly was the lead signatory for the Comanches, followed by Queen-a-sha-no (the War Eagle) and then Taba-queena. Signing for the Wichitas were Kano-sto-wah (the Man Who Doesn't Speak) and Ko-sha-rok-ah (the Man Who Marries His Wife Twice).

According to the pact, the tribes would forgive and forget injuries from others and pay for injuries committed by themselves. They would return property stolen by their members; the prairie tribes would permit other tribes to hunt freely west of the Cross Timbers; and all the tribes would maintain perpetual peace and friendship with the United States. This first attempt to establish a lasting peace with the prairie tribes would ultimately prove to be a failure, the pact soon being renounced by the Comanches. It did, however, bring about a tenuous cessation of the long warfare between the Comanches and the Osages.

At the same time that the council was being held at Camp Holmes, the authority of the United States was being extended on the northern edge of the Comanchería at Bent's Fort. Col. Henry Dodge, who the year before had visited the Comanches and Wichitas, led a 125-man exploring expedition out of Fort Leavenworth. Marching westward up the Platte, Dodge had stopped to hold councils with the Pawnees, Otos, and Arikaras. Wishing to end their war with the Cheyennes, the Pawnee chiefs sent a peace party of 100 men with Dodge. They accompanied him on his march to the mountains and then south past the site of present Denver to the Arkansas River.

Near the site of present Pueblo, the expedition met a camp of fifty Arapahos. The Arapahos had been warring with the Utes, from whom they had recently stolen some two hundred horses. Continuing downstream, Dodge encountered a band of Cheyennes headed out on a foray against the Comanches. Another large war party had been out in the same direction for some time.

Dodge found the Cheyennes to be friendly. But the band was in a seriously depraved state because their principal chief, High-Backed Wolf, had recently been killed in a family quarrel. Their people were also badly debauched by whiskey obtained from Taos traders. Dodge was told that the order in which the Cheyenne warriors valued the goods of the world was whiskey first, then tobacco, guns, horses, and, lastly, women.

The Cheyennes stated that they were at war with the Comanches, Kiowas, Pawnees, and Arikaras. Despite these conflicts, a band of Kiowas, known as the Upper Band, and the Plains Apaches, numbering about two thousand, also frequented the areas around Bent's Fort, as did northern tribes such as the Blackfeet, Arikaras, and Gros Ventres.

On August 16 Dodge helped effect a peace between the Cheyennes and the Pawnees. The Pawnees presented fifty guns to the Cheyennes, and the Cheyennes gave a hundred horses to the Pawnees. Peace between the two tribes was ill-fated, however, as long as the Pawnees continued to hold the Cheyennes' Sacred Medicine Arrows. As for the United States, Dodge told the chiefs that the great American father had no wish to take any of their land, that he wished only for the tribes to stop their warfare and be friends.

Earlier in the summer, the Osages had paid a visit to the Cheyennes and made peace with them. It was reported also that a band of Osages had visited the Comanches on the Red River to confirm peace agreements made during the Leavenworth-Dodge expedition of 1834. Before the Dodge expedition left the area, the trader William Bent arrived back at his post from a trip to the Red River. He said that he had visited among two thousand Comanches, who had treated him kindly.[18]

After the Treaty of Camp Holmes, Maj. P. L. Chouteau, the brother of Col. A. P. Chouteau, made a near-heroic effort to locate the Kiowas. He went first to Coffee's trading

A painting by George Catlin of High-Backed Wolf, the much-re-spected principal chief of the Cheyennes, who was killed by his own people during a family quarrel. (Smithsonian Institution)

post on the Red River, then westward to Cache Creek, without success. After two days' travel on up the Red, he located bands of Tawakonis and Wacos, who directed him to a Wichita village. The Wichitas said he could find the Kiowas to the south in Texas. Chouteau headed off to the headwaters of the Colorado, scouring the region until his horses were almost worn out. Finally he stumbled onto a combined camp of Comanches, Kiowas, and Plains Apaches. The tribes were just starting on their seasonal journey northward to hunt buffalo after conducting raids against the Texans and the Mexicans.[19]

Moving with them back to Cache Creek, Chouteau held talks with the chiefs. Though skeptical of the idea, the Kiowas reluctantly agreed to send emissaries to Fort Gibson in early May of 1836. They failed to do so, however, and continued their raiding to the south and against other nations.[20] During the winter of 1836–37, Chouteau sent his son Edward and four others to contact the tribes in their winter camps below the Red. Edward reported that the Comanches, realizing that other tribes had been given free access to their hunting grounds, were very angry and hostile. They had, in fact, burned their copy of the Camp Holmes treaty and were threatening to attack the trading post that Col. A. P. Chouteau had established near the Camp Holmes treaty site.

The Comanches, Kiowas, and Wichitas were carrying on extensive raids against the Texas frontier, taking many prisoners. The Comanches, Edward Chouteau estimated, held some thirty to forty captives. During the spring of 1837, a Comanche war party brought three white prisoners in to Camp Holmes to show their desire for peace. In April Colonel Chouteau, for whom the Indians had great regard, was prevailed on to make an effort at bringing in the prairie tribes, particularly the Kiowas. He did so, arriving at Fort Gibson in May with chiefs of the Kiowas, Tawakonis, and Plains Apaches. A treaty involving those tribes, the Osages, and the United States was initiated, its principal item being the freedom of all Indian nations to hunt and trap on the prairie.

After shaking hands with and embracing the Osage chief Clermont, the Kiowa chief Titche-toche-cha told him: "I have shaken hands with you. . . . The road is now open to all our Red Brethren. They shall come to us in safety and we will receive them with open hearts."[21]

The government had asked Col. A. P. Chouteau to gather a delegation of Comanches and Kiowas and escort them to Washington, D.C. Chouteau, however, died before he could carry out the mission.[22] In the spring of 1839, frontiersmen Jesse Chisholm and John Conner gathered a delegation of Comanche and Kiowa chiefs and took them as far as the Choctaw Agency at Skullyville, Indian Territory. However, flooded rivers and lack of food stymied them there. The chiefs were given presents of blankets, knives, tobacco, and cloth and escorted back to the Plains.[23]

The Hamilton, Tennessee, *Gazette,* observing the ruthless removal of the Cherokees to the Indian Territory in 1838, had clearly foreseen the continuing press of whites westward, observing: "This is not all; another and another wave of emigration by the whites will continue to roll around the Indian frontiers, until its surge shall overlap its bounds."[24]

Already the trails to Oregon and Santa Fe were becoming more and more crowded with wagons and other American transportation. However, the first Anglo-American challenge to Indian dominance of the southern Plains would be made by the Anglo-Texans.

CHAPTER 11

The Texas Frontier Wars

EVEN while under Mexican rule, Anglo-Americans in Texas were often in conflict with the tribes native to the area. One such clash was reported by Razin P. Bowie during a visit to Philadelphia. By his account, he lead eleven Americans who left San Antonio in November 1831 for the San Saba mission, where they hoped to locate a lost Spanish silver mine. One of the group was Razin's brother, James Bowie, who was destined to die at the Alamo five years later.

En route they were met by two Comanches and a Mexican captive who had stolen a drove of Tawakoni and Waco horses. The Americans gave the three some powder, lead, and tobacco and continued on. The next morning the Mexican reappeared. He had been sent by his Comanche master to warn them that 124 Tawakonis and 40 Wacos were on their trail. Indeed, while they were camped at a spring only six miles from the abandoned San Saba fort, the small band of Americans came under attack.

The men were forced to dismount and build defensive fortifications. Although their situation was desperate, they managed to hold off their attackers and exact a heavy toll during eight days of seige. When the Indians finally withdrew, the Americans made their way back to San Antonio having suffered one man killed and three wounded.[1]

The Indian policy of Texas, both as a republic and as a state, followed a wavering path of conciliation and pacification on the one hand and a course of ruthless extermination on the other. Most early Texas settlers and many Texas leaders held a bitter hatred for the Indians, who raided homes, murdered settlers, stole stock, and carried off women and children into captivity. Yet, for many years, Texas Indian policy was set by a man who had a great understanding and compassion for the Indian.

Sam Houston had lived among the Cherokees as a boy in Tennessee and later on the Arkansas River of Indian Territory before coming to Texas. After an unfortunate marriage that had caused him to resign as governor of Tennessee, Houston had come west to Fort Gibson. There he operated his Wigwam Neosho trading post and cohabited with a half-Cherokee, Diana Rogers.[2] In 1833 he headed south; three years later he found fame as the leading figure in the Texas Revolution and became the first president of the new Republic of Texas.

Houston's sincere affection for the Cherokees had a strong influence on the Indian policy of Texas. However, even his unceasing efforts to find peaceful resolutions to the Indian problems of Texas were not enough. The hatred and fear that Texas whites held for Indians and the settlers' determination to take over the land were too powerful. Within twenty-five years after winning their independence in 1836, Texans had driven every major Indian tribe from their soil.

The Cherokees were not native to Texas; a small group under Chief Bowl had entered Texas in 1819 or 1820, eventually settling in the forested lands of East Texas well ahead of any white colonists. Houston had done everything he could to validate the Cherokee claim to the land on which they resided, even signing a treaty with them in 1836 verifying the claim. But white resentment of the Cherokee presence inside Texas was fanned to bloody resolution in 1838 and 1839.

In October 1838 eighteen members of the Killough family in Cherokee County were massacred. Despite a lack of evidence that the Cherokees were responsible, Texans held them to blame.[3] The rancor against the Cherokees rose even higher when it was learned that Mexican authorities had contacted Bowl and his chiefs in the hope of stirring them to an uprising. But most damaging to the Cherokees' situation, perhaps, was the election of the Indian-antagonist Mirabeau Buonaparte Lamar as president of the Republic of Texas in November. Lamar had come to Texas from Georgia, where the Cherokees had been severely abused by whites.

Houston had been restraining an army under Gen. Thomas Jefferson Rusk, who had advanced on the Cherokee settlement to quell the threat of six hundred Mexicans in the area. But when Lamar took over the presidency from Houston, he initiated a determined policy to rid Texas of the Cherokees. Ignoring the Houston treaty, Lamar appointed a commission to issue an ultimatum to Chiefs Bowl and Big Mush.

The Cherokees were to abandon their homes in Texas and join the main body of Cherokees in present Oklahoma. They were to be paid a fair price for their property. The eighty-three-year-old Bowl, knowing the danger that a fight with the Texans meant to his women and children, might have agreed had it not been for a couple of the terms of the agreement.

The Cherokees did not wish to be escorted out of Texas as if they had been defeated and were prisoners under guard. Also, the warriors rejected point-blank the demand that they give up their gunlocks, fearing the Texans would kill them the moment they were disarmed. When Bowl refused to sign the treaty, the Texas army moved against the Cherokee camp. It was empty, but the Indians' trail was clear. The Texans set out in pursuit. Late in the afternoon of July 14, they encountered a group of Cherokee warriors who held a hilltop.

The warriors charged Rusk's advance several times without effect before taking cover in a thicket at the bottom of a ravine on the Texans' left. Rusk now brought his main force forward and advanced on the thicket, repulsing a Cherokee attack on the right flank. Shortly before sunset the Cherokees were driven from the field, leaving behind eighteen of their dead as well as five valuable kegs of gunpowder, 250 pounds of lead, and much of their livestock and supplies. The Texans had three men killed and five wounded.

Rusk continued his pursuit the following morning. In the afternoon his advance force contacted the Cherokees, who were strongly entrenched in a ravine near the Neches River. The Texans dismounted to fight on foot. As they were doing so, the Indians attacked, killing one man and several horses. Despite a stout resistance by the Cherokees, the Texans made a relentless advance. After a fight of an hour and a half, the Cherokees were routed. Their losses this time were much larger, with an estimated one hundred killed and wounded.

Among the Cherokee dead was Chief Bowl. Riding a beautiful sorrel horse with blazed feet, wearing a black military hat, silk vest, and sash, and wielding a sword—all gifts presented to him by his close friend Sam Houston—the elderly leader had made a conspicuous figure on the battlefield. Even the Texans were impressed with the courage and defiance of the Cherokee leader.

When his mount was shot from under him, Bowl rose and began walking away with great dignity. It was then that a Texas bullet struck him in the back. One admiring Texan went forward to protect him from further harm, but not in time to stop a militia captain who ran up and shot Bowl in the head, killing him instantly. It was said that later the Cherokee's body was scalped and that strips of hide were cut from his back to make bridle reins for a victorious Texan.[4]

The defeated Cherokees fled in all directions, many to Indian Territory, some to Arkansas, and one group to Mexico. The Texans pursued for several days, destroying cornfields and burning houses wherever found. Chief Big Mush survived the ordeal, escaping to Indian Territory, where he lived out his life on the Canadian River.

The Texas victory was complete; it had rid the republic of resident Cherokees. But there were still other tribes, principally the Comanches, to be dealt with. Even as the Texas army was attacking the Cherokees in northeastern Texas, rangers and volunteer forces of the republic were conducting search-and-slaughter expeditions against the Comanches of central and western Texas.

The Comanches posed an even greater threat to Texas sovereignty than the Cherokees. They had begun to strike back against the Anglo-Americans and European immigrants who were moving up from the coastal region beyond San Antonio and westward onto the Edwards Plateau. The result was a series of conflicts—in reality, an undeclared war—between the Texans and the Comanches and other tribes that stood in the path of Texas advancement.

The Comanches had long conducted wholesale war against the Mexican rancherias and settlements. By the start of the eighteenth century, the warrior strength of the Comanche Nation was overwhelming throughout the province of Texas. With the Spanish colonies reflecting the deterioration of the Spanish crown, the mission-presidio system of military and civilian administration in the Mexican north country collapsed. Despite the increasing Anglo-American thrust into western Texas, the Comanches enjoyed a virtually unopposed concourse directly into Mexico.[5]

As a result, the pueblos and haciendas became regular targets of brutal raids by the Comanches. For nearly half a century these Indians looted, destroyed, murdered, and scalped, stealing mules and horses and taking captives with impunity. Their mastery of the defenseless Mexicans misled the Comanches into the belief that they could run roughshod over any non-Indian.

Certainly they had no great concern about the growing body of whites, mostly descendants of southern frontiersmen, whose settlements were beginning to spread up along the Brazos and Colorado rivers into the Comanche raiding path to Mexico. However, an intense hostility between these two vastly different peoples soon began to develop. A clash was inevitable.

The first significant event occurred in 1836 on the Navasota River near Mexia, Texas, where a Tennessee family named Parker had settled and constructed a log stockade-fort. During the spring of that year, the fort was approached by a large band of Indians comprised mostly of Comanches. Benjamin Parker, the titular head of the settlement, went out to talk with the war party, only to be surrounded and lanced to death.

Before the inhabitants had time to close the gates, the shrieking Indians rode their horses inside the stockade and began a bloody melee. They killed and mutilated the men and raped the women. When Lucy Parker attempted to escape with her four children, mounted warriors took them captive. She and two of the children were saved by the brave action of David Faulkenberry, but the other two children were carried off. These were John Parker, age six, and his nine-year-old sister, Cynthia Ann, who was destined to become legendary on the plains as the mother of Comanche chief Quanah Parker.[6]

This tragedy, which seared a deep hatred into the souls of Texans, was essentially the beginning of the Comanche-Texas war—a war in which white, and occasionally black, settlers became the frontline victims. There were many more people to be killed and many more women and children to be taken captive before the Texans could put up effective resistance.

Disadvantaged by the slowness of their workhorses as well as by their poor horsemanship, single-shot pistols, and muzzle-loading hunting rifles, the settlers were no match for the well-mounted Comanche warriors, who attacked by surprise. The Indian could fire numerous arrows while the Texan was attempting to reprime his clumsy weapon. It was only when the hard-riding, aggressive Texas Ranger force was provided with the repeating Colt revolver that the Comanches' superiority in battle was threatened.[7]

As a part of Lamar's tough punitive policy, in early 1839 an expedition of rangers, volunteers, and Indian scouts was organized to make a strike against the Comanches. The force of sixty-three Texans and sixteen Lipan and Tonkawa scouts set out from La Grange in late January under the command of Col. John H. Moore. Riding with the group was Andrew Lockhart, whose daughter Matilda had been captured by the Comanches.

After marching up the Colorado River for over two weeks, they were finally rewarded when scouts reported that they had located a Comanche village on Spring Creek, a tributary of the San Saba. Leaving their baggage train behind, the Texas force slipped up on the village and surrounded it during the night. In the cold predawn of February 15, they charged into the village on foot, catching the Indians completely by surprise. Jerking open the flaps of tipis or simply pulling the lodges down, the Texans killed the occupants even as they still lay in their buffalo-robe beds. The camp erupted in a pandemonium of gunfire, screaming women and children, and barking dogs.

When the Comanche warriors counterattacked, Moore ordered his men to fall back. He later said he did so because the gunsmoke made it difficult to define targets and because his men needed to reload their weapons. However, the Lipan chief Castro was so disgusted at Moore's action that he took his men and departed. The rangers retired to where their horses were being held, only to find that the Comanches had driven off forty-six of them. As a result, many of the men were forced to make the long return home on foot.[8]

Shortly after the battle, the Comanches sent an emissary, a Lipan woman, under a flag of truce to talk with the Texans and arrange an exchange of prisoners. The move was too late—the Lipans had already murdered the captured Comanches. As a result, it was impossible to rescue Matilda Lockhart and the four other white captives held by the Comanches.[9]

The continuing depredations against frontier settlements along the upper Brazos, Colorado, and Trinity rivers caused the Texas congress to authorize the formation of several Texas Ranger units for three months' service. One company of fifty-nine men was raised in Austin under the command of Capt. John Bird. In late May 1839, Bird and his men were camped on the Little River north of Austin when a Comanche hunting party chased a buffalo herd through their camp.

The rangers pursued what they thought to be a small group of Indians, only to end up pinned down in a ravine by a force of 240 warriors. During the fracas, the Indians formed a long battle line and made a war-whooping charge on the rangers. The gunfire of the Texans beat them back, with a considerable loss of men. Afterward, the warriors broke off the engagement and departed, leaving the rangers to count their own dead—seven lifeless rangers lay scattered about, among them Captain Bird.[10]

Just how much the Comanches were influenced by Lamar's policy of attacking their camps is debatable. But early in 1840, the Comanches sent three chiefs to San Antonio to suggest a peace council. The Texans agreed, on the condition that the Comanches bring in all of their white captives. The Comanche emissaries departed San Antonio, leaving the small mission settlement of Texans, Mexican laborers, and garrison troops to wait anxiously for the arrival of their prairie guests with the captives. Finally, on the morning of March 19, 1840, a guard spotted a long line of horsemen moving across the land swells toward the town.

Immediately the alarm was sounded. Many of the Mexican inhabitants, who had long known the dread of Comanche raiders, fled to their homes to watch with trembling fascination as the tribesmen rode single file into the public square. The Texans stood with weapons close at hand as they prepared to greet the visitors.

The Comanches, indeed, presented an imposing sight. Their bronze bodies were decorated with paint. Their long, black braids floated in the breeze as they sat their

This sketch of San Antonio de Béxar shows the settlement as it was in 1840 when the Comanche chiefs were massacred there. (Western History Collections, University of Oklahoma)

prancing, well-trained horses. Their arrow-filled quivers and the lances atilt over their heads proclaimed their readiness for war if necessary. At their lead was a tall war captain, Chief Mook-war-ruh (or the Spirit Talker), whose stately bearing, unflinching gaze, and fierce countenance clearly revealed that he and his people had come to talk peace not out of weakness or fear but as the defiant masters of the Comanchería.

Through an interpreter, the commissioners representing the Republic of Texas invited the Comanche leaders to dismount and enter the courthouse. The Texans also asked that the visitors lay aside their arms. The Comanches ignored the request. They carried their bows, arrows, and knives with them as they entered the council room and seated themselves in a circle on the dirt floor of the small building.

The Comanche chiefs had felt secure enough under the truce to bring their families with them and set up camp inside the San Antonio plaza. Instead of returning all of their captives, as requested, they had brought only one. This was sixteen-year-old Matilda Lockhart, whose scarred body and face evidenced her abuse by the Indians. Her condition and story aroused the seething hatred imbedded in the Texans.

The Texas leaders had already determined that if all the prisoners were not brought in, they would hold the chiefs as hostages. When Chief Mook-war-ruh attempted to barter other Comanche captives for goods, the Texans made their move. Guards surrounded the chiefs while the interpreter, with great trepidation, informed them that twelve of them were to be held as prisoners against the return of the captives.

The Comanches, infuriated by this betrayal of the truce and by no means willing to be taken without a fight, leaped into action. Sounding their war cries, they rushed the guards in an effort to escape, showering the room with arrows and fighting hand-to-hand with knives as they made their way to the door. Emerging into the courtyard, they were met by a barrage of gunfire for which their weapons were no match.

Most of the Comanche chiefs were killed in the plaza, but one escaped to the shelter of a stone house and fought from behind a grated window. With him was his wife, a woman who dressed much like a Comanche male and carried a long knife in her waistband. Together the two put up such fierce resistance that they could not be dislodged from the house. Finally a Texan climbed on top of the building, cut a hole in the roof, and dropped a ball of burning turpentine onto the Indians. The warrior and his wife dashed ablaze into the street, where they were cut down by rifle fire.[11]

In the melee all of the chiefs were killed, along with several Comanche women and children—thirty-three in all. About that many more women and children, many of them wounded, were captured. Seven Texans had been killed, and ten more were wounded. One of the captured Indian women, the wife of a chief, was put on a horse and sent back to her people to warn them that if the other white captives were not released in twelve days, the Comanches held at San Antonio would be executed. It was a sad miscalculation by the Texans. Instead of releasing the captives, the enraged Comanches tortured many of them to death.

A force of some three hundred Comanche warriors then descended on San Antonio looking for battle and hoping to rescue their kindred. They screamed insults and challenges at the Texans, who remained behind the Alamo mission walls and withheld their fire. It was not the Comanches' style of fighting to assault a fortification, and they finally gave up and rode back to their camps.

But they had not given up in their desire for revenge. A new war leader, Pochenaquaheip (Buffalo Hump), had risen to prominence among the southern Comanches. Under the command of this shrewd tactician, a large, well-armed Comanche force was organized on the Edwards Plateau west of San Antonio. There would be no attempt to storm the fortified mission town; instead Buffalo Hump aimed his strike at the defenseless Texas settlements scattered south and east of San Antonio.

Silently bypassing the town at night, the Comanches reached the coastal town of Victoria. There they killed several people—whites and slaves—speared cattle to death, and set some buildings ablaze before being driven off by the gunfire of the townspeople. From there Buffalo Hump's raiders swept on toward Port Lavaca, leaving behind a trail of dead settlers and burned homes. At the small port town of Linnville the Comanches came across a warehouse stacked high with goods awaiting transfer. The colorful bolts of cloth, women's wear, high hats, and umbrellas immediately caught the attention of the Indians.

Loading these and other goods aboard some of the many horses and mules they had captured, the jubilant Comanches headed back for their home camps. Now encumbered with the loot as well as their prisoners and the large herd of stolen animals, Buffalo Hump chose to return by a more direct route, to the north of San Antonio. This proved to be a fatal mistake. Waiting for him at Plum Creek was a

Tonkawa chief Placido, *left*, highly regarded as a peacemaker in Texas, was killed during the Wichita Agency massacre of 1863. *Right*, Caddo Indians, such as this warrior, who originally occupied East Texas, were among other Texas Indians that were driven north of the Red River into the Indian Territory. (Homer Thrall, *A Pictorial History of Texas* [St. Louis, 1879])

force of Texas Rangers and Tonkawa Indians under Capt. Ben McCulloch. In the engagement that followed, the Comanches were badly mauled and routed. After killing many of their prisoners and abandoning their loot, the Comanches fled. They left behind over eighty of their dead.

Nor was this the end of the trouble. In September and October 1840, Moore conducted another Indian-hunting campaign up the Colorado River, deep into the Comanchería. This operation was considerably more successful than his first. With a command of ninety volunteers and twelve Lipan scouts, Moore made a foray through the country west of present Abilene, Texas. After nearly three weeks of scouring the mesquite prairie of West Texas, he located a Comanche village camped in a bend of the

Colorado River three hundred miles west of Austin. The camp was estimated to contain sixty families and well over a hundred warriors.

Again waiting until daybreak, Moore's command charged the Comanche camp, this time on horseback. Most of the Indians not killed on the initial charge were picked off by rifle fire or were chased and either shot or cut down with sabers. Moore later claimed that forty-eight dead Comanches were left on the bloody battleground while some eighty more were either killed or drowned in the river as they attempted to flee. The Texans suffered only two men wounded. After burning the village and its equipage, Moore and his triumphant force returned to Austin with five hundred captured horses plus some of the goods taken at Linnville the preceding summer.[12]

In 1841, Texas fought a border war with both Mexican troops and Mexican bandits. This limited but did not stop its warring efforts against the Comanches. During the summer, Capt. Jack Hays, with a force of thirty-five men, attacked a small group of Indians near Uvalde Canyon west of San Antonio, killing ten and taking two prisoners. Returning to San Antonio, Hays recruited several more men, plus ten Lipan guides, and headed west in search of more Indians. On the Llano River he found a Comanche village on the move with packhorses and travois. When some one hundred warriors placed themselves between their families and the rangers, Hays attacked with twenty-five men. A running fight ensued, with several Indians being killed.[13]

Campaigning against the Indians was restrained during the remainder of the summer, in part because of the capture of the Lamar-sponsored Texas Expedition to New Mexico. The purpose of this large group of merchants, military men, and adventurers was to establish trading relations with Santa Fe—and, if things went well, to establish Texas authority over New Mexico in accordance with the treaty signed by Santa Anna after his defeat at San Jacinto. The disastrous results of the grueling march through northern Texas and the expedition's imprisonment in Mexico were a severe distraction from Indian matters.

In late 1841 Sam Houston was reelected as president of the Republic of Texas. Dismayed and angered by Lamar's Indian policy, he immediately reinstituted efforts to establish peace with the frontier tribes, whom he knew Texas was in no position to control militarily. During the four years preceding Texas statehood, the Houston administration would make several efforts to pacify the Indians through peace councils and treaties. He also asked for help from the United States in this effort.

Eliciting the assistance of the half-Cherokee Jesse Chisholm and other Cherokee and Delaware frontiersmen, who scoured the prairie to "talk in" the scattered bands, Houston arranged for a council at Tehuacana Creek, eight miles above Torrey's Trading Post, which had just been founded near present Waco. At the time, this point essentially marked the start of the northern frontier in Texas. The meeting site soon became known as Council Springs.

Texas was represented by Gen. G. W. Terrell. The Cherokee agent Pierce M. Butler, a former governor of South Carolina, came from Fort Gibson with an entourage to represent the United States. Among Butler's group was the western artist John Mix Stanley, who painted the scene at Council Springs. The meeting was attended by most of the prairie tribes who were then residing in Texas: the Caddos, Delawares, Shawnees, Anadarkos, Tawakonis, Wacos, Wichitas, and Kichais.[14]

The Comanches refused to respond to Houston's peace overtures. The San Antonio courthouse massacre had occurred only three years before, and a burning hatred and distrust of the Texans still gripped the tribe. The smaller tribes felt the same sense of betrayal, as the Waco chief Kakakatish (the Shooting Star) indicated in a speech to the commissioners: "The soil I now stand upon was once mine; it is now the land of the Texans. I am now here on this soil, where in my young days I hunted the buffalo and red deer in peace, and was friendly with all, until the Texan came and drove me from my native land. . . . The wild fire of war has swept over the land, and enveloped my home and people in smoke."[15]

Gifts were issued to the Indians, speeches were made by Terrell and by the various chiefs, and a letter from President John Tyler was read. Eventually a pact was signed, both sides agreeing to stop the warfare in Texas and arranging for the Indians to conduct trade at Torrey's. Everyone knew, however, that without participation by the Comanches, the agreement meant little. Arrangements were made for another treaty in the fall.[16]

During the summer of 1843, Houston dispatched the Texas superintendent of Indian affairs, J. C. Eldridge, on a hazardous and difficult journey onto the prairie to locate the Comanches and persuade them to attend the forthcoming council. Accompanied by Thomas Torrey and guided by the Delaware scout John Connor, Eldridge embarked on what would prove to be an extended journey.

Eldridge and Torrey traveled northward looking for the Comanches, eventually crossing the Red River into present Oklahoma. Finally, near the Wichita Mountains, they came upon the village of the Comanche principal chief Pahhahuco (or the Amorous Man). Despite the return of two Comanche children captured in 1840 at San Antonio, angry relatives of the chiefs slain in the courthouse fight clamored to kill the Texans. They were saved only when the portly Pahhahuco mounted his horse, rode through the camp, and in a commanding voice issued his orders that, as was the Comanche custom to protect their guests, the visitors were not to be harmed or their horses stolen.[17]

Despite the chief's protection, Eldridge and his party still could not persuade the Comanches to attend a peace council. Again, the tribe was noticeably absent when other bands convened at Bird's Fort, seven miles north of present Arlington, Texas, in late September 1843. And once again, without them, the treaty efforts were meaningless.[18]

Still another attempt to conciliate the Comanches was made by Agent Butler in November. Again as a representative of the United States, he led a delegation from Fort Gibson to the mouth of Cache Creek on the Red River south of the Wichita Mountains. He went into camp across the Red from the large, double-log fort of trader Abel Warren. The fort was surrounded by a fifteen-foot-high picket palisade with parapets at each corner.[19] Butler was again accompanied by Stanley, who produced several canvas portraits and scenes of Comanche life. Butler's effort to work out a treaty was doomed, however, by an incident of Comanche warfare.

Though the famed Comanche war chief Buffalo Hump was present, Principal Chief Pahhahuco could not attend, being in mourning for his son who had recently been killed in a raid on the Mexicans. Beset with sorrow, the chief had killed most of his horses and mules, burned five of his six magnificent lodges, thrown away ornaments and wearing apparel, and headed north to the salt plains to mourn. When three of his scouts were late in returning from a reconnaissance, having gone farther than ordered, Butler feared the worst and departed.[20]

Houston continued his efforts to secure a pact with the Comanches the following spring. Chisholm, Connor, and other emissaries toured the vast prairie, contacted the tribes, and invited them to another council. But when it was held on May 13, 1844, at Council Springs, the Comanches were again conspicuously absent.[21]

It wasn't until the following October that the long-hoped-for meeting with the Comanches was achieved. Houston's promise to attend the council in person and the efforts in the field by Chisholm and others finally persuaded the reluctant chiefs to come to Council Springs.[22] When the tribes had all arrived, the Texas president made his appearance mounted on a fine horse and dressed in the full uniform of a general in the Texas army.

Houston tried his best to work out an agreement with Buffalo Hump. He apologized for the courthouse massacre, saying: "The peace was kept until a bad chief took my place. That chief made war on the Comanches and murdered them at San Antonio."[23]

But there was still no resolving the territorial claims of the Comanches and the Texans. No agreement could be found for establishing a dividing line between the two, a line along which Houston wished to establish a series of forts. Though a friendship pact was signed, it did not stop the Comanches from raiding into Mexico or against the extending Texas settlements, and it did little to end the conflicts caused by the migration of settlers onto the Comanchería.

With the advent of Texas statehood in 1845, another major treaty effort was conducted under the auspices of the United States, which wished to secure safety for Americans traveling the plains and to rescue captives held by the Indians. Early in 1846, the commissioners Pierce Butler and Col. M. G. Lewis led a large expedition from Coffee's trading post to the site of Comanche Peak, Texas, where they arranged for a treaty council with the prairie tribes.

At the request of the tribes, however, the treaty parties moved on down the Brazos to Council Springs to hold their talks. This time the Comanches were in full attendance, headed by Chiefs Pahhahuco, Mopechucope (Old Owl), Buffalo Hump, and Santa Anna. On May 15, after many delays and a long, arduous process, the Treaty of Comanche Peak was signed.

By it, the Comanches and other prairie tribes accepted the sovereignty of the United States and agreed to trade only with U.S. citizens. They promised to release all prisoners, deliver up Indians who committed crimes against any citizen of the United States, and return stolen stock. Further, they accepted military posts and Indian agencies on their borders and promised to remain at peace.

In return, the United States would reward the tribes with ten thousand dollars in gifts and would send blacksmiths, schoolteachers, and preachers among them.[24] Then, in hopes of impressing the Indian leaders with the enormity, grandness, and military might of the United States, the Americans took a delegation of chiefs from the various tribes on a trip to New Orleans, up the Mississippi River, and then overland to Washington, D.C. Headed by the Comanche chief Santa Anna, the delegation toured the city, went to the Capitol, and visited President James Polk at the White House.[25] The trip, however, did little to end the conflict that was daily increasing between the advancing Texas settlers and the Indians who resided in their path.

Many Comanche bands had now moved their camps north of the Red River for the protection of their families. When Lt. James W. Abert led an exploring party back from the Rocky Mountains along the Canadian and Washita rivers in the fall of 1845, he met bands of both Kiowas and Comanches. The Kiowas warned Abert to beware lest the Comanche chief Red Jacket, who was camped near the Antelope Hills, might think the party to be Texans, for whom the chief held a great hatred.[26]

During the decade of the 1840s, the Republic of Texas pushed its Indian population farther and farther northward. The oppressive regime of President Lamar had massacred the Cherokees in East Texas and the Comanches at San Antonio. Its ranger force and newly established army posts had made central Texas unsafe as a home camping ground for the Indian tribes. Further, the rapid advance of white settlements was taking away much of the range that the Comanches and other tribes had once roamed freely.

The United States made still other treaties with the Texas Indians, including one conducted on the San Saba River in 1850. A huge caravan of wagons carrying treaty goods and supplies proceeded from Fort Martin Scott to the Spring Creek tributary of the San Saba. The frontiersmen Jesse Chisholm and John Connor had assembled the Caddos, Lipans, Quapaws, Tawakonis, Wacos, and Comanches there. Buffalo Hump was again the principal chief at the council.

With the head commissioner, John R. Rollins, seriously ill and virtually on his deathbed, the Texas agents Robert S. Neighbors and John S. Ford did most of the negotiating. Eventually, agreements were made for the tribes to turn over members who had committed crimes against whites. Both white and black prisoners, some of whom were run-

Sam Houston, president of the Republic of Texas, met with the Comanches and other tribes at Council Springs, near present Waco in 1844. (Eugene C. Barker Texas History Center, University of Texas at Austin)

U.S. and Texas officials relied on Jesse Chisholm to persuade the Comanches to talk peace after the San Antonio courthouse massacre of 1840. (Archives and Manuscript Division, Oklahoma Historical Society)

away slaves, would be released; the whiskey trade among the tribes would be abolished; and general friendship and peace would be established. The United States would provide annuities and send traders, blacksmiths, schoolteachers, and missionaries to the Indians.[27]

Also, Buffalo Hump now accepted that a line be drawn between the Comanches and whites. It would follow the military post line along the Colorado River and run west from that river to the headwaters of the Llano River. The Comanche also turned over a number of captive children,

John Connor (*front, third from left*), a Delaware chief and frontiers-
man, was hired to remove the remaining Indian tribes from Texas.
Black Beaver stands second from left. (Western History Collections,
University of Oklahoma)

mostly Mexican, to Chisholm and Connor. Some children,
however, had become attached to their Comanche families
and refused to be rescued.

The San Saba pact failed to end the troubles in northern
Texas. Indian raiders continued to strike the intruding
Texas homesteads and settlements, driving off horses and
other stock. Furthermore, Indians residing north of the
Red River—Delawares, Shawnees, Seminoles, Cherokees,
Creeks, and Kickapoos—came into the area armed with
the latest guns, killing the diminishing game, stealing
horses and robbing frontier homes. Some of these bands
settled in Texas, and in 1853, U.S. authorities hired John
Connor to round up the splinter bands of Delawares,
Shawnees, Quapaws, Cherokees, and Seminoles and escort them back across the Red River to Indian Territory.[28]

With the rapid depletion of the buffalo, the Texas tribes became more and more impoverished. Starvation haunted many of the Comanche bands as well as the smaller tribes. It was little wonder that the Comanches hated the intruding bands almost as much as they did the Texans. As a result, a huge party of fifteen hundred Comanche, Kiowa, Prairie Apache, Osage, Cheyenne, and Arapaho warriors collected at the Pawnee Fork of the Arkansas River. They planned to hunt and wipe out all non–Plains Indians found on the prairie. Riding eastward, they met a small band of Sauk and Fox Indians, who took refuge in a ravine. The Iowa tribe was well armed and put up such a stout defense that the Plains tribes were forced to retreat, leaving many of their dead behind.[29]

Finally, in 1854, in an effort to stop the accelerating horse thefts, murders, and other depredations on the Texas frontier, the United States established two large reservation areas on the upper Brazos under the Indian agent Robert Neighbors. Some Indians came in and accepted reservation life, but many others simply retreated north of the Red River into the sanctuary of Indian Territory.

Some Texans were still not satisfied and were determined to rid the state of the last remaining vestiges of tribal life, even that on the Brazos reserves.

CHAPTER 12

Invasion of the Comanchería

BY the end of the 1830s, the domain of the southern Plains Indians had been reduced by Texas colonization from the south and American advancement from the east. The Santa Fe Trail along the Arkansas River had cut into its northern sphere, bringing an ever increasing number of wagon trains traveling between Missouri and New Mexico. It was still a vast, unknown, dangerous country. But now more and more whites were daring to venture forth onto the plains for trade in furs, buffalo hides, or horses; and with them came military posts and soldiers.

In 1843 Capt. Nathan Boone and a detachment of dragoons from Fort Gibson made a military reconnaissance past the salt plains to the Santa Fe Trail, encountering only an Osage hunting party, which proceeded to steal some of their mules. Two years later Abert led his exploring expedition from Bent's Fort eastward down the Canadian River. The Americans met bands of Kiowas and Comanches, who were friendly and helpful when they learned that the visitors were not the Texans they hated so fiercely. The Indians were congenial, also, with the thousands of California gold rushers who traversed the land along the Canadian River route during 1849 and 1850.

Responding to public demands that military escort be provided for the gold seekers, General Arbuckle appointed Capt. Randolph B. Marcy to the task. In the spring of 1848, Marcy and a command of dragoons accompanied a large gold-rush party to Santa Fe, opening a new trail along the Canadian River. Later he led a military exploration through the little-known country of north Texas and still another up the Red River to its source in the Palo Duro Canyon of the Texas Panhandle.

By mid-century, the entire complexion of the struggle for supremacy on the plains had been drastically altered by the entry of a new player, the U.S. Army. New military posts were being established all across the southern plains: Fort Mann and Fort Atkinson on the Santa Fe Trail; Fort Arbuckle just north of the Arbuckle Mountains in Indian Territory; Forts Belknap, Phantom Hill, and Chadbourne across north-central Texas.

Still, the old habits and traditions of warriorship were not easily changed. Intertribal enmities, horse-stealing forays, the capturing of slaves, sporadic murders, and scalp taking had become integral parts of the Plains Indian war culture. These would continue even as the tribes faced a far more potent threat to their homelands and way of life than ever before.

The hostility of Texans toward the Indians rose to a fever pitch, and a great public clamor called for military action against the tribes. However, trying to defeat elusive war parties in the field was an impractical, virtually impossible task. Texas military men agreed with the suggestion made by Lt. Gen. David Twiggs, commanding the U.S. Texas Military District, to send troops into the Indians' country and strike their villages and homes—even if it meant invading the treaty-protected sanctuary inside Indian Territory.[1]

The Texas governor, Hardin R. Runnels, authorized the formation of a special company of rangers. He assigned its command to Capt. John S. Ford, a former frontier doctor, Texas legislator, Mexican War veteran, and Indian agent. Ford, who came to be known to his men as "Old Rip," immediately prepared for an expedition beyond the Red River to invade the homeland of the Comanches.

Gathering a force of 102 frontier-seasoned rangers, he reinforced them with 113 Brazos reservation warriors under Capt. Shapley P. Ross. The Indians were mostly Tonkawas, but they also included Anadarkos, Caddos, Kichais, Wacos, Delawares, and Shawnees. The rangers were well mounted, and each was equipped with a good rifle and one or two Colt revolvers.[2]

On April 22, 1858, with two wagons, an ambulance, and fifteen pack mules, Ford left Camp Runnels some sixty miles south of present Wichita Falls, Texas. He marched north, with his Indian allies, some of whom were on foot, scouting a broad path in advance for Comanche signs. Though he had no authority to enter federal lands, Ford did not pause when he struck the Red River just west of present Frederick, Oklahoma. Pushing on north, the rangers continued their advance along the east side of the one hundredth meridian separating the Texas Panhandle and the Indian Territory.

On reaching the valley of the Washita River, the group picked up and followed a travois trail. Then, on the evening of May 10, scouts came in with two Comanche arrowheads they had taken from a recently wounded buffalo. Feeling certain that a large Comanche encampment was near, Ford concealed his wagons and animals in a draw and sent his scouts to spy out the area. They returned to report that they had seen Comanches running buffalo in the distance. In addition, the direction in which the Indians were hauling off the buffalo meat had given the scouts a good idea as to the location of the Comanches' camp.

Leaving a small guard to watch his wagons, Ford cautiously moved on northward, keeping to ravines and low ground until he reached the Fort Smith–Santa Fe road that ran along the south bank of the Canadian River. From there the Texans could see figures moving about on the far side of the river. At dusk Ford made a fireless camp and waited out the night in the wilds of western Indian Territory.

When daybreak came on May 11, the Texas Ranger–Indian command set forth at a gallop, ready to do battle. After a short march they passed the buttes of the Antelope Hills, which protruded high above the floodplain of a huge northward loop of the Canadian River. There a small camp of five Indian tipis was discovered and easily taken.

Two inhabitants of the camp escaped on horseback toward a much larger encampment that could be seen on the north bank of the willow- and cottonwood-lined river. Leaving the Tonkawas behind to take charge of prisoners and destroy the lodges, Ford and his ranger force plunged headlong after the fleeing pair. The Comanches crossed the river without pause, unwittingly revealing a good fording point.

The Indian village was nestled in a comfortable bend of Little Robe Creek not far from where it empties into the wide-bedded Canadian River from the northwest. The tops of the Comanche lodges some three miles away glistened brightly in the first light of the spring morning, looking almost like white birds against the greening prairie pastures. Only a few trails of smoke from lodge fires drifted lazily skyward.

Once on the north bank, Ford paused to organize his attack. He knew there was no time to waste if he wanted to keep the advantage of surprise. As Ross drove his Indians between the village and the river, Ford brought his ranger unit to a halt and hurriedly aligned them into a cavalry charge formation. He then quickly gave the signal, and the ranger line swept down on the Comanche camp.

The sleepy Comanche village burst into frantic activity. Warriors dashed pell-mell from their lodges to secure their ponies, stringing their bows as they ran. Other villagers— the women, children, and old ones—scurried like alarmed coveys of quail into ravines and thickets to the northwest of the camp, ahead of the ranger attack. Ford and his men drove through the terrified village, shooting at anything before them. In his report on the battle, Ford detailed the action:

The fight was now general, and extended very soon over a circuit of six miles in length, and more than three in breadth. Squads of rangers and Indians were pursuing the enemy in every direction. The Comanches would occasionally halt and endeavor to make a stand, however their efforts were unavailing, they were forced to yield the ground to our men in every instance. The din of the battle had rolled back from the river, the groans of the dying, cries of frightened women and children, mingled with the reports of fire-arms and the shouts of men, as they rose from hill-top, from thicket, and from ravine.[3]

While the rangers were engaged in their massacre of the camp inhabitants, their Indian allies were observing a lone, gorgeously attired Comanche chief. With his lance tilted above his bonneted head, he rode out from the Comanche encampment on an iron-gray steed. At the top of the lance fluttered a white flag of truce. The Comanche appeared to be amazingly impervious to the barrage of bullets poured fourth at him. He rode forward a short distance, made a circle with his horse, and expelled his breath with great force. He reached the end of the line without a sign of injury, erect and unscathed.[4]

The reservation Indians looked at the smoking barrels of their rifles and exclaimed in disbelief. But then, as the Comanche was leaning into his turn at the end of the line, he jerked, straightened in his saddle, and crumpled from his horse onto the prairie. A resounding shout of success went up along the line of reservation Indians. A second chief rode forth, only to be killed by a bullet from the rifle of a Shawnee war captain.

Later, when the fighting was done, the village burned, and captives taken, the corpse of the first chief was examined. The rangers were amazed to discover that the Comanche chief, Pohebits Quasho (or Iron Jacket), had worn an ancient breastplate of Spanish mail beneath his buffalo robe. Only when a bullet had rammed up beneath a metal scale during the Comanche's turn had Iron Jacket been felled. The rangers later cut up the armor for souvenirs, sending one piece to Governor Runnels.[5]

The fighting was not yet over. Another Comanche encampment was located a few miles up the Canadian. On hearing the gunfire, warriors from this village swarmed forth. They did not charge the ranger force but held forth on a hilltop and issued taunts and dares directed in particular at the reservation Indians. Ford described the "mimic battle" that followed:

> Our allies proposed to draw them out, and requested me to keep my men in line to support them if necessary. The Comanches descended from the hill to accept their proffered invitation. With yells and menaces, and every species of insulting gestures and language, they tried to excite the reserve Indians into some act of rashness by which they could profit. A scene was now enacted, beggaring description. It reminded me of the rude and chivalrous days of knight errantry. Shields and lances, and bows and head dresses, prancing steeds and many minutiae were not wanting to complete the resemblance. And when the combatants rushed at each other with defiant shouts nothing save the piercing report of the rifle varied the affair from a battle field of the middle ages. Half an hour was spent in this without much damage to either party.[6]

Finally, Ford ordered his rangers to attack, but their jaded horses were no match for the Comanche ponies. The rangers' assault on the Comanche encampment and the ensuing engagements had resulted in the capture of a number of women and children and some three hundred horses and mules—not one of which was identified as being a stolen animal.

Ford claimed that the actual count of the Comanche dead was seventy-six, undoubtedly with women and children among them. All of the lodges of the village were burned, and the camp paraphernalia was destroyed. The ranger loss was two killed—a Waco Indian and a ranger private, Robert Nickels, who had perished at the end of a Comanche lance—and three wounded.

From a Comanche captive woman it was learned that Buffalo Hump, with a strong force of warriors, was twelve miles below on the river. Fearing for the safety of his supply wagons, Ford ordered his force back to camp. On May 13 the rangers began their return to Camp Runnels, arriving there after thirty days in the field. Their victory at the Battle of Little Robe Creek was roundly applauded by citizens throughout Texas. "The rangers, with the assistance of friendly Indians, killed seventy wild Indians," one Texan exulted. "When did the soldiers ever do so much?"[7]

Another incursion into western Indian Territory was made a month after Ford's fight. With U.S. troops withdrawn from Forts Washita and Arbuckle to help put down the Mormon rebellion in Utah, the immigrant tribes felt imperiled. In an effort to show that the "woods" Indians could and would protect themselves, the Chickasaw agent Douglas H. Cooper led a sizable force of Chickasaws, Choctaws, and Cherokees into Comanche country.[8]

Guided by the famous Delaware frontiersman Black Beaver, Cooper's force scoured the country west along the Red River and the Wichita Mountains area. The expedition found no Comanches. They met only a U.S. surveying party that was daringly working its way northward along the one hundredth meridian. Cooper also found some deserted Wichita and Waco villages on Cache Creek.

Eventually, they located a Wichita village of some 150 straw huts with over one hundred acres of corn under cultivation on Rush Creek. The chief of the village assured Cooper that there were no Comanches south of the Canadian, the main body being at the salt plains. Seven Comanche bands had leagued together, the Wichitas said, to conduct a war of revenge for the Ford attack.

Cooper asked about a trail, headed to the south, that he had crossed. He was told that it had been made by Comanches who were ashamed to return to their people until they had gone to Texas and committed reprisals for the Ford attack. With his horses badly jaded, Cooper turned back to Fort Arbuckle, little knowing that very soon another conflict between white soldiers and the Comanches would take place there at the peaceful Wichita village.

The Battle of Little Robe Creek was significant in that it extended whites' warring potential into the heart of Comanche country. It also established a method of warfare against the Plains Indians: attack whatever village of Indians that could be found, regardless of indication of guilt, strike it without warning or without giving chance for surrender, and unmercifully kill any occupants without consideration of age or sex.

Gen. George A. Custer, who would pass by the Antelope Hills ten years later on his way to the Washita River, would use this same tactic in attacking Black Kettle's Cheyenne village. It was also the warring technique that would be used against the Comanches by Maj. Earl Van Dorn of the Second Regiment of U.S. Cavalry. Ford's victory, highly praised despite any evidence of guilt on the part of the Comanche band, drew the envy of the U.S. military in Texas, who had been dismally unsuccessful in their Indian-fighting efforts.

The command of the Texas-based Second Regiment, which had been formed especially for frontier service, listed such names as Albert Sidney Johnston as its commanding colonel and Robert E. Lee as its lieutenant colonel. Many of its officers were destined to become famous as Civil War generals. Further, its horses were prized saddlebred animals purchased at high cost in Kentucky. Each trooper was armed with carbines, Colt revolvers, and the cavalry saber.[9]

After the Texas Ranger victory, General Twiggs ordered a battalion of the Second Cavalry under the command of Van Dorn, a West Point graduate from Mississippi, to establish a base inside Indian Territory for a campaign against the Comanches. A force of Caddo and Tonkawa Indians from the Brazos reserves under twenty-year-old Sul Ross, later a governor of Texas, was sent ahead into Indian Territory to locate a military site.

Ross selected a spot on Otter Creek just west of the Wichita Mountains. Van Dorn soon followed with four companies of cavalry and one of infantry. They built a stockaded military post, named Camp Radziminski in honor of a Polish-born officer of the unit who had died recently.

The Wichita Indians were now settled peacefully on Rush Creek near the present site of Rush Springs, Oklahoma. After the Ford strike, federal authorities had urged the Wichitas to persuade the Comanches to come in to nearby Fort Arbuckle for a peace council. Reluctantly the Wichitas had gone to the Comanche camps and convinced their former warring allies that the whites sincerely wanted peace. They also issued an invitation for the Comanches to visit them on the way and feast, as in the old days, on corn, beans, and pumpkins. The hungry Comanches accepted, bringing a large party of several hundred tribesmen and their families to the Wichita village in late September 1858.

The arrival of the Comanche entourage was discovered by Caddo and Tonkawa spies working for Van Dorn. He later insisted that he knew nothing of the U.S. efforts to make peace with the Comanches. When the spies arrived at Camp Radziminski with the information, Van Dorn saw his opportunity. Ordering his four troops of Second Cavalry into the saddle, Van Dorn set out on a grueling seventy-five-mile ride eastward, skirting the northern rim of the Wichita Mountains. After a thirty-six-hour march, the last part conducted continuously through the night, Van Dorn and his force reached Rush Creek at daybreak.[10]

A hurried reconnaissance revealed the Comanche camp spread along the foggy creek bottom. No sentinels had been posted at the camp or with the nearby horse herds. Van Dorn sent one troop under Capt. N. G. Evans to advance against the lower end of the village. He ordered the Indian allies under Ross to stampede the Comanche ponies while he led the other three troops against the upper end. Evans, who had been given instructions to deploy and charge as soon as he came in sight of the village, initiated the battle. When his gunfire was heard, Van Dorn's bugler sounded the call for the remainder of the mounted troops to go into action.

The Comanches, again caught completely by surprise,

were forced to fight on foot—a severe handicap for the best horsemen on the plains. Further, their weaponry was mostly bows and arrows, pitted against the pistols, carbines, and sabers of the cavalrymen. Still, with the numerous ravines and trees impeding the cavalry charge, the Comanches put up a fierce resistance in the brief encounter, fighting from tree to tree and hand to hand. Soon the fighting was spread throughout the river valley as the desperate Indians scurried for the protection of the hills.

When it was over, the Comanches had suffered another severe loss. Some fifty-seven or fifty-eight of their people had been killed, their 120 lodges burned, and their valuable horse herd lost. They had exacted a small retribution. A Comanche arrow had pierced the heart of Lt. Cornelius Van Camp, killing him instantly. He was one of five Second Cavalry dead. Four arrows had struck Van Dorn. One had entered the right side of his body and passed up through his stomach and lung to protrude from his left side. He, however, would live. A good many soldiers were wounded, some seriously enough that they died later.

For a second time, the Comanches had seen the safety of their homes and camps in Indian Territory violated by a surprise and, to their mind, unwarranted attack. They were now unable to believe the whites, who talked of peace on the one hand and killed on the other.

The peaceful, generous Wichitas suffered every bit as much, if not more, than the Comanches. Though they lost only two of their people in the melee, afterwards Van Dorn's took all their corn, saying they would be reimbursed at Fork Arbuckle.

Wichita chief Toseqosh claimed that the morning after the battle, the troops began killing the Wichitas' dogs and chickens and broke some of their brass kettles. Worse still, the Comanche leader told the Wichitas, "You lying Wichitas, you see what you have done, got all my people killed and it won't be long we will wipe you all out."[11] The unfortunate tribe was forced to flee their Rush Creek homes and seek safety at Fort Arbuckle, living there in near starvation because the post had scant food for the

574 Wichitas and 61 Kichais, not counting infants who arrived.

In December 1858 the Pawnees came to within twenty or thirty miles of Fort Arbuckle to steal large numbers of ponies from the Kickapoos. When they learned that the Kickapoos were in pursuit, the Pawnees hid in the channel of a creek. They were discovered, and five were killed. When the commander of Arbuckle learned of this, he sent out invitations for the Kickapoos to come to the fort and hold a scalp dance. However, the band could not be located.[12]

The war of the prairies continued into February 1859, when a Fort Arbuckle command of fifty soldiers and fifty Wichitas made a scouting probe westward. Twenty miles from the fort, the group met a large party of Comanches, and a battle resulted. Two Comanches were killed and two soldiers wounded before the Indians withdrew.

Later, when rumor reached Fort Arbuckle that the Comanches were coming in force to take the fort, fifty cavalrymen under Capt. Eugene A. Carr were sent south from Fort Leavenworth, Kansas. The troops found no Indians; however, another fight occurred near Arbuckle between a Comanche party and troops under Lt. D. S. Stanley. Eight Indians were killed and several more wounded. The troops reportedly lost one man and had two more slightly wounded.[13]

During the winter, Van Dorn had returned to his home in Mississippi to recuperate from his wounds. The Camp Radziminski troops, many of them new recruits, drilled, carried out camp chores, and hunted the abundant game of the area. The winter, a severe one, was difficult for the tent-housed soldiers, even though some of the men improved their abodes by adding sod or log walls.[14]

After making a rapid recovery, Van Dorn returned to his command in the spring of 1859, joined by Capt. Edmund Kirby Smith and Lt. Fitzhugh Lee, both future Confederate generals. All of the garrison yearned for another campaign against the Comanches and looked forward to the end of

April, when the spring grass would be high enough to sustain the cavalry horses and mules on the prairie.

Through the help of Shapley Ross, now the agent at the Lower Brazos reserve, fifty-eight Caddos, Kichais, Tonkawas, Delawares, and Shawnees were secured as scouts and trailers. They were headed by the Delaware Indian Jack Harry and Shawnee Jim, an intelligent veteran of the Texas Revolution who spoke excellent English.

On April 30, Van Dorn led six companies of Second Cavalry out of Radziminski on a march to the north, making his way up Elk Creek to the Washita and Canadian rivers through what are now Kiowa, Beckham, and Roger Mills counties. The Indian scouts rode as far as ten miles in advance and as flankers. On the fourth day in the field, one of the scouts captured a Comanche boy. Under threat of death, the boy was forced to lead the cavalry command to his village.

The Canadian River was in flood stage when the troops crossed it thirty miles downstream from the Antelope Hills. Parking his wagon train under guard, Van Dorn continued ahead with pack mules across present Woodward and Harper counties without encountering the Indians he sought. The Kansas border was crossed at its intersection with the Cimarron River, and soon after a small band of Indian buffalo hunters was spotted. A running fight ensued, with one Indian, a Comanche, being killed. Now large, recently abandoned campsites were seen regularly.

Swinging to the northwest across present Clark County, Kansas, Van Dorn followed a fresh trail made by a small band of Indians. During a noontime halt, three Indians were discovered as they crept up on the Second Cavalry horse herd. While giving chase to the Indians, Lt. William B. Loyall discovered and captured a large herd of horses not far from a Comanche village. When Van Dorn was notified of this, he immediately ordered his troops back into their saddles and attacked the camp.

Again deprived of their principal fighting implement,

their horses, the defiant Comanches took up positions among the bushes and trees of Crooked Creek and poured a barrage of arrows and gunfire from their concealment. Van Dorn positioned two mounted troops on each side of the river, dismounted two more, and formed a line that swept down through the river valley.

The disadvantaged Comanches were routed, forty-nine of them being killed and thirty-six taken prisoner. One trooper was lost, and Lieutenant Lee suffered an arrow driven through his chest and right lung and protruding from his back. Captain Smith received a bullet wound in the thigh. Both would recover, soon to take up arms for the Confederacy. These Comanches were thought to be part of Buffalo Hump's band, the same group that Van Dorn had mauled at the Wichita village.

In Texas, meanwhile, frontier hysteria and foment against the Indians of the Brazos reserves were building. Settlers wanted the last tribes of the state to be removed to north of the Red River—a move that would effectively shift the center of the Indian conflict directly into Indian Territory. Despite the counterclaims of men such as Ford and Neighbors, the reservation Indians were blamed for virtually all frontier depredations.

Texas vigilante parties committed murders of innocent Indians and agitated for action against others. An old Comanche man was killed by four white men for his horses; the camp of some peaceful reserve Indians led by Choctaw Tom was attacked at night, and several people were murdered. Fear of retaliation created a frenzied desire among white settlers to hunt down and kill other Indians. In May 1859, the former Comanche agent John R. Baylor led a party of 250 men onto the Brazos reservation and attacked some of the Indians, killing one old man before the Indians and U.S. troops drove the vigilantes off.[15]

It had become more than apparent to Neighbors, now the supervising agent for all Texas Indians, that removal of the Brazos reserve Indians to Indian Territory was vital for their protection. He pressed the matter with U.S. government officials, who agreed. A treaty was negotiated

As a child of nine, Cynthia Ann Parker was taken prisoner at Parker's Fort, Texas, in 1836. She eventually became the wife of the Comanche warrior Peta Nacona and the mother of Comanche chief Quanah Parker. (Western History Collections, University of Oklahoma)

Texas Indian agent Robert S. Neighbors (shown here with his wife) was shot from ambush and killed by whites for defending the Indians of his Brazos Indian Agency. (Western History Collections, University of Oklahoma)

with the Choctaws and Chickasaws to lease a large tract of land near the Wichita Mountains for the resettlement of the Indian tribes of Texas and western Indian Territory. After helping to select a site suitable to both the tribes and the government, Neighbors began the removal.

On August 1, 1859, the two Brazos Indian reservations were closed, and the exodus was begun. Some fourteen hundred Indians moved northward in a caravan of wagons, Mexican carts, army ambulances, cattle, horses, and dogs to a small creek named for the Comanche agent Matthew Leeper. Two months later Maj. William H. Emory arrived with units of the First Cavalry and First Infantry to establish Fort Cobb three miles from the agency.[16]

The attacks in 1858 and 1859 had severely punished the Comanches, but by no means was the tribe's fighting force destroyed. There would still be raids into Texas and battles with whites. On December 18, 1860, the Texas Rangers under Capt. Sul Ross attacked a small Comanche village below the Red River in present Foard County, Texas. Several Indians were killed, including chief Peta Nacona, husband of the elusive Cynthia Ann Parker. She was recaptured and taken to Austin, where she died in 1870. Her son Quanah Parker became a leading Comanche chief.[17]

The Comanches and Kiowas also harassed the tribes of the Leased District, whose warriors were not reluctant to take an occasional scalp in return. To the north of the district was the Santa Fe Trail, where American immigration flowed westward virtually unprotected. The Comanches, still with the country of the Texas Panhandle and present western Oklahoma as a refuge, would have their revenge. However, a momentus new factor was about to have a drastic effect on all the tribes in Indian Territory.

CHAPTER 13

The Immigrant Indians in the Civil War

WHEN the American Civil War erupted in the spring of 1861, Indian Territory stood as an island surrounded by the deep conflicts between Union and Confederate loyalties. To the east and south were the strongly pro-Southern states of Arkansas and Texas. To the north and west were the Union-aligned state of Kansas and the territories of Colorado and New Mexico. All of these areas were organized under unifying governments that, even though their citizenry might be divided on secession, controlled their military affiliation.

Indian Territory had no such single government, and it was mainly populated by Indian people whose loyalties were as divided as those of the whites between North and South. Many of them had been removed from the South. These Indians were attached to Southern traditions, the most singular being the practice of slavery. Many of the part-Indian, part-white tribal leaders, as well as full-bloods, were slave owners. They not only had a mind-set sympathetic to Southern whites but also shared a fear of losing valuable slave properties.

Bitter resentments and hatreds still festered within some of the nations over the loss of their native home-

Scalping and other old war habits practiced by the rebel Cherokees at the Battle of Pea Ridge brought an end to the use of Indians as integrated Civil War combatants. (*Leslie's Illustrated Newspaper*, March 29, 1862)

lands, which had often been achieved through bribery of Indian leaders by the United States. This was particularly true among the Creeks and Cherokees, where the issue of giving up their southern lands had resulted in intense animosities, assassinations, and intratribal divisions. It was to be expected that these opposing factions would take different sides in the war. Neutrality, they would find, would be impossible.

There was also the factor of subsistence. All of the tribes had treaties with the United States by which they were owed payments and other benefits. Most of them had become dependent to some degree on the food and other goods supplied by the government. This dependency influenced many of the Indians, who had doubts as to the ability of the South to help them.

Indian Territory was looked on by both North and South as a buffer zone against military invasion by the other. The Indians, therefore, became important pawns in the war, and their loyalties were much sought by both sides. The use of Indians as soldiers was also a factor, though many whites were reticent about the "barbarous" manner of Indian fighting.

At the very start of the war, the Union abdicated military control of Indian Territory to the South; in doing so, it also abandoned its responsibilities to the Indians there. The North had little choice, however. Fort Gibson had been closed for some time, and the U.S. garrisons at Fort Washita, Fort Arbuckle, and Fort Cobb were far too small and too isolated to stand against any organized force.

In March 1861, Col. William H. Emory had been dispatched from Washington, D.C., to assume command at Fort Cobb, with discretionary orders regarding the disposition of troops within Indian Territory. While en route, he learned at Fort Washita of an impending attack from a regiment of Texas volunteers. Abandoning Washita and taking the garrison with him, Emory headed for Cobb. He was joined by troops from Arbuckle, who were also fleeing before the Texans.[1]

A courier, Lt. William W. Averell, who carried orders for the complete evacuation of Indian Territory troops to

Fort Leavenworth, also overtook Emory. Near the site of present Minco, Oklahoma, Emory found the Fort Cobb garrison already in flight and added them to his procession, taking a course toward Kansas.

The exodus was guided by a Leased District resident, Black Beaver, who during the march told a Kansas newspaperman: "Bad white man and fool red man talk about seceding and raise Texas flag and swear he scalp Yankee Indian." The post commander at Cobb had advised Black Beaver: "Let [your] cattle go to hell and save your scalp."[2]

The retreating troops reached Fort Leavenworth without being attacked by the pursuing Texas units, who occupied the abandoned posts. Now began the Confederacy's tenure of military control of Indian Territory. With it came sponsorship for the Indian tribes of the region, with whom the Confederacy immediately sought to arrange alliances. Heading this effort was the Arkansas lawyer Albert Pike, who would ultimately be appointed the brigadier general in command of Indian Territory for the Confederacy.[3]

In late May 1861, while serving as a commissioner for the Confederacy, Pike visited the Cherokee capital at Tahlequah in an effort to sign a treaty with that nation. He found the Cherokees severely split between a group of predominantly full-bloods known as Pins, who were supporters of the Union, and half-bloods, who favored secession. Pike was unable to dissuade Chief John Ross, a slave owner, from his stand of neutrality.[4]

Continuing on, Pike met with the Creeks, who after a long council signed a treaty with the Confederacy on July 10. Among the signers of the treaty was Chief Chilly McIntosh; but notably absent was Opothle Yahola (Oh-poth'-le Yah-ho'la), a leading Creek full-blood who was thought to have played a part in the murder of William McIntosh, the chief's father. Pike also made treaties with the Choctaws and Chickasaws before moving up the Canadian to the Seminole Agency and initiating a pact with that tribe. He later traveled on to the Wichita Agency to work out agreements with the prairie tribes.

John Ross, undoubtedly affected by the rebel victory

over Union forces at Wilson Creek in Missouri, eventually came around to aligning the Cherokee Nation with the Confederacy. In October, Pike returned to Tahlequah to meet with Ross and representatives from the Osages, Quapaws, Senecas, and Shawnees. Treaties were signed with each of those tribes. But even as the agreements were being made, events were taking place that would lead to the first battle of the Civil War in Indian Territory.

Opothle Yahola, though no longer a Creek chief, was a highly regarded leader. He represented the view of many Creeks and other Indians who wished to stay out of the white man's war. Opothle Yahola was also greatly concerned about the welfare of his people with the Union forces withdrawn. During the spring and summer of 1861, he and others traveled to the Antelope Hills and the salt plains to discuss the matter with the prairie tribes and their close friend Jesse Chisholm, who now resided on the North Canadian River.

After a meeting of Creek loyalists at Talasi, near the mouth of Little River, a delegation was sent to federal officials in Kansas. In a letter from Opothle Yahola and others to the president, the Indians asked for protection: "You said that in our new homes we should be defended ... now the wolf has come, men who are strangers tread our soil, our children are frightened & the mothers cannot sleep for fear."[5]

Northern promises of help were of little reassurance as the hostility of the rebellious factions in the territory became more and more threatening. The only course, Opothle Yahola decided, was to lead his followers north to the protection of the Union. A call was sent out to all who wished to follow him north to gather at his home near present Eufaula at the mouth of the North Canadian River. His Creek followers, mostly full-bloods, arrived, as did a contingent of loyal Seminoles and eventually a large group of former slaves.

Hurriedly, the Indians gathered stock, slaughtered pigs for the journey ahead, and stowed goods aboard wagons. The assembled caravan included a long train of wagons,

Opothle Yahola and his loyal faction of Creeks and others had to fight their way to Kansas during the Civil War. (Western History Collections, University of Oklahoma)

people on horseback and on foot, and herds of livestock. Both Creek and Seminole men were in war gear, "stripped and painted" as an indication that they were prepared to fight if necessary.[6]

Breaking camp on November 5, the loyalists headed north up the Deep Fork River. Confederate forces were well aware of Opothle Yahola's movement and were determined to stop him. Col. Douglas Cooper, the former U.S. agent for the Chickasaw Nation and an avid proslaver, now commanded the rebel military in the territory. Under him were some fourteen hundred men, including his own Choctaw and Chickasaw regiment plus units of secessionist Creeks and Seminoles and a detachment of Texas cavalry.

Arriving at Opothle Yahola's deserted camp on November 15, Cooper set out in pursuit, following the Creeks' trail up the Deep Fork and across to the Cimarron River. On the nineteenth, the camp of Opothle Yahola's rear guard was seen and charged by seventy men of the Ninth Texas Cavalry. Finding that the scouts had already fled, the Texans pursued them until the main camp of loyalists was discovered near a large knoll known as Round Mountain south of present Sand Springs, Oklahoma.[7]

They were met by heavy fire that forced them to retreat, but in support the Chickasaw and Choctaw units were brought forward and dismounted as skirmishers. With night having fallen, the two forces exchanged gunfire in the dark until the loyal Indians withdrew from the field. Six of Cooper's men were killed in the Battle of Round Mountain. The number of Opothle Yahola's dead is not known, but when the Rebels entered the abandoned camp the next morning, they found the chief's buggy, wagons, valuable foodstuff, many horses, and other livestock.[8]

With his horses badly jaded and short of forage, Cooper broke off his pursuit and went into a rest camp at Tulseytown (now Tulsa) before resuming his march up the Verdigris River to Bird Creek. There he joined with a detachment of five hundred Cherokee Mounted Rifles that had been stationed at Coody's Bluff. The Cherokees were under the command of Col. John Drew, a prominent half-blood merchant.

Opothle Yahola, in camp only six miles down the creek near present Turley, sent word that he desired to make peace. However, when Cooper's emissary visited the refugee camp, he found the Creek and Seminole warriors painted for battle and threatening attack that night. This news had a severe effect on the Cherokees, many of whom were still unsure of their desire to secede but very sure that they did not wish to war with the Creeks. During the night such large numbers defected, many to the loyalists, that Drew was left with only twenty-eight men in his command.[9]

Opothle Yahola did not attack as expected; however, on the following morning, as Cooper pushed forward to engage the Indian leader's main force, some two hundred warriors struck the rebel rear. These were beaten back, and now Cooper's army began closing in on the position Opothle Yahola had taken in a horseshoe bend of Bird Creek. The precipitous walls of the creek at the battle site gained it the Indian name of Chusto Talasah, or the Caving Banks. There the loyalists took up fortified positions behind fallen logs in the heavy timber and thick undergrowth inside the loop on the west bank.

Cooper struck from the east across the creek during the afternoon of December 9. The four-hour battle that lasted until dark was a series of attacks, flanking movements, and countermoves, the Rebels sometimes charging on horseback but largely pressing forward as skirmishers from position to position until the lines were close. For nearly half an hour before sunset, the fighting became especially intense. It was only when a fresh detachment of Creeks under Col. Daniel N. McIntosh arrived and took up the battle against their brothers across the stream that the loyal Indians were forced to retreat. Cooper withdrew nearby to camp for a night, and when morning came he found that Opothle Yahola had retreated up Hominy Creek into the hills to the north.

Burying his fifteen dead, Cooper again withdrew from

the chase. Not only was he short of ammunition but he had also learned that more than a hundred Cherokees from Fort Gibson had joined the loyalists. Retiring back down the Arkansas to Fort Gibson, which the Confederates had reactivated, Cooper sent a call for reinforcements. Col. James McIntosh (no direct relation to the Creek McIntoshes)—a West Point graduate who had served with the U.S. Army at Arbuckle, Cobb, and Gibson before joining the Confederacy when the war began—responded with fifteen companies of Texas and Arkansas cavalry from Van Buren, Arkansas.

When Cooper was held up by the desertion of his Indian teamsters, the eager McIntosh would not wait. Moving forward with his force of thirteen hundred men, he made contact with Opothle Yahola's warriors on the evening of December 25 but did not pursue. On the following day, McIntosh's forward elements crossed Hominy Creek. As they did so, they came under fire from loyalists posted on a rugged, oak-covered hill, which would eventually become known as Patriot's Hill, a few miles northwest of present Skiatook, Oklahoma. Seminoles under Chief Halleck Tustenuggee were posted at the base of the hill behind trees and rocks. At the top of the hill was another line of defense, while the mounted Creeks were held in reserve. The loyalist force was estimated at seventeen hundred.

McIntosh readied his forces, and at high noon he ordered his bugler to sound the charge. Yelping their battle cries, the Texas and Arkansas troops surged forward, overrunning the Seminole positions and driving them up the hill to its summit. There, in desperate hand-to-hand combat, Opothle Yahola's men were put to rout and sent fleeing into the ravines and hills, with the rebel forces in pursuit.

A final stand by the refugees was made at their camp, but there too they were quickly overrun. By four o'clock that afternoon, the Confederates stood as "victors in the center of Opothle Yahola's camp."[10] About the Rebels lay the wounded, dying, and dead of the loyalists as well as the main portion of their supplies, food, clothing, and other belongings. McIntosh reported a loss of only 8 men and claimed that more than 250 loyalists had been killed in this fight, now known as the Battle of Chustenahlah.

On the following morning, Col. Stand Watie arrived at the battle site with three hundred Cherokees and joined in the pursuit of the now desperate Indians and blacks. After marching twenty-five miles, Watie overtook a body of some five to six hundred Creek warriors and, with half of his command led by Col. E. C. Boudinot, attacked. The Cherokees claimed that in the running fight that followed, about 20 of the loyalists were killed. As McIntosh repaired to winter quarters, Cooper conducted mopping-up exercises that, he claimed, netted 6 more of Opothle Yahola's party killed and 150 prisoners, mostly women and children.

By now intensely cold, sleet-driven weather gripped the country as the remnants of the exodus struggled on toward Fort Roe, a makeshift camp on the Verdigris River in Kansas. Many died on the way; others arrived with toes and fingers frozen. All were destitute of clothing, shelter, fuel, cooking utensils, and food. Union authorities would attempt to help them in their terrible plight, but it would be many months before the loyalists who survived would know any of the comforts they had left behind in Rebel-dominated Indian Territory.

On November 22, 1861, Albert Pike was named commanding general of Indian Territory for the Confederacy. Establishing his headquarters at Cantonment Davis, just across the Arkansas River from Fort Gibson, Pike attempted to reorganize his Indian units into a more effective fighting force, developing four regiments, two battalions, and some lesser detachments. However, Pike's authority in the territory was diminished when the Confederacy created the Trans-Mississippi District under Maj. Gen. Earl Van Dorn. Strong animosity existed between Van Dorn and Pike over Pike's public criticism of Van Dorn's 1858 attack against the Comanches at the Wichita village.

Pike saw his Indian force as being essentially a home guard. However, when Union forces in Missouri arose from their Wilson Creek defeat and began a new advance to the south, Van Dorn ordered Pike to move forward—out of Indian Territory—in support of Gen. Ben McCulloch in northwest Arkansas. Pike complied, giving orders to his commanders, but his Indian troops were in no hurry to involve themselves in the white man's war. The Creeks, Choctaws, and Chickasaws lingered in the rear, and the mostly half-blood Cherokees arrived a day late for the three-day Battle of Pea Ridge, Arkansas.

Though the Cherokees missed the skirmish at Bentonville on March 6, they did fight well in the following day's battle at Leetown.[11] Their part in the battle was to become highly controversial. Mounted on ponies, armed with a hodgepodge of personal rifles, shotguns, bows and arrows, and tomahawks, the Cherokees knew little military discipline. Given permission by Pike to fight in their own fashion, they quickly dismounted and fired from behind and up trees.

To the white soldiers, the Indian war whoop was a hideous, barbaric sound—it may well have inspired the famous rebel battle yell. But generating the greatest criticism was the scalping and mutilation of the dead on the field. Further, it later surfaced that men under John Drew had conspired to kill some of the Confederate white soldiers during the battle. Even though Col. Stand Watie's Cherokee Mounted Rifle battalion rendered additional service by helping to cover the retreat of the defeated Confederate army, white prejudice against the Indians as soldiers would cause Pea Ridge to be the last time the Confederates would integrate Indian with white combat units.

Northern leaders held similar misgivings about the use of Indians as soldiers. Many northern Indians had indicated a desire to fight on the Union side, as had the refugee Indians who had fled to Kansas and now lived in dire conditions on the Verdigris. Opothle Yahola and many others were anxious to be armed for a return invasion of Indian Territory. When efforts were made to organize an

Indian expedition for this purpose, Maj. Gen. Henry W. Halleck, commanding the Department of the Missouri, authorized the use of Indian troops only against other Indians or in defense of their own territory.[12]

Two Indian regiments, or "Indian Home Guards," were organized at Humboldt, Kansas, to be incorporated into two brigades of white troops under the Indian expedition commander, Col. William Weer. The First Indian Regiment consisted of eight companies of Creeks and two of Seminoles—about one thousand men. The Second Indian Regiment enlisted about the same number of Quapaws, Cherokees, Delawares, Kichais, Caddos, Ionis, and Kickapoos.

Although Opothle Yahola asked for "wagons that shoot"—artillery—they were given mostly worthless guns that would not fire. It was intended that the Indians would be used for scouting ahead into the Indian country, not for regular fighting. Still, the refugee Indians held their traditional war dances in preparation for battle.[13]

After the rebel defeat at Pea Ridge and the deaths there of both McCulloch and James McIntosh, Pike had become the ranking Confederate officer in Indian Territory. Taking the main portion of his bedraggled forces, Pike had retreated deep into Choctaw country, where he built Fort McCulloch on the Blue River. Watie, Cooper, and Drew were left to operate in the northeast, virtually as guerrillas and as an advance guard against Union intrusion.

Watie and his Cherokee Mounted Rifle unit were situated at Cowskin Prairie. On April 26, 1862, he attacked a force of two hundred federal cavalry advancing toward Arkansas, driving them back to Neosho, Missouri. On May 31, Watie staged a surprise attack on the Neosho force, routing it. The Cherokee Rebels then entered the town and tore down the U.S. flag that waved from atop the courthouse.[14]

However, Watie and his troops were the first to feel the sting of Weer's six-thousand-man Indian expedition, which had begun its march down the Grand River from Fort Scott, Kansas, on June 28. When a strong advance

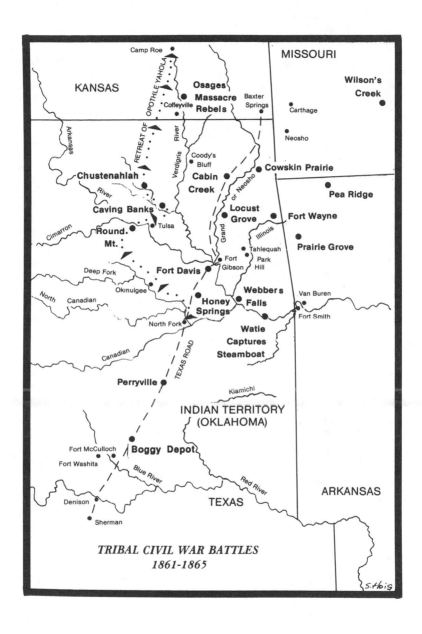

KANSAS

Camp Roe

MISSOURI

Wilson's
Creek

Osages
Massacre
Rebels

Coffeyville

Baxter
Springs

Carthage

Arkangas

RETREAT OF OPOTHLE YAHOLA

Verdigris River

Neosho

Coody's
Bluff

Cowskin Prairie

Chustenahlah

Cabin
Creek

Grand or Neosho

Pea Ridge

River

Caving Banks

Tulsa

Locust
Grove

Fort Wayne

Cimarron

**Round.
Mt.**

Illinois

Tahlequah

Prairie Grove

Deep Fork

Fort Davis

Fort
Gibson

Park
Hill

North Canadian

Okmulgee

**Webbers
Falls**

Van Buren

**Honey
Springs**

Fort Smith

North Fork

**Watie
Captures
Steamboat**

TEXAS ROAD

Canadian

Perryville

Kiamichi

**INDIAN TERRITORY
(OKLAHOMA)**

Fort McCulloch

Boggy Depot

Fort Washita

Blue River

Red River

ARKANSAS

Denison

TEXAS

Sherman

*TRIBAL CIVIL WAR BATTLES
1861-1865*

S.tbis

force unexpectedly engaged Watie near Cowskin Prairie, the Cherokees retired south to Spavinaw Creek to await support from Pike. But Pike, disillusioned and preparing to resign, refused to send aid. He did order Douglas Cooper, now a general, to take command of Confederate troops north of the Canadian—even as Col. J. J. Clarkson was assigned to the same task by Gen. Thomas C. Hindman, the department commander at Little Rock.

On July 3 Clarkson was encamped at Locust Grove with a force that included Drew's Cherokee regiment. At sunrise they were attacked by detachments of the First Indian Regiment and the Tenth Kansas. Most of the fighting was done by the Creeks and Seminoles, who charged through the underbrush and timber while whooping and firing. They sent Clarkson's force fleeing. Clarkson himself was captured, as was his entire wagon train. Weer moved on to take Fort Gibson.[15]

The main effect of Weer's victory, however, came when Drew's Cherokees defected almost as a body; they soon were serving in the Union ranks as the Third Indian Home Guard. Later, Chief John Ross—by his willing consent, many think—was taken prisoner at his Park Hill home near Tahlequah. Weer's Indian expedition, beset by fear of being cut off and by dissension among its officers, lost its steam and pulled back. Ross went with it, taking the funds of the Cherokee treasury and spending the remainder of the war in the East with his family.[16]

The loyalist Indian regiments were stationed on Grand River above Tahlequah as Union vanguards. On July 27 a four-hundred-man scouting unit of the Third Indian Home Guard under Maj. William A. Phillips—many of them Cherokees who had recently deserted from Drew's command—attacked Watie's Cherokees at Bayou Menard. A good many of the secessionist Indians were killed or taken prisoner before their unit was driven from the field by their fellow Indians and former comrades.[17]

The Confederates gained some revenge against Phillips's Cherokees on September 30 at Newtonia, Missouri. The Chickasaws and Choctaws under Cooper helped defeat the Union force. However, in the face of an advancing Union army under Maj. Gen. James Blunt, Cooper was forced to fall back to Fort Wayne in Indian Territory. Early on the morning of October 22, after an all-night march, Blunt made a slashing cavalry attack on Cooper's First Choctaw and Chickasaw and First Cherokee regiments, sending them reeling southward below the Arkansas River.[18]

Following this victory, the Indian regiment consolidated the Union hold on Indian Territory north of the Arkansas River, taking and destroying Cantonment Davis. The North advanced in Arkansas, also, by virtue of Blunt's victories over Hindman at Cane Hill and Prairie Grove, Arkansas, during November and December. Union Indian troops fought effectively in both battles, as did Stand Watie's Confederate Cherokees until forced to retreat with the rest of Hindman's army.

In February 1863 the pro-Union Cherokee council voted to renounce its ties with the Confederacy. The Cherokees still loyal to the South elected Stand Watie as their principal chief. Learning of this, Phillips and his Third Indian Regiment made a night march on April 25 to attack and rout the rebel camp. Watie attempted to retaliate on May 28 by ambushing a Union supply train just north of Fort Gibson, but he was chased back across the Arkansas River by federal troops.[19]

Stung but not subdued, Watie joined with other rebel forces in a sortie across the Arkansas, striking northeastward through Tahlequah and on up the Grand River. When Union pressure forced him to head back, he found himself blocked by the Grand and Arkansas rivers, which were in flood stage during this rainy summer. On June 16 the First Indian Regiment caught up with Watie at Greenleaf Prairie south of Tahlequah. It was only after a series of inconclusive charges and countercharges that the Cherokee officer and his men were able to escape across the Arkansas at Webbers Falls.

When the movement of a large Union supply train from Baxter Springs to Fort Gibson was discovered by the Con-

Stand Watie, leader of the mixed-blood Cherokee faction that favored the South, rose to the rank of a Confederate general. (Western History Collections, University of Oklahoma)

federate command, plans were made to take it. Stand Watie was dispatched with five hundred men to the Cabin Creek crossing of the road above Gibson. He was ordered to hold the train there until reinforcements arrived. When the commander of the wagon train escort discovered the trap, he parked the train under a secure guard and advanced against Watie. Because of the flooded Grand, the expected rebel reinforcements were unable to reach the scene. Supported by heavy artillery fire, a Union force comprised of Indian, black, and white troops was able to overcome a stubborn defense of the ford and drive the Rebels from the field.[20]

The stage was now set for the largest and most decisive Civil War battle in Indian Territory. The hard-pressed Confederates, hoping to regain their control north of the Arkansas, laid plans to move against Fort Gibson. The Indian and Texas troops under Cooper would be joined by those under Brig. Gen. William L. Cabell from Arkansas, forging a seven-thousand-man army that could overwhelm the much smaller Union force. The place of rendezvous would be Cooper's camp at Honey Springs on Elk Creek twenty miles south of Fort Gibson.

When General Blunt in Missouri learned of the rebel plans from civilian spies and refugees, he decided to attack Cooper's forces quickly, before the Confederates could unite. Hurrying to Fort Gibson with the First Kansas Colored Volunteer Infantry Regiment, Blunt organized a two-brigade strike command of some three thousand effectives. Wisely foreseeing the problems caused by swollen streams, Blunt ordered rafts to be constructed for ferrying troops and supplies across the Arkansas.

At midnight on July 15 Blunt himself led 250 cavalry troops and supporting artillery on a diversionary course to the north of Fort Gibson before turning west, ferrying across the Grand, and following back down its west bank to secure a selected ford of the Arkansas south of Gibson. Early on the sixteenth, Blunt's men were on the opposite side of the ford and waved across the main force, which had moved directly from Gibson to the crossing. All that day was spent in rafting Blunt's army and its equipage across the river.

Blunt had no intention of stopping there. When the crossing was finally completed at 10:00 P.M., he ordered his army forward along the route of the Texas Road until, at daylight, his advance guard located the rebel forces deeply entrenched along Elk Creek. Cooper's pickets had observed the crossing but were uncertain whether the troops were a large scouting party or the advance of a major attack.

When Blunt's forward elements appeared, a brisk exchange of fire erupted. Blunt's men were repelled, but the dampness of the misty morning seriously affected the poor-quality ammunition of the Rebels. The situation was made even worse for them when it began raining heavily, rendering many of their arms useless and forcing them to fall back to new positions where they could obtain better ammunition.[21]

Meanwhile, the Union army poured heavy artillery fire into the rebel lines preparatory to a rifle and bayonet charge at the center by the First Kansas Colored Regiment. Cooper's artillery in turn made large holes in the advancing line, but other Union regiments, including the Second Regiment of refugee Indians, moved up in support. This regiment, the Second Indian Home Guard, rushed into battle anxious to avenge their ordeal of 1861. In doing so, they placed themselves in the field of fire between the two lines.

When a Union officer issued orders for the soldiers to temporarily halt the firing and for the Second Regiment to fall back, the Confederates mistook it for a general retreat. They rose en masse to press their advantage with a charge, yelling victoriously as they rushed pell-mell into deadly volleys of Union fire.

With the rebel ranks now ripped apart, Blunt's men poured across Lee's Creek all along the mile-and-a-half front, sending their enemy fleeing and taking Cooper's camp, which they burned. Among their captured loot were iron shackles, which the Rebels had planned to use on captured black soldiers of the Union army.[22]

Blunt lost no time in pressing his advantage. After a brief rest and refitting, he quickly pushed on south to North Fork Town just behind the retreating rebel army. From there he moved on south along the Texas Road to Perryville (three miles south of present McAlester), wiping out scattered elements of resistance along the way. After driving away the Perryville defenders, the Unionists found a Confederate storehouse of arms and ammunition, clothing, food stocks, and other goods. The entire place was burned to the ground.

Blunt now turned east toward Fort Smith. After occupying Webbers Falls, he sent Col. W. F. Cloud of the Second Kansas Cavalry ahead to advance on Fort Smith. They found that the important river town and longtime military post at the very edge of Indian Territory had been abandoned by Confederate Gen. William Cabell, who feared the entrapment of his command there. Union forces occupied Fort Smith on September 1.

Blunt, who had been ill, started back to Kansas in September, confident that his forces were in control of Indian Territory. However, the hard-striking officer suffered an unexpected disaster. The infamous Confederate border-raider William C. Quantrill, who had earlier attacked the military post at Baxter Springs with a strong four-hundred-man force, ambushed Blunt's approaching entourage. Some eighty-five men of Blunt's escort were killed in the October 6, 1863, massacre.[23]

By the end of 1863, the Confederate presence in the territory was extremely weak, with rampant defection of Indian soldiers. Only the aging but determined Stand Watie now remained as a viable Confederate military threat. On October 29, he and his disaffected Cherokees rode into Tahlequah, killing several Union soldiers. He then went to nearby Park Hill and burned the home of John Ross—for whom Watie held an intense hatred—taking several of Ross's slaves.

Teaming with Quantrill on December 16, Watie attempted to capture Fort Gibson. Repelled by the garrison troops there, he returned to Park Hill and created more havoc. Two days later, units of the Third Indian Home Guard engaged Watie on the Barren Fork of the Illinois River. Once again it was Cherokee against Cherokee as the Union contingent forced the Confederates into the rocks and trees of a hillock and finally drove them from the field in disarray.[24]

In January 1864, William Phillips, now a colonel and in command of Union troops in the territory, launched a daring invasion south of the Arkansas River down the Texas Road. With patrols sweeping aside light resistance ahead of him, Phillips attacked a Confederate post at Boggy Depot, routing it and moving on toward Fort Washita. When his supply lines became overextended and rebel resistance intensified, Phillips ended his invasion and returned to Fort Gibson. He left behind some 250 dead Confederates and a wide path of destruction.[25]

To this point, Northern forces had had the upper hand in the area, but this was to change during 1864. In April, two Choctaw regiments of the Confederate Second Indian Brigade fought well in defeating federal forces at Poison Spring, Arkansas. The Union loss in killed and wounded was six times that of the Rebels. At the same time, two regiments of Cherokees, Creeks, Chickasaws, and Seminoles were taking part in a Confederate strike eastward along the Arkansas River, harassing Union outposts.

In June Stand Watie, now a general, won a major Confederate success by sinking an Arkansas River steamboat, the *J. R. Williams.* The boat was carrying a valuable load of Union military supplies upriver from Fort Smith. Though most of the goods that Watie's men had stacked on a sandbar washed away during a cross-river standoff with federal troops, the supplies were, at least, denied the Union forces at Gibson. Moreover, the incident did much to boost morale for the Rebels, causing an increase in Indian enlistments in the territory.[26]

During July, Confederate troops advanced against Fort

Smith, successfully driving the Union soldiers back and badly mauling them with artillery fire before retiring. During this encounter, Stand Watie's Cherokees and other Indian troops were involved in much of the fighting. In August, Watie with five hundred men attacked a Union haying party at Gunter's Prairie, killing twenty of the guard detail of over four hundred men. At the same time, a Confederate raiding party attacked and burned a Union supply train on Lee's Creek and followed that with an ambush of a mail-wagon escort, killing forty-three of the sixty-man escort.[27]

An overwhelming Watie-led force of nearly two thousand men fell on another haying party at the Flat Rock Ford of the Grand River north of Fort Gibson in September. The Union haying guard, consisting of more than one hundred white and black troops, put up stout resistance. They knew well enough that with black troops in their force, the Rebels would take no prisoners. Only four of the black soldiers escaped the massacre, in which the federal party lost over a hundred men while Watie suffered only three wounded.[28]

The inability to resupply Gibson by steamboat had made the Texas Road a vital northern link for the Union forces. Knowing that a large wagon train from the north was on its way to the fort, the Confederates set out to locate and waylay it. A scouting force was sent ahead to the Cabin Creek crossing of the road, where nearly two hundred Second Indian Regiment troops defended an L-shaped log stockade and hayricks.

During the night of September 17, Watie moved his eight-hundred-man Indian brigade into position along the south bank of Cabin Creek, west of the trail. Gen. Richard Gano, with his twelve-hundred-man Texas army, took up a line of battle east of the trail. They were ready and waiting when the Union caravan—an immense train of three hundred well-burdened wagons—arrived at Cabin Creek early in the morning of the eighteenth. The military escort, which included Cherokees of the Second Indian Regiment, plus the Cabin Creek garrison and a newly arrived company of Third Regiment Cherokees, added up to a little over six hundred Union effectives.

There was no delaying until morning. Under the cover of darkness, the Confederate lines began advancing on the Union position. The Union troops held their fire until the Rebels were within three hundred yards. At that point both sides commenced a heavy exchange all along the line. But the Confederate's six artillery pieces created great havoc with the animals of the Union wagon train. The terror-stricken mules, still in their harnesses, attempted to stampede, causing a melee of entangled, screaming animals, some pulling their wagons off the steep bluffs at the river's edge. Many of them were cut loose and taken by fleeing civilian teamsters.

Having accomplished their main goal of stopping the train, the Rebels withdrew for the night. But when morning came the attack was renewed, the stockade defenders were quickly routed, and the prize was taken—a highly valuable booty of guns, ammunition, clothing, blankets, liquor, wagons, and mules. Both sides lost about fifty men in the engagement; for the Rebels it was a small price for their gain in matériel and morale.

The Rebels were pursued by a federal brigade, and a brief standoff was held at Pryor's Creek before Gano and Watie slipped away at night, crossing the Arkansas River near Tulseytown. In Richmond, Virginia, the Confederate Congress honored the daring feat with a joint resolution of commendation.

Despite these successful maraudings in Indian Territory, major defeats in the East prevented the Confederacy from attending to secondary concerns in the West. Unable to obtain horses and supplies and demoralized by the South's all-too-apparent lost cause, the rebel immigrant Indians of the territory held a grand council on June 10, 1865, and agreed to surrender as independent nations.

The last Indian troops of the Confederacy to surrender were the Chickasaw and Caddo units on July 14, 1865.[29]

The whites' war in Indian Territory was over. The Civil War had decimated the tribes, as it had the nation. Now came the difficult task of rebuilding tribal unity, which had been as badly wounded as the unity of the United States.

CHAPTER 14

The Prairie Indians in the Civil War

WHEN, at the start of the Civil War, federal troops abandoned their commitments in Indian Territory and abdicated to the Confederates, most of the prairie tribes were alarmed. Particularly affected were the Leased District Indians, who lived in great fear of the Texans. Vanishing in the dust cloud of Emory's retreat were all of the assurances of protection that had been faithfully promised them, as well as any hope of receiving the much-needed annuity rations that the federal government owed them by treaty. Further, they had few arms and little ammunition with which to procure food or protect themselves from either the Texans or the often belligerent Comanches and Kiowas. For a people who had been assured over and over that their Great Father in Washington would protect and care for them and who had placed their entire welfare in the hands of the federal government, the outbreak of the war was a foreboding event.

Some twenty-five hundred Indians—remnants of the Wichita, Caddo, Anadarko, Kichai, Tawakoni, Waco, Ioni, and Tonkawa tribes, plus a few Shawnees and Delawares—were gathered together in the Leased District under the supervision of the Wichita Agency and the protection of Fort Cobb. In addition there were some Comanches who had come in, though the majority of that tribe and the Kiowas still remained on the prairie beyond the confines of the district. The Tonkawas, who were accused of cannibalism by other tribes who disliked them, alone were on good terms with the Texans.

When the Texans replaced the Union soldiers at Fort Cobb, many of the Leased District Indians fled to the prairie. However, they were persuaded to return in August 1861 by emissaries of their old acquaintance Albert Pike. Pike had ordered the Texan Charles B. Johnson, a former beef contractor for the Union, to continue the issue of rations. Escorted by a guard of Creeks and Seminoles with whom he had just signed treaties, Pike arrived at the Wichita Agency on August 6 to find all of the tribes, with the exception of the Kiowas, waiting.[1]

In a council held on August 12, Pike promised the western Indians that the Confederate States would continue to protect and feed them, requiring in return that the tribes place themselves under the authority of the Confederacy. The Texas troops would be withdrawn south of the Red River.[2] Accordingly, the small force of Texans then located at Fort Cobb left. Matthew Leeper, the former U.S. agent who was now the Confederate Indian agent, recruited thirty or so Indians as agency guards.[3]

The Indians at the agency became strongly displeased with Leeper, partly because of his disagreeable attitude but also because of the Confederacy's constant failure to live up to Pike's promises. Many Indians left the reservation to fend for themselves. Some, encouraged by the Delawares, went north to Kansas to seek refuge. The Comanches, in particular, were angry with Leeper over the failure of the agency to supply the food and goods due under their 1861 treaty.

Buffalo Hump and his warriors treated Leeper and other agency personnel with scorn and insolence. Leeper reported, "They have destroyed pretty much all of the poultry belonging to Dr. [John] Shirley, have shot arrows into his milk cows, killed several of the beeves belonging to the contractor."[4]

The young Comanches held war dances at the agency and bragged of their agility in stealing horses and taking scalps. They were also proud of the attention given them by young Comanche women. Three warriors who entered Shirley's trading post made an effort to invade his wife's bedroom, but they desisted when the trader scuffled with them. When an interpreter, Horace P. Jones, tried to admonish Buffalo Hump, the old chief gave him a severe tongue-lashing.

Matters began to deteriorate badly. Rumors were heard that some of the Indians who had gone to Kansas were planning to send down a war party to attack the agency. When Leeper heard reports that nonagency Indians had been seen lurking about the area, the frightened agent took his family and departed, leaving Jones in charge. Representatives of the agency tribes went to Jones and requested that he write Leeper and ask him not to return.[5]

The rumors and signs of trouble proved to be valid. A heavily armed band of seventy Delawares and twenty-six Shawnees had arrived on the Washita River from Kansas under the leadership of a Delaware named Ben Simon. Infiltrating the various bands still residing outside the reservation area, the Delawares and Shawnees incited the reserve Indians to revolt against the Confederates operating the agency. Adding to this fomentation was a rumor, circulating among the tribes, that the Tonkawas, the detested friends of the Texans, had recently killed a Caddo boy and were about to feast on him.[6]

Spies were sent to the agency to size up the situation there in preparation for an attack. After dark had fallen on the evening of October 23, a large and well-armed band of Shawnees, Delawares, and warriors from the other tribes moved onto the agency grounds and surrounded the headquarters building. Jones was fortunate. Hearing the agency dogs barking, he went outside to investigate. Standing by the building, he saw forms moving about in the dark. Then his ears picked up the click of rifles being cocked as the attackers approached. Without sounding the alarm to his employees, Jones jumped on his horse which was tied up nearby and fled to the safety of Fort Arbuckle.

When the Indians charged, the other four whites at the agency resisted as best they could. One Delaware was shot dead, and a Shawnee was wounded. Infuriated, the Indian mob killed all of the men. After looting the agency files, the attackers torched the building, burning it to the ground along with the bodies of the four men. For some time both Union and Confederate officials erroneously thought that Leeper had been among those killed.

The murdering was not yet done. During the night the Tonkawas, hearing the gunfire, were frightened and left the reservation en masse. When morning came, their trail was discovered and followed to a grove of trees in which they had attempted to hide. The Tonkawas had only their bows and arrows, whereas the attacking party was well supplied with guns and ammunition. It was nothing less than a slaughter. The Tonkawas were completely surrounded before the firing began. Out of some 390 men, women, and children, only about 150 managed to escape. Among those killed was Chief Placido, a highly respected Indian leader.

After the fury of the attack on the agency had subsided, it was reported that Chilly McIntosh was on his way with a large party of Texas and Indian troops. The Wichitas and other Leased District Indians now had no choice but to flee north to Kansas. Before the agency building had been destroyed, many of its papers had been seized. These, along with letters to Placido from Texas leaders such as Sam Houston, Mirabeau Lamar, and General Rusk, were wrapped in a Confederate flag and taken along.

After a difficult journey, the agglomeration of some seven hundred Wichitas, Caddos, Tawakonis, Kichais, and Shawnees reached Walnut Creek in southern Kansas. Leaving their people there, a delegation of chiefs and warriors went on to Leroy, Kansas, to meet with Union officials. They carried with them the flag, papers, twelve hundred dollars in Confederate money, and a large number of scalps taken during the Wichita Agency massacre.[7]

These tribes would remain in southern Kansas throughout the war and beyond, living in severe destitution. Scantily fed and cared for by the United States, many died from cholera and other diseases before finally being returned to their Leased District homes in 1867. Some served with the Indian Guard units.

The Comanches and Kiowas remained on the prairie, enjoying the happy respite as the attention of the whites was diverted to the Civil War. Their warriors still conducted raids against frontier settlements and transportation routes in Texas and along the Santa Fe Trail of western Kansas. But neither Texas nor the Union could divert the resources and fighting men necessary to mount any effective resistance as long as the war continued.

The Osages, now located on a large reservation area in southeastern Kansas, aligned themselves with the Union. Though they did not become involved in the struggle in any organized military way, warriors of the tribe fought a little-known but bloody battle with Confederates on the Verdigris River in the spring of 1863. It was one of the more bizarre incidents of Indian involvement in the war.

On the morning of May 23, a small band of Osage warriors spotted a party of about twenty heavily armed and uniformed white men, each towing a pack mule behind, riding from east to west across the Indians' land between the Neosho and Verdigris rivers east of present Cherryvale, Kansas. Union officials had instructed the Osages to disarm and arrest any unknown persons found on their land and to take the prisoners in to the military post at Humboldt.[8]

Accordingly, the Osages intercepted the strangers, demanding that they give up their weapons and go with the Indians to Humboldt. Instead of complying, the black-bearded leader of the group pulled a revolver and shot the Osage spokesman from his saddle, killing him. The remainder of the intruders then began firing. The Osages, outnumbered and outgunned, fell to the side of their ponies and raced back to their camp, where a force of some two hundred fighting men was quickly mustered.

About five miles east of the Verdigris River, the Osages overtook the invaders, who were dismounted and eating their noon meal. The whites quickly remounted, and a running fight followed. Two of the intruders were knocked from their saddles. The remainder of the group reached the river and took up a defensive position in a wooded bend of the stream. They displayed a white flag, but it was ignored by the incensed warriors.

Being well armed, the white men put up a stout defense before the overwhelming Osage force drove them back from the trees along the bank and onto a sandbar of the stream. Unfortunately for the defenders, the bank on the opposite side was too high and precipitous to be passable. They found themselves pinned in the riverbed. They were at the mercy of the Osage riflemen, whose fire quickly mowed them down.

When the last resistance ceased, the Osages rushed forward with their knives and battle-axes to scalp and behead their victims. The victorious Indians returned to their village with the scalps stretched umbrella-wise on the ends of sticks. They also had with them the guns, horses, sabers, saddles, and other paraphernalia they had captured. Additionally they carried some blood-stained papers taken from the pockets of their victims.

Being unsure just whom they had killed, the Osages were reluctant to report the matter to the Union officials. Finally, however, they were persuaded by an Indian trader to send word to Humboldt. Capt. Willoughby Doudna, commanding the Humboldt garrison, immediately took a company of troops out to investigate the matter. He found a gory scene of decomposed, headless bodies bearing the uniforms of Confederate cavalry. Doudna's men undertook the loathsome task of digging a trench and dragging the bodies into it with long sticks.

The papers retrieved by the Osages revealed the identity of the dead Confederates. Their leader was Col. Charlie Harrison, formerly a saloonkeeper in Denver, Colorado

Territory, and a noted gunman of the early West. Harrison—who liked to brag that he had killed twelve men in gun duels—had been evicted from Denver by Union men at the beginning of the war. He had quickly risen in the Confederate ranks during the bushwhacker war of southwestern Missouri, reportedly riding with Quantrill for a time. Another of the dead Confederates was the hot-tempered W. P. McClure, Denver's first postmaster, who had been involved in a duel and another shooting fracas before leaving Colorado. All of the men were rebel officers—three colonels, one lieutenant colonel, one major, four captains, and the remainder lieutenants.[9]

It had been Harrison's idea to return to Colorado, raid the lucrative gold-mine routes, and recruit men to serve with the South. The venture ended tragically for him and most of his party. However, it was later learned that two of the Rebels had managed to escape from the Osages by following the cover of the riverbank, eventually making their way back to Missouri.

During the spring and summer of 1864, the Comanches and Kiowas launched numerous attacks on the transportation along the Santa Fe Trail of western Kansas and eastern Colorado Territory. Ravaging wagon trains was popular with the warriors. It offered them the chance of great reward in horses, mules, and loot, with very little risk. They could ride north from their refuge in Indian Territory and the Texas Panhandle and patiently lay in wait for a slow-moving train. When one appeared, they could fall on it with a sudden, shrieking attack, often stampeding the teams and causing the runaway wagons to overturn.

Nor did the frontier of Texas escape its share of infliction. After the Brazos Reserve Indians were removed, the region above Fort Belknap attracted a scattering of settlers and cattlemen. With the Civil War having drawn away much of the protective manpower by 1864, this frontier region was virtually defenseless and ripe for an Indian attack.

On October 13, it came. A huge force of Comanche and

Kiowa raiders—more than 250—struck the settlements along the valley of Elm Creek, a tributary of the Brazos ten miles above Fort Belknap, in present Young County. A Confederate patrol organized as Bourland's Border Regiment was attacked, and five of the fifteen men were killed.

The Indians invaded the ranch home of Elizabeth Fitzpatrick, a widow, and killed a woman and a young black boy. After looting and burning the house, the raiders made off with Mrs. Fitzpatrick and six other captives. The youngest of these, eighteen-month-old Milly Durgan, would grow up among the Kiowas and marry a chief named Goombi.[10]

The Indians also attacked a fortified ranch known as Bragg's Fort, killing two men; they also raided every homestead along Elm Creek, taking horses and stock at will. In total, they killed eleven settlers, wounded several others, and made off with seven captive women and children. An important sequel to this raid was the heroic efforts of a slave, Brit Bailey (or Johnson), who repeatedly risked his life in going among the Kiowas to rescue not only his wife and daughter but two other children and Mrs. Fitzpatrick as well.

Another engagement, which involved a combined force of Confederate troops and Texas militia, took place on January 8, 1865, west of San Angelo in present Tom Green County, Texas. The 170-man force impetuously attacked a much larger force of Kickapoos who were migrating to Mexico. It was a mistake. Though the Texans were said to have killed 14 of the Kickapoos, they lost 22 killed and 19 wounded themselves.[11]

In an effort to end the Santa Fe Trail raiding, during the fall of 1864 the United States organized a force whose aim was to invade the Comanche-Kiowa sanctuary and punish the tribes. The military expedition consisted of units of the New Mexico First Cavalry and First Infantry and the California First Cavalry and First Infantry. The 14 officers and 321 enlisted men were supported by two 12-pound mountain howitzers mounted on prairie carriages. Additionally, 72 friendly Utes and Apaches were recruited. The commanding officer was the famed frontiersman Col. Kit Carson.

The small army rendezvoused at Fort Bascom, New Mexico Territory, marching from there on November 6. Trailed by its long baggage train, the command headed eastward down the north bank of the Canadian River. For over two weeks, Carson's expedition scouted for Indians along the river. Finally, signs of a large Indian encampment on the move were discovered on November 24 at Mule Creek.

Carson ordered his cavalry on ahead, keeping the infantry to guard the wagon train. A Kiowa village of 176 lodges was soon found and immediately attacked. The surprised Kiowas retreated along the Canadian to just below where Fort Adobe (also known as Adobe Walls) sat roofless and crumbling on the north bank. The post had been established around 1840 by traders from Bent's Fort on the Arkansas to barter for horses and mules with the prairie tribes. The isolated site had been abandoned when the tribes of the region had become too threatening.

Near the old ruin, the Kiowas joined a large Comanche village of some five hundred lodges. The Kiowa and Comanche warriors put up a stiff resistance that halted the cavalry drive. A number of the Indians fought on foot as skirmishers in the tall grass, their excellent marksmanship making it hot for the troops, who had also dismounted. Another larger group, mounted and wearing their war dress, "charged continually across our front from right to left and *vice versa*, about 200 yards from [Carson's] line of skirmishers, yelling like demons, and firing at intervals."[12]

The artillery had been slowed by the rough terrain. When it came up, the none-too-military Carson waved his hand toward a large body of warriors who appeared to be gathering for a charge. He suggested to the artillerymen, "Fling a few shells over thar." This was done, driving the Indians out of firing range.[13]

Now facing nearly a thousand well-mounted and well-armed Indians, Carson fell back to Fort Adobe, where his horses would be protected by the walls of the ruin. Concerned about the safety of the wagon train, he retreated up the river to the deserted Kiowa village. The troops were harassed all the way by the Indians, who burned the dry prairie grass for a smoke screen from which to shoot into the columns.

After looting and burning the village, Carson's army headed back for Fort Bascom, content with having destroyed the Kiowas' lodges and winter provisions. The claim of the expedition was nearly a hundred Indians killed and that many and more wounded. Two soldiers had been killed, and two or three more of the twenty-one wounded would eventually die. One Ute had been killed and four wounded. One scalp had been taken by Carson's men—by a Mexican youngster who had outshot a Comanche whom he had suddenly faced through the smoke of the prairie fire. The Apaches and Utes purchased it from the boy to use for a scalp dance.[14]

Though the Southern Cheyennes and Arapahos had won the right to range south of the Arkansas River, during the period of the Civil War their principal range remained western Kansas and eastern Colorado Territory. After the Colorado gold rush of 1858–59 and the resulting colonization of the territory, conflicts soon developed between the two tribal allies and whites who saw them as a threat to contacts to the east. The situation became particularly tense in Colorado Territory, which was under the civil administration of Gov. John Evans and the military-district command of Col. John M. Chivington. During the spring of 1864, after the murder of a family near Denver by a Northern Arapaho party, a sense of crisis pervaded the region.

A series of attacks on unsuspecting Indian camps along the South Platte and Arkansas rivers by Colorado troops followed. The most serious incursion into the Indian country took place in May, when Lt. George S. Eayre led an eighty-four-man, mounted detachment, equipped with two mountain howitzers, from Denver into Kansas with Chivington's orders to burn villages and kill Indians.

Cheyenne chief Lean Bear is seated, *far left*, in this White House photograph, in which Mrs. Abraham Lincoln stands, *far right*. Although carrying a letter from President Lincoln, Lean Bear was shot down by U.S. troops on the Kansas plains the following year. (Courtesy Lloyd Ostendorf)

On the Smoky Hill River, the unit came onto a large buffalo hunt that was being conducted by Cheyennes under Lean Bear, a chief who only the year before had visited Washington, D.C., and conversed with Pres. Abraham Lincoln. On seeing the troops, Lean Bear and a Cheyenne named Star rode forth to meet them and display a letter from the president indicating that they were friendly Indians. Eayre's command opened fire, shooting both Cheyennes from their ponies and killing them.[15]

The transportation lines and frontier settlements of Kan-

This famous photograph, made in Denver in 1864, shows Cheyenne chief Black Kettle, *seated, center*; White Antelope, *seated, far left*; and a young Bull Bear, *seated, second from right*. Standing, *third and second from left*, are the famous frontiersman John Simpson Smith and his son Jack. Maj. Edward W. Wynkoop, cigar in mouth, is squatted directly in front of Black Kettle. (State Historical Society of Colorado)

sas, not Colorado Territory, suffered bloody retaliation by the Cheyennes. A state of undeclared war existed through the summer of 1864, until in late August, Principal Chief Black Kettle sent a letter to Maj. Edward W. Wynkoop, commanding Fort Lyon in southeastern Colorado Territory. In it he stated the desire of the Cheyennes to make peace.[16]

In response, Wynkoop daringly led an expedition to the Republican River to meet and council with the Cheyennes. The officer was able to persuade Black Kettle and six other chiefs to accompany him to Denver for peace talks. There they were assured by Colonel Chivington, commanding the Military District of Colorado, that if they would take their people in to Fort Lyon, they would be protected.[17]

Maj. Scott J. Anthony, commanding at Fort Lyon, was quick to join Colonel Chivington in attacking the Cheyennes at Sand Creek. (Denver Public Library Western Collection)

Capt. Silas S. Soule was later assassinated in Denver for his testimony and defense of Black Kettle's Cheyennes at Sand Creek. (State Historical Society of Colorado, Denver)

Black Kettle complied, leading his small band to Fort Lyon. But the main body of Cheyennes remained on the Republican with the still suspicious Dog Soldiers. During the interim, Wynkoop was relieved of his command by army superiors because of his pacifist policies. He was replaced by Maj. Scott J. Anthony, with whom he had fought when the Colorado First Cavalry had defeated the invading Texas Confederate army under Col. Edward R. S. Canby at La Glorieta Pass, New Mexico, during the spring of 1862.

Anthony told the Indians that he had no food with which to feed them. He instructed Black Kettle to go to the bend of Sand Creek some thirty miles north of Lyon and camp where his men could hunt and procure their own food. Anthony assured the Cheyenne leader that he and his people would be safe from U.S. troops there. It was, after all, on land assigned to them by the Treaty of Fort Wise in 1861.

In Denver, meanwhile, a hot political race had heightened citizens' alarm over a rumored "war of annihilation" against whites. Chivington had recruited a regiment of one-hundred-day volunteers, the Colorado Third Regiment of Cavalry, from the streets of Denver. As time passed and they saw little action, other Coloradans nicknamed them "The Bloodless Third." Chivington feared their enlistment would come to an unfruitful end. He and Governor Evans concurred on using the volunteers in a punitive strike against the Indians. Chivington decided to attack the Indians on Sand Creek.

In mid-November, at the same time that Carson was afield in the Texas Panhandle, Chivington ordered the Colorado Third on a march through severely cold and snowy weather south to Pueblo, then eastward along the Arkansas to Fort Lyon. There he ran into opposition from Capt. Silas Soule and other officers who agreed with Wynkoop's views. They considered it a betrayal to attack the Cheyenne camp. Anthony, however, readily agreed to add the Fort Lyon First Colorado garrison to Chivington's command.

Chivington lost no time in heading north to attack the Cheyenne encampment at Sand Creek. The troops marched through the night without stopping, arriving at the bend of Sand Creek at sunrise on November 29. Without pausing to parley or to demand a surrender, Chivington sent his army forward against the sleeping village.

It was a rout—a massacre by any definition of the word. As some of the cavalry units drove between the village and the Cheyenne horse herds, others dismounted into skirmish lines and began firing into the now panic-stricken village. These riflemen were supported by two pieces of field artillery, which began lobbing grapeshot and canister into the encampment.

Despite some effort at resistance, the Indians were

Col. John M. Chivington betrayed his own promise of safety by attacking the Cheyennes under Black Kettle at Sand Creek, Colorado Territory, November 29, 1864. (State Historical Society of Colorado)

quickly put to headlong flight. Chivington sent his cavalry in hot pursuit of the fleeing Cheyennes. Any who were caught or found hiding were cut down without regard to age or sex. Among those killed was Chief White Antelope, who at the first had approached the troops and attempted to persuade them to stop. He was shot to death in the middle of Sand Creek.

Another victim was Jack Smith, the blond, half-blood son of the trader John Simpson Smith. The two had been visiting the camp. The boy (who as a crying baby had been quieted by pouring icy water on his head, as mentioned earlier) was ruthlessly murdered after the battle for defying the troops. His corpse was victoriously dragged about the camp behind a horse. Though threatened, John Smith was not harmed. Some of the Colorado Third men had bragged about taking scalps, and now they did so. Some even cut breasts from dead women and testicles from men, supposedly to make into tobacco pouches.

Chief Black Kettle managed to escape. His wife also lived through the ordeal, but only after her body was riddled with nine bullets. Soldiers had potshot her as she had lain on the ground, finally leaving her for dead. Somehow she survived and made it to the Cheyenne camps to the north.[18]

Chivington claimed a great victory in his attack on the Sand Creek village, citing thirty-eight Indians killed while losing nine of his troops. However, both the reaction of the prairie Indians to what they considered to be a base betrayal and the critical response of the American public caused the massacre at Sand Creek to become a symbol of white duplicity. The incident also prompted the wrath and power of the war element among the Cheyennes, Arapahos, and Sioux.

In the days ahead, innocent white citizens, most of them in Kansas, would pay dearly for Chivington's act.

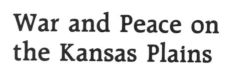

CHAPTER 15

War and Peace on the Kansas Plains

THE half-Cheyenne George Bent, son of William Bent of Bent's Fort, and his brother Charlie were among those who fled the Sand Creek village, heading north to the Dog Soldier camps on the headwaters of the Smoky Hill River. There, during December, George Bent observed turbulent councils in which the Cheyennes decided to send to the Arapahos and Sioux inviting them to a war against the whites.[1]

Warriors of those tribes readily accepted the offer. It was unusual to start a war during winter, when forage was poor and blizzards threatened, but the warriors were very angry. They talked of "war to knife" and said they would run the white man out of the country. But they knew that was impossible. The Indian campaign against whites along the Platte Road was carried out purely for revenge of Sand Creek.[2]

Some two thousand warriors from these three tribes began gathering on the Republican River while their chiefs and war captains conducted councils to plan a coordinated counterattack. Early in January 1865 the Indian force made its move. Shifting their camps closer to the South Platte trail that cut down across the northeast corner of

Colorado Territory, the Dog Soldiers and their allies started operations on January 6.

Acting as a decoy, a small party attacked a wagon train near Valley Station, killing twelve men. Under the cover of darkness, just before dawn, the greater mass of warriors took cover in the sand hills a short distance from Fort Rankin and nearby Julesburg. Daylight had barely broken when the Cheyenne chief Big Crow slipped up to the fort and made a rush on the sentinels stationed outside the walls.

Quickly enough a troop of cavalry came charging out of the fort in pursuit. Once the sixty-man unit was clear of the fort, the Indians sprang their trap. More than a thousand whooping warriors swarmed out of the sand hills to cut the cavalrymen off from the fort.

The deadly fire of the Indians began to empty cavalry saddles. Some soldiers dismounted to fight but were quickly overrun, and all but the few who managed to return to the fort were killed. The remaining garrison, civilian workers, and stagecoach riders prepared to defend the fort. But charging a fortified position was not the Indians' way. Instead they raced a mile up the South Platte to undefended Julesburg.

There they looted and plundered at will while the troops at Fort Rankin fired harmlessly with howitzers. Along with foodstuff and forage for their horses, the attackers discovered a strongbox that an army paymaster had left behind in his haste to reach the fort. Most of the Indians tossed the green paper into the air and let it blow away, but not George Bent. He stuffed as much of the currency as he could into his pockets.[3]

Another massive force of warriors returned to Julesburg on February 2, burning and looting the town along with wagon trains that had taken refuge there. The exultant Indians held their victory dance in sight of the Fort Rankin garrison, which dared not venture out. The Platte Road had become a war zone, its transportation and stage stations constant prey to swooping attacks by war parties.

The U.S. military responded with punitive strikes, and

a series of small but bloody conflicts occurred in the summer of 1865. On July 25 the Indians launched an attack on a post known as Platte River Bridge in Wyoming. After falling on an approaching wagon train, the Indians cut off and killed twenty-nine men in a rescue force under Lt. Caspar Collins. During the fight, Collins lost control of his horse and was carried head on into the attacking Indians. An arrow struck him in the forehead. His body was later found wrapped in telegraph wire, his hands and feet cut off and his heart and tongue cut out. The dead troopers were pinned to the ground with lances and similarly mutilated.[4]

Clashes between U.S. troops and the Indians north of the Platte continued into September, when warriors belonging to the Southern Cheyenne and Arapaho bands began moving south toward the Arkansas. Minor incidents had been taking place during the spring and summer of 1865 along the Santa Fe Trail as well. Even as the army and Congress had started investigating Chivington's attack on Black Kettle's camp, there had been raids on stage stations, wagon trains, and even military posts. Stock had been stolen, and two military couriers had been killed and scalped between Fort Zarah and Fort Larned.

Military men such as Gen. Grenville M. Dodge, as well as most white citizens in Kansas, argued the cause of putting troops into the field to defeat and punish the Indians. But there were others, such as the Comanche-Kiowa agent Jesse H. Leavenworth and the Cheyenne-Arapaho agent Edward Wynkoop, both former military men, who were convinced that the Plains Indian problem could be solved by peaceful means. Congress agreed, authorizing funds for a treaty council. It was hoped that with a new treaty, the prairie tribes could be removed to below the Arkansas River and the raiding of the wagon roads across Kansas could be ended.

Leavenworth dispatched Jesse Chisholm, who during the war had retreated into Kansas along with the refugee Indians, to Indian Territory to bring in the leaders of the Plains tribes residing there. Chisholm was successful in persuading most of the important chiefs to attend. Some were peace-minded chiefs, and some were war leaders of their tribes. Most were significant figures in the annals of plains warfare.

Attending for the Cheyennes were Black Kettle, Seven Bulls, Little Robe, Black White Man, Eagle's Head, and Bull That Hears. Importantly, however, none of the leaders of the Cheyenne Dog Soldiers, who were still north of the Arkansas River, were present. The absentees included important war leaders such as Bull Bear, Tall Bull, Roman Nose, and others who would play major roles in future conflicts on the plains.

The Arapahos were represented by the cigar-smoking Little Raven, along with Storm, Big Mouth, Spotted Wolf, Black Man, Chief in Everything, and Haversack.

The Kiowas attending included Little Mountain, Sitting Bear (Satank), Lone Wolf, Black Eagle, Big Bow, White Bear (Satanta), Kicking Eagle (or Eagle Who Lands With His Talons Out, better known to whites as Kicking Bird), Pawnee (or Poor Man), Bear Runs Over a Man, Plumed Lance, and Stinking Saddle Cloth. Their small associated tribe, the Plains Apaches, was led by Poor Bear, Iron Shirt, Old Fool Man, Crow, and Wolf Sleeve.

The Comanche signatories of the treaty represented the five divisions of the tribe at the time. Signing for the Yamparika (Root Eaters) were Iron Mountain, Ten Bears, Over the Buttes, Rising Sun, and Female Infant. Milky Way signed for both the Penetaka (Sugar Eaters) and Kotsoteka (Buffalo Eaters) bands. Buffalo Hump and Silver Broach also signed for the Penatekas. Eagle Drinking and Horse's Back headed the Nokonis (Go-abouts), and Iron Shirt (not the Plains Apache) represented the Denavi (Liver Eaters) band.[5]

The delegation of peace commissioners that met with these chiefs at the mouth of the Little Arkansas in October was comprised of Maj. Gen. John B. Sanborn, Maj. Gen. W. S. Harney, James Steele of the Bureau of Indian Affairs, Agent Leavenworth, and two of the most famous names on the Western frontier, Kit Carson and William Bent.

This one rare photograph exists of Kiowa chief Tohawson (Little Mountain) and his wife, Aun-kee-mah. Tohawson signed treaties with the United States at Fort Gibson in 1837, at Fort Atkinson in 1853, and at the Little Arkansas in 1865.

Chief of the Penateka Comanches, Tosh-a-wah (or Silver Broach) signed treaties with the Confederacy in 1861 and with the United States in 1865 and 1867. (Both photographs from the Western History Collections, University of Oklahoma)

Also present were numerous other traders and frontiersmen along with teamsters, clerks, scouts, and tribespeople who intermingled among the grass huts, tipis, tents, wagons, horses, and mules that were accumulated on the site of present Wichita, Kansas.

Talks got under way on October 12. The Indians were treated with presents, and the usual promises and speeches of goodwill were made. Black Kettle still felt the pain of his betrayal at Sand Creek: "Your young soldiers I don't think they listen to you. You bring presents, and

George Bent—shown with his Cheyenne wife, Magpie—was the half-blood son of fur trader William Bent of Bent's Fort on the Arkansas River. George Bent was personally involved in the Cheyenne wars and later provided much valuable information to historians.

Comanche chief Horse's Back signed both the Treaty of the Little Arkansas, in 1865, and the Treaty of Medicine Lodge, in 1867. (Both photographs from the Western History Collections, University of Oklahoma)

when I come to get them I am afraid they will strike me before I get away. When I come in to receive presents I take them up crying. Although wrongs have been done me, I live in hopes. I have not got two hearts. . . . My shame (mortification) is as big as the earth."[6] The Cheyenne leader expressed doubts about signing a treaty, saying that there were so few of his people present that it would not look right to make a treaty for his whole nation. He also requested that Cheyenne children taken by Chivington's troops at Sand Creek be returned.

Little Mountain of the Kiowas issued his tribe's claim to most of the buffalo range and the goods found there:

The Kiowas own from Fort Laramie and the north fork of the Platte to Texas, and always owned it. That [includes] all the branches, creeks, rivers and ponds that you see; all the deer and buffalo, wolves and turtles, all belong to him—were given to him by the Great Spirit. White men did not give it to him. . . . I want to tell you again and again to throw away the soldiers, and I will get all badness out of my heart, so that we can all travel kindly together.[7]

The Comanche chief Eagle Drinking agreed, saying that he loved the land he was born on and did not want to give up any more of it. The white man, he said, had taken enough of his land. "We don't want any of the Comanche lands," Commissioner Sanborn solemnly insisted.[8]

The issue of captives was central to the treaty discussions. The commission insisted on the return of prisoners being held by the Comanches and Kiowas. By agreement, a party with an army ambulance was sent into Indian Territory. It eventually returned with twenty-six-year-old Caroline McDonald of Fredericksburg, Texas; her one-year-old daughter, Rebecca; her seven-year-old nephew, James Taylor; her three-year-old niece, Dorcas Taylor; and seven-year-old James Burrow of Georgetown, Texas.[9] Eagle Drinking reminded the commission that Kiowa and Comanche children, who had been taken captive by the Texans and by Van Dorn during his attack on the Wichita village, were still being held by whites.

In a treaty signed with the Cheyennes and Arapahos on October 14, the two tribes accepted a temporary reservation located between the Arkansas and Cimarron rivers and covering sizable areas of land straddling the Kansas-Indian Territory line. In doing so, they were required to give up all claim to the vast region between the Platte and Arkansas rivers, land that had originally been assigned to them by the 1851 Treaty of Fort Laramie.[10]

The treaty initiated on the eighteenth with the Comanches, Kiowas, and Plains Apaches designated a vast reservation area including most of present western Oklahoma and its panhandle area and all of the Texas Panhandle to the southeast corner of New Mexico. The government promised each tribe money, annuity goods, and other assistance.

Eventually the chiefs reluctantly signed the pact, and all went their way. But the Treaty of the Little Arkansas was doomed from the start. The reason was simple. Only Black Kettle's peace faction had represented the Southern Cheyennes at the Little Arkansas council. The Dog Soldiers knew nothing of the treaty, had signed nothing, and still fiercely held their claim to the hunting grounds on the Republican, Solomon, and Smoky Hill rivers of western Kansas. The recent opening of a stage route along the Smoky Hill through the very heart of their country had reignited their anger over the Sand Creek attack and white intrusion.

As warrior bands moved south from the Platte River during early November, barely two weeks after the Little Arkansas treaty had been concluded, the Indians fell on five relay stations along the Smoky Hill, burning them and killing six people.[11] However, with winter setting in, the Cheyenne warriors joined camps below the Arkansas and became quiet. During this interim, the government assigned Agent Wynkoop the task of persuading the Dog Soldiers to make a peace arrangement.

Wynkoop met with the Cheyennes at Bluff Creek, Kansas, in February. Black Kettle was present, along with two Dog Soldier chiefs, Medicine Arrows and Big Head. When Wynkoop asked them to sign the recent treaty agreement, they strongly objected. They argued that even more whites would come onto their hunting grounds and drive away the buffalo. But Wynkoop, who had been outspoken in his condemnation of Chivington's actions at Sand Creek, eventually persuaded them to accept the treaty stipulations. With the help of John S. Smith, he also effected the rescue of sixteen-year-old Mary Fletcher, who had been taken captive on the Platte.[12]

The Dog Soldiers remained peaceful during the spring and summer of 1866, but they were not happy. Even as ratification of the Little Arkansas treaty waited for congres-

Despite their army guards, work crews for the Kansas and Pacific Railroad were constantly harassed by the infuriated Cheyenne Dog Soldiers. (*Harper's Weekly*)

sional approval, the war leaders renounced it. They vowed they would never give up their Smoky Hill hunting grounds and forced Black Kettle to repudiate his agreement. This created great concern in Washington, for a vital new development was under way. The Kansas Pacific Railroad was preparing to build its line west to Colorado Territory. Its route would follow the Smoky Hill River.

Wynkoop was given urgent instructions to contact the Indians and pacify them with an issue of annuity goods. The agent met with Black Kettle and other chiefs at Fort Zarah in August and found them in an agreeable mood. But from the Smoky Hill River came reports that the Dog Soldiers planned to close the Smoky Hill to white travel as soon as the Indians finished holding their Medicine Arrow ceremonies. Their hostility had been further inflamed by the wares of white whiskey traders.[13]

An initial warning of their intentions came when the

horse herd at Fort Wallace was stampeded by Cheyennes. This was followed with an attack on the Chalk Bluff stage station by forty Dog Soldiers. They burned the station and killed two men who worked there.[14] These actions added weight to the military's argument that force was the only way to deal with the Plains tribes. Fully convincing proof came on December 21, 1866, when the Sioux and Northern Cheyennes lured Lt. Col. William J. Fetterman out of Fort Phil Kearny in Wyoming Territory and killed him and eighty-one of his men.

In Kansas, two new participants had arrived on the scene. One was Maj. Gen. Winfield Scott Hancock, who assumed command of the military division that included Kansas and Indian Territory. The other was Gen. George Armstrong Custer, commanding the Seventh Cavalry as a part of the new Indian-fighting army that had been organized at Fort Riley, Kansas. Hancock decided that a show of American force and, if need be, use of it would intimidate the Cheyennes.[15]

Accordingly, in March 1867, a sizable expedition of Seventh Cavalry, infantry, artillery, and some Delaware scouts marched southwestward from Fort Riley to Fort Larned at the mouth of the Pawnee Fork of the Arkansas. From there scouts located a large encampment of Cheyennes and Sioux forty miles up the Pawnee Fork. By invitation, a delegation of chiefs, fully decked out with ornaments and their finest wear, arrived to council with Hancock despite a late-season snowstorm.[16]

Around a flickering campfire that night, the chiefs listened as Hancock promised them peace and assistance if they behaved, but severe punishment if they did not. When Hancock indicated he was going to march to the Indians' camp, the Dog Soldier chief Tall Bull advised against it. His people, he said, still remembered Sand Creek all too well.

Ignoring this, as well as Wynkoop's concurring advice, Hancock began his march up Pawnee Fork, with the Seventh Cavalry in advance. They were soon halted, however, when they came face to face with an impressive army of

Maj. Gen. Winfield S. Hancock antagonized an already-explo-
sive situation by burning the lodges of a Cheyenne-Sioux camp
on the Pawnee Fork of the Arkansas River in March 1867. (U.S.
Signal Corps photo no. 111-B-5365, Brady Collection, National
Archives)

warriors spread across their line of march. The warriors, decked in full battle array, calmly sat their ponies with their weapons poised. Among their lead was the magnificently built Cheyenne war captain Roman Nose. Four revolvers protruded from his belt, a carbine hung to one side of his pony, and he held ready his bow and several arrows. There was no doubt that he and the others were primed to fight.[17]

As Hancock and Custer brought their columns into battle formation, Wynkoop went forward and prevented what would have been a major conflict. Assured by Hancock that he would not attack, the Indians returned to their camp. Hancock followed and bivouacked nearby. He was greatly chagrined when he later discovered that the frightened Indians had deserted their camp and fled.

Hancock ordered Custer to overtake the Indians and bring them back. Custer put his Seventh Cavalry in hot pursuit, guided by the half-blood Ed Guerrier. The Indian trail kept breaking into three on the prairie. Each time, Custer stayed with the middle trail, until it simply disappeared. With no Indian tracks to pursue, Custer, an avid sportsman, went buffalo hunting.[18]

Meanwhile, Hancock, who had vacillated on burning the Indian village, finally decided to do so, against the counsel of Wynkoop. The act, the agent argued, would only further anger the Indians and do them no real harm. In the days ahead, he would be proven all too right. Further exacerbation of the situation came when a squad of troops attacked and killed six Cheyennes west of Fort Dodge without any valid reason.[19]

Still, the work crews and the advancing rails of the Kansas Pacific Railroad along the Smoky Hill River were the ultimate cause of renewed warfare. Dog Soldier leaders such as Tall Bull, Bull Bear, Roman Nose, Grey Beard, and White Horse were strong-minded fighting men who were determined to resist to the death this intrusion of their hunting grounds. Their resolve resulted in a series of bloody incidents along the Smoky Hill during the spring and summer of 1867.

Railroad surveyors, engineering parties, and work crews, as well as stage stations and workers, were attacked. Killings, scalpings, and sometimes torture became almost commonplace as the Cheyennes conducted a hit-and-run campaign of terror. On one occasion, Seventh Cavalry troops under Capt. Albert Barnitz were decoyed into an ambush near Fort Wallace. In a three-hour fight, Barnitz lost six troopers and had eight others wounded. One of them was Sgt. Frederick Wyllyams; photographs of his nude, slashed, and arrow-spiked corpse were later displayed in eastern journals.[20]

In July, Custer and the Seventh Cavalry again took the field with the intention of locating and punishing the Indians. But Custer's difficult march through the harsh cactus-studded country of northwestern Kansas and Colorado Territory netted him only one brief, inept encounter with a Sioux war party under Chief Pawnee Killer. Custer found that his heavy army mounts were no match for the light, quick ponies of the Sioux. When he reached the Platte road to the Colorado gold fields, six of his men deserted. On Custer's orders they were pursued; three were shot, and one died.[21]

During the return march to Fort Wallace, buzzards were seen circling in the distance. Riding to the spot, Custer found the bodies of 2d Lt. Lyman S. Kidder, his ten troopers, and a Sioux scout who had been carrying orders for Custer to take command at Fort Wallace. They had all been killed, scalped, and mutilated. The scalp of Red Bead, the scout, had been left discarded beside his corpse as a statement of contempt. Because of this, it was believed that Pawnee Killer's Sioux were responsible for the murders.[22]

Custer, anxious to see his wife, who was at Fort Hays, left his post at Fort Wallace, where he had been assigned, and made a dashing trip under military escort back up the Smoky Hill. This abandonment of his post and the shooting of the deserters resulted in Custer's court-martial and temporary suspension from command, rank, and pay. He returned to his former home at Monroe, Michigan, leaving behind a dismal record in his Indian-fighting efforts.[23]

While Custer had been unsuccessfully scouring the prairie for Indians to fight, the newly created Eighteenth Regiment of Kansas Volunteer Cavalry had seen duty along the Santa Fe Trail, largely as stage and wagon train escorts. The little-trained, poorly mounted volunteers, who suffered badly from an epidemic of cholera that was sweeping the area, also saw few Indians.[24]

In August one company under Capt. George B. Jenness had just joined the wagon train of Capt. George A. Armes of the Tenth Cavalry north of Fort Hays when a large force of Indians made an assault. Surrounded, the Kansas volunteers and the wagon guard defended themselves while ahead Armes also busily fought off Indian attackers. After a parley the Indians withdrew, and the troops headed back for Hays with three dead and thirty-five wounded. They claimed that at least fifty Indians had been killed.[25]

Despite these failures to inflict serious damage on the Indians, many whites still argued that military force was the only way to deal with the militant tribes. Peace treaties had been equally futile, but Leavenworth, Wynkoop, and the Indian Bureau insisted that a peaceful, less expensive, and more humane answer could be found. Once again Congress responded by approving funds for another treaty effort. The Indians recommended Medicine Lodge Creek in southern Kansas as the council site.

The Treaty of Medicine Lodge in October 1867 was one of the largest events of the southern plains, even though in the end it would prove to be another failure. The massive undertaking featured a grandiose gathering of Indian, military, and frontier notables along with a sizable corps of newspaper correspondents. Here the white and the Indian met to reside side by side for an extended period, make speeches, and interact with one another. It was also an opportunity for the many journalists to pen detailed pictures of Indian life for newspapers around the nation.

An Indian orator addresses the peace commissioners at Medicine Lodge Creek before making a new treaty. (*Harper's Weekly*)

The commission was composed of Gen. William S. Harney, Gen. Alfred H. Terry, and Gen. C. C. Augur; N. G. Taylor, commissioner of Indian Affairs; the Missouri senator John B. Henderson; Gen. John B. Sanborn, now with the Interior Department; and Samuel F. Tappan, formerly an officer with the First Colorado Cavalry and a severe critic of Chivington's Sand Creek attack. Augur had been named to replace Gen. William T. Sherman, who had publicly referred to the treaty effort as a "humbug."[26]

Holding talks first with the Comanches and Kiowas, the commissioners heard a powerful speech from Satanta. The Kiowa stated his love for the freedom of the prairie, concluding his remarks by saying, "I have no little lies hid about me, but I do not know how it is with the commissioners."[27] The Comanche Silver Broach indicated that his people had still not forgotten the San Antonio massacre of their chiefs twenty-seven years earlier.

Eventually the Comanche and Kiowa chiefs agreed to sign a treaty document that placed them on a large reservation area in present southwestern Oklahoma. They pledged to keep the peace on the frontier. In return, the government would provide the tribes with houses plus buildings for an agency, hospital, school, warehouse, and other needs. Additional help would be provided in the form of teachers, a blacksmith, a carpenter, a sawmill operator, and an engineer.[28]

The tribes signed the treaty only after a clause was introduced giving them the right to continue hunting along the Big Bend of the Arkansas River as well as in the Texas Panhandle. This was of great importance to the Indians, but it was a serious flaw in the pact, for it ensured future conflicts with white settlers in those areas.

Attempting talks with the Cheyennes, the commissioners were kept waiting for several days until the Cheyennes completed the rituals of renewing their Sacred Medicine Arrows. When they did appear, it was with an intimidating show of military strength that caused other Indians to flee in fear and sent chills down the spines of the commissioners. One correspondent, Henry M. Stanley, later of African fame, described the arrival of the Cheyennes:

> Then a blast of the bugle was heard, followed by a thousand voices, chanting the maddening Indian war saga. Slowly they advanced in five columns, crashing through the timber, plunging through the tall weeds that choked up every space, singing, and firing pistols as they came. While they were yet in the timber we could see the silver crosses and medals on their breasts gleaming in the noonday sun, then the outline of their forms, and lastly they appeared in full sight on the double trot. Five columns of a hundred men each, forty paces apart, dressed in all their gorgeous finery. Crimson blankets about their loins, tall, comb-like headdresses of eagle feathers, variegated shirts, brass chains, sleigh bells, white, red and blue worked moccasins, gleaming tomahawks, made up the personnel of a scene never to be forgotten.[29]

The Dog Soldiers played a commanding role in the negotiations. Bull Bear signed first, even ahead of Black Kettle—a sure indication that the war element was in control of Cheyenne destiny at the time. The war chief Tall Bull refused to sign the treaty document, which placed them on a reservation south of the Arkansas River. He and others

Bull Bear, longtime leader of the dreaded Cheyenne Dog Soldiers and head Cheyenne signatory of the Treaty of Medicine Lodge, was among the first to send his children to the whites' school. (Smithsonian Institution)

Yamparika Comanche chief Ho-wear (or Gap in the Woods) attended the grandiose but unsuccessful treaty council at Medicine Lodge in 1867. (Western History Collections, University of Oklahoma)

finally made their marks on the paper only after Senator Henderson had orally promised that they could continue to hunt along the Smoky Hill and Republican rivers of western Kansas.[30]

The treaty papers signed by the Cheyennes and by the government, however, did not make any such stipulation. Once again, the Treaty of Medicine Lodge failed in its primary objective of removing the troublesome Indians from the path of American advance in Kansas. Stanley called it a mock treaty, claiming that not a word of the treaty had been interpreted for the Indians and that the chiefs signed it merely as a matter of form. "How then," he asked his readers, "can the treaty have been a success?

Bull Bear and Buffalo Chief, even while they signed, said, 'We will hold that country between the Arkansas and the Platte together. We will not give it up, as long as the buffalo and elk are roaming through the country.' Do the above words seem anything like giving up all claims to that country?" Stanley predicted that when whites came, believing they had the perfect right to settle there, it would be a "burning brand—a signal for war." Events would soon prove him to be a worthy prophet. The war for western Kansas was far from over.[31]

Virtually forgotten by the government during this postwar period were the loyal refugee tribes—the Wichitas, Caddos, Absentee Shawnees, Kichais, Wacos, Anadarkos, Delawares, Tawakonis, and Ionis who resided in the vicinity of the Little Arkansas River. In 1865, after the Treaty of the Little Arkansas, the government had held a council with these tribes almost as an afterthought.

Still extremely destitute and plagued by illness, these small remnant bands were so impoverished that members were dying of starvation. Charges were made that they had been neglected, poorly supplied, and cheated by their agent, Milo Gookins.[32] After visiting a Wichita camp, one participant in the Little Arkansas treaty concluded that the coming winter "would likely finish them up."[33]

The tribes all expressed a strong desire to return to their homes in the Leased District of Indian Territory. Yet the government did nothing during the winter of 1865 and 1866, and the refugees struggled through the cold. Good rains promised a bountiful harvest during the spring of 1866, but the rain did not stop during June. The Little Arkansas and other streams overflowed, washing away the Indians' crops.[34] The refugees' situation was made even worse by the Cheyenne Dog Soldiers, who drove them from the hunting range.

Maj. Henry M. Shanklin arrived at the Little Arkansas in July 1866 to replace Gookins. He distributed some of his own supplies among the ill and aged and arranged to provide the 1,888 Indians with flour, beef, salt, and medicine. During the spring of 1867, Congress approved thirty-seven thousand dollars for returning the refugee tribes to the Leased District. However, this seemingly simple task was complicated by a series of events. Once again, heavy rains flooded the streams of the area, causing a delay in the removal until late June. But then another calamity befell the Indians. The dreaded cholera, which was spreading throughout Kansas, struck the camps at the Little Arkansas. In a five-day period, eighteen Wichitas died. The others refused to leave until they had had time to harvest the corn that the Great Spirit had given them the strength to plant that spring. If they did not protect their seed corn, they said, the Great Spirit might not give them that strength again.[35]

However, on August 3 a group of 313 Absentee Shawnees, 98 Caddos, 58 Delawares, and 8 Ionis headed south for the Leased District under the direction of Special Agent J. J. Chollar. These Indians were in apparent good health when they started, but once on the trail they too were hit by cholera. While encamped near present Enid, Oklahoma, the group was devastated by the disease. The Shawnees lost fifty of their members and the Caddos forty-seven, including several headmen.[36] Those still living struggled on south to their former reservation.

William Mathewson, an Indian trader from Kansas, was returning up the trail from the south and encountered the tragic exodus. He reported that the Indians had died and been left along the trail like "rotten sheep."[37] The bones of the dead would later cause Ephraim Creek to be renamed Skeleton Creek.

On October 15, as the Treaty of Medicine Lodge was getting under way, Shanklin finally began moving the Wichitas southward. On the trail they were soon victimized by a tragedy of another kind. Philip McCusker, who had lived among the Comanches and worked as an interpreter for Agent Leavenworth, reported:

> When the Indians got over to Cow Skin Creek a great many of them were very sick, and two of them about to die. These the Indians would not abandon, and as the agent would not

wait for them, they remained in camp on Cow Skin about 5 days. When these two Indians died, they buried them right at the Crossing and then moved over to the Ninnescah.

The night they encamped on this stream, the prairie fires were burning in all directions, but the Indians did not consider them dangerous. But toward morning the wind changed 'round to the north, a terrific gale bringing the fires down on the Indian camp with the speed of a race horse.

They made every effort to save their stock, but in spite of all exertions they lost one hundred and thirty-one saddle horses, besides mares and colts. A great many of those saved were so badly burned that I think they cannot live through the winter. This is the worse thing that could have befallen these people as they depended entirely upon their horses for supplies of meat and buffalo robes.[38]

Moving on by foot, the desperate Wichita survivors finally reached the Leased District. In 1868 C. F. Garrett, a special Indian commissioner, reported them to be "decimated by disease and hardship . . . wholly destitute of everything except the scant supplies furnished by the United States."[39] Once a numerous, powerful tribe, they had been reduced not by war but by circumstances and maltreatment. Now they would watch as the Cheyennes, Arapahos, Comanches, and Kiowas fought against impossible odds to retain their freedom and way of life.

CHAPTER 16

The Sheridan-Custer Campaign

ON September 7, 1868, a large military expedition forded the Arkansas River at Fort Dodge, Kansas, and headed south toward Indian Territory. Commanded by Brig. Gen. Alfred Sully, it consisted of nine companies of Seventh Cavalry under Maj. Joel Elliott and one company of Third Infantry. Three frontiersmen who were married to Indian women—John Simpson Smith, Amos Chapman, and Ben Clark—rode as guides and scouts. The purpose of the expedition, under the orders of Maj. Gen. Phil Sheridan, was to invade Indian Territory, attack the home villages of the Indians, and capture their stock.[1]

On arriving to take command of military affairs in Kansas during the spring of 1868, Sheridan had made a tour of the Kansas military bases to size up the situation. He was particularly angry that Agent Wynkoop had issued the Indians arms and ammunition under the agreements of the Medicine Lodge Treaty. It was not long after the issuance that a group of young Cheyennes, along with some Arapahos and Sioux, committed a series of depredations—murder, rape, and kidnapping—against white settlers on the Saline and Solomon rivers of central Kansas.

An infuriated Kansas populace demanded punishment of the Indians.

In response, Sheridan decided to send a formidable military force into Indian Territory to make a punitive strike against the homes and families of the tribes. Command of the expedition was assigned to Sully, a son of the famous portrait painter Thomas Sully. Having won distinction as a Union commander during the Civil War, Alfred Sully had also earned a reputation as an Indian fighter by putting down the Sioux in Minnesota during an 1863 uprising.

Sully hoped to surprise the Indians. He issued orders that no bugle calls would be sounded and that the troops would observe strict silence.[2] There was no way, however, to silence the trumpeting brays of the expedition's jackasses. Two companies of Seventh Cavalry rode ahead as advance guard, two more rode on each flank, and two followed behind as rear guard for the long, two-abreast wagon train that carried supplies, ammunition, and forage for the stock. The remaining troop was detailed as the headquarters guard. As soon as the march was under way, the soldiers of the Third Infantry disappeared into the backs of the wagons. The officers of the Seventh Cavalry were disgusted that Sully chose to ride in a covered army ambulance.

The caravan moved slowly southward, the cumbersome wagon train finding it hard going over a countryside of deep ravines, creeks and rivers, and sand hills. Sully ordered four companies of the Seventh to search ahead for Indians. The Indians, however, found him first. Three days into the march, the expedition was moving along the north bank of the Cimarron, with the three guides riding in advance. A squad of Indians—Cheyenne Dog Soldiers, it was thought—suddenly appeared from over a rise, cutting off the scouts from the main caravan.

The frontiersmen were able to hold the Indians off until a detachment of cavalry arrived. Sully later claimed that in the exchange of gunfire, two of the Indians were killed. That night, as the command was in camp at the conflux of

Maj. Gen. Philip Sheridan put into effect the strategy of attacking the Plains Indians in their home villages in order to defeat their warriors. (U.S. Signal Corps photo no. 111-B-2520, Brady Collection, National Archives)

Gen. Alfred Sully commanded a cumbersome and inept expedition into northwestern Indian Territory in 1868. (U.S. Signal Corps photo no. 111-BA-313A, Brady Collection, National Archives)

the Cimarron and Crooked Creek, the Indians harassed the troops with rifle fire and arrows.[3]

Then, on the following morning, as the last of the wagons were pulling out from the campsite, the Indians made a lightning move against two soldiers, a cook and his helper, who were still harnessing their mess-wagon team. A band of yelping warriors poured out of a draw and swooped down on the pair. The Indians jerked the hapless soldiers across the backs of their ponies, snatched the reins of the team, and dashed away.[4]

The soldiers' cries for help alerted the two troops of the Seventh Cavalry riding as rear guard. They immediately gave chase, pouring a barrage of pistol fire at the fleeing Indians. But as they began to close in on the two double-loaded ponies, one of the Indians shot his captive and dumped the soldier, badly wounded, to the ground. The other kidnapper made his escape with his victim still screaming to be rescued. Sully, upset by the breach of formation, sent a staff officer to order further pursuit halted, much to the continued unhappiness of the Seventh Cavalry officers.[5]

The expedition continued its march on south to where Beaver Creek and Wolf Creek join to continue southeastward as the North Canadian River. They were paralleled all the way by warriors who rode the distant ridges, jeered, and sometimes stood on the backs of their ponies to thumb their behinds at the soldiers. Intermittent charges were made by the Indians against the rear-guard units. The attacks were repulsed by gunfire.[6]

The soldiers spotted the twin ruts of Indian travois leading into the sand hills east of the mouth of Wolf Creek. Thinking he was on the trail of an Indian village, Sully ordered his command to pursue. Soon his wagons were embedded axle-deep in the loose sand, virtually unable to move. Finally, it was realized that the Indian warriors had been dragging double poles weighted with stones behind their ponies.

Taunting Indians appeared atop sand hills ahead; but when cavalry units were sent in pursuit, the warriors vanished, only to appear atop still another hill, luring the troops onward. Sully's situation became so hopeless that there was no choice for him but to give the order to turn about and return to Kansas. In his report on the expedition, he optimistically claimed that he may have killed some twenty-two Indians to compensate for his casualties of three dead (counting the kidnapped man) and five wounded.[7]

There had been no battle, only distant skirmishing. Sully's effort to use a large, heavily encumbered wagon expedition to surprise the Indians in their home lodges had proved to be a gross failure. The Indians had made him look foolish, and he had done them no appreciable damage.

Sheridan would have to find another way to make war

Maj. George A. Forsyth led a force
of fifty civilians, most of them totally without frontier experience,
deep into Indian country, where
he very nearly lost them all at
Beecher's Island. (Kansas State
Historical Society, Topeka)

against the Plains tribes. In fact, he had another effort
under way even as Sully was in the field. He had authorized Maj. George A. Forsyth and a small force of frontier
scouts to foray into the Indian stronghold of western
Kansas.

Forsyth selected as his second-in-command a young
lieutenant who had been winning laurels as an officer and
scout on the Kansas frontier. He was 1st Lt. Frederick H.
Beecher, a nephew of the famous New York clergyman
Henry Ward Beecher. Also assigned to the group were Dr.
John H. Mooers, as the company surgeon; W.H.H. McCall,
a former Civil War brevet brigadier general, as first sergeant; and Abner T. "Sharp" Grover, a tough, seasoned
frontiersman, as head scout. However, many of the fifty-

Lt. Fred Beecher, nephew of Henry Ward Beecher, was killed on the Arikaree along with the famous Cheyenne war leader, Roman Nose. (Kansas State Historical Society, Topeka)

three members, who styled themselves as the "Solomon Avengers," had little or no Indian-fighting experience.[8]

Outfitted with good horses, Spencer rifles, Colt revolvers, and other equipment, the scouts rode west out of Fort Hays on August 29, 1868. Each man had 140 rounds of rifle ammunition, 30 rounds for his revolver, and seven days' rations. The scouts beat out the country between the Smoky Hill and Republican rivers without seeing more than abandoned Indian camps and old trails before they went in to Fort Wallace. While resting there, they received word of an Indian attack on a freighter's wagon train. Galloping to the scene, they picked up the trail of some twenty-five war ponies. They followed the tracks northward only to find that the trail became dimmer and dimmer until finally there was none at all.

An artist visualized the Battle of Beecher's Island for *Harper's Weekly* magazine, October 17, 1878. (Kansas State Historical Society, Topeka)

They had now ridden well into the heart of the Cheyenne and Arapaho hunting grounds of northwestern Kansas. Both Grover and McCall advised Forsyth against continuing on with such a small force, but the zealous officer would not listen. Pushing ahead, the scouts reached the Republican River, there picking up another Indian trail. This one led to the west up the Arikaree Fork of the Republican into Colorado Territory.

They began to see more and more fresh Indian signs, and there was a growing awareness that they were deep in hostile Indian country. On the evening of September 16—at the same time that Sully was making his way back to Kansas—the scouts went into camp on the bank of the Arikaree. The men were just beginning to stir the following morning when the sentry sounded the cry of "Indians! Indians!"[9]

Several warriors rushed the scouts' horses, war-whooping and waving blankets in an effort to stampede the animals. At the same time, hundreds of other Indians, mounted and afoot, suddenly appeared from all quarters. A barrage of gunfire drove the surprised scouts back, forcing them onto a sandbar in the center of the stream. In the excitement of the moment, they committed a critical error by leaving behind the pack mules with all of the rations and medical supplies.

The scouts took up positions behind trees and in scooped-out sandpits for protection against the heavy fire. They soon began to suffer casualties. Forsyth himself was the first wounded when he was hit in the right thigh. Soon afterward, a shot shattered the bone of his left leg. Dr. Mooers dragged Forsyth to the safety of a hole he occupied, but then the surgeon himself was struck in the center of the forehead by a bullet. Mooers would lie mortally wounded for three days before dying.[10]

The Indians were Cheyennes, and at their lead was the magnificent Roman Nose, who appeared downstream astride his war pony. Stripped to the waist, his face daubed with paint and his long multicolored warbonnet trailing behind, the Cheyenne war leader marshaled his excited followers into the creek bed in preparation for a rush against the embattled scouts. When he sounded his war whoop, the charge was on.

The pounding tide of warriors flooded down the channel, but the steady fire of the scouts with their Spencer rifles (carrying six shots in the magazine in addition to one in the barrel) broke the momentum of the attack. Several such charges were repulsed. Eventually, however, the determined Roman Nose and his pony made it through the fusillade of bullets. It was just after his pony had jumped over the position of one of the scouts that a bullet caught Roman Nose in the back. He rode to his camp and lay down, and on the following morning he died.[11]

During one charge, Lieutenant Beecher was hit in the side by a bullet that went on to sever his backbone. The young officer writhed in pain until sundown, when he died. The death of Roman Nose had quieted the desire of the other warriors to overrun the island defenders. Now they began to shoot the scouts' horses, picking the animals off one by one until all were killed. After another weak dash or two, the Cheyennes gave up their siege and faded away, leaving the field to the badly cut-up remnants of the scouting force.[12]

Four of the scouting party were dead, and twenty-seven were wounded. Their only food was the flesh of the dead horses. The stench of death under the blazing autumn sun became almost unbearable, and the wounded men suffered badly from infection and maggots. Four of the scouts managed to slip away, two at a time, to go for help. Finally, on the ninth day after the attack began, a relief column reached the desperate group. The survivors were loaded into army ambulances and taken to Fort Wallace.

The Cheyennes had failed to wipe out the small force of embattled scouts, their mass charges proving ineffective against the firepower of the Spencer repeating rifles and Colt revolvers. At the same time, Forsyth had been foolish to invade the Indian heartland with such a small force. He and most of his men had barely escaped annihilation, and the message to Sheridan was clear. This too was no way to fight Indians.

Sheridan now decided on a different military tactic—a winter's campaign that would strike the home villages of the tribes who had retreated into the sanctuary of Indian Territory. This time he would establish a supply post closer to the Indians and attack with freshly mounted troops. The tribes had been drawn south for the winter by the reactivation of old Fort Cobb on the Washita under the command of Maj. Gen. William B. Hazen. Cobb served as an agency post for the issuance of annuities to the hungry tribes who came there for food and subsistence.

Sheridan's campaign involved a three-pronged drive into Indian Territory: one pushing southeastwardly from Fort Lyon, Colorado Territory, under Maj. Gen. Eugene A. Carr; one marching east from Fort Bascom, New Mexico, under Maj. A. W. Evans; and one moving south from Fort Dodge, Kansas, under General Sully and Maj. Gen. George

A. Custer. The Fort Lyon and Fort Bascom units would serve as "beater-in" units to drive the Indians before them toward the Fort Dodge force. Sheridan himself would accompany the Dodge expedition.[13]

Custer, a favorite of Sheridan's from Civil War days, had been recalled from his home in Michigan, where he was languishing and writing his memoirs. He was restored to the command of the Seventh Cavalry, which had been led in the interim by Maj. Joel Elliott.

With Custer commanding the Seventh Cavalry and Sully in charge of the march, the huge train of wagons, infantry, and cavalry departed Fort Dodge on November 12, 1868, and headed back to the Beaver and Wolf juncture. It was planned that the expedition would be joined there by troops of the Nineteenth Regiment of Kansas Volunteer Cavalry under the former Kansas governor Samuel J. Crawford, marching from Topeka. Crawford, the commander of a Union black regiment during the Civil War, had resigned his governor's post to lead the Nineteenth.

Sully, meanwhile, arrived at his destination and put his infantry men to work building a fortification that would become known as Camp Supply (later designated as a fort). Friction had already developed between Sully and Custer over field command. When Sheridan reached Camp Supply a few days later, he quickly opted in favor of Custer—who had greeted him on his arrival and had serenaded him with the Seventh Cavalry band. Sully was sent back to Kansas with the wagon train. Sheridan also lost no time in putting Custer and the Seventh Cavalry in the field. Sheridan's orders were typically harsh: "Proceed south, in the direction of the Antelope Hills, thence towards the Washita River, the supposed winter seat of the hostile tribes; . . . destroy their village and ponies; . . . kill or hang all warriors, and bring back all women and children."[14]

Custer was anxious and ready. Undaunted by a snowstorm that struck on the evening of November 22, Custer had his troops in their saddles early the following morning. With a foot of snow on the ground, he headed along

Bvt. Maj. Gen. George Armstrong Custer is considered by many Plains Indians to be the white arch villain for his massacre of Black Kettle's village on the Washita on November 27, 1868. (Western History Collections, University of Oklahoma)

Maj. Joel Elliott, second in command of the Seventh Cavalry, was still unaccounted for when Custer retreated from the Battle of the Washita. Later his mutilated body was recovered. (Kansas State Historical Society)

Camp Supply was constructed at the conflux of Beaver and Wolf creeks in present northwestern Oklahoma as a supply base for Sheridan's winter campaign of 1868–69. (*Harper's Weekly*, February 27, 1869)

the southwesterly course of Wolf Creek—following the
same route that his old Civil War foe "Jeb" Stuart had used
in searching for Indians in 1860. Between present Gage
and Shattuck, Oklahoma, Custer abruptly swung southward from Wolf Creek toward the Antelope Hills.[15]

On reaching the Canadian River, Custer dispatched
three of his eleven companies of Seventh Cavalry under
the command of Major Elliott to scout westward along the
river for what should have been a clear sign left in the
snow-covered ground by any Indian war party. With his
wagons and remaining cavalry waiting at the foot of the
Antelope Hills, Custer and his staff officers rode to the top
of one of the buttes for a panoramic view of the countryside. It was from there that he spotted a horseman riding
from the west, moving like a black dot in the snow.

It was a courier from Elliott bringing the exciting news
that the recently made trail of a war party had been discovered. Elliott had already crossed the river and was following the trail southeastward. Exactly what orders Custer
had given Elliott are not known, but it is certain he did
not want his subordinate taking off on his own to engage
the enemy. Custer moved quickly. Parking his baggage
train with an eighty-man guard and taking only seven
ammunition wagons, he headed the remainder of his regiment at a fast pace directly south on a line that would
intercept Elliott.

The lead position of the march was changed constantly
to relieve the tired horses who broke the path through
heavy snowdrifts. Custer's force pushed forward from
midmorning until late in the evening before finally finding
and joining Elliott's trail. Custer sent a special detail on
ahead with orders for Elliott to hold up and wait; and it
was well after dark before the main command overtook
Elliott's detachment on the Washita.

There was no thought of making a camp for the night.
Custer's forte during the Civil War had been long, fast
marches that let him suddenly appear where the enemy
did not expect him. After a brief rest, the reunited Seventh
Cavalry was in the saddle, with the Osage scouts in the

van, plunging ahead eastward along the river—a snaking column of shivering men and laboring horses winding silently under a bright moon along the snow-whitened banks of the Washita.

The first indication that they were nearing an Indian camp came when the Osages reported they smelled smoke. Soon after, they found the dying embers of a campfire thought to have been left by Indian boys guarding a horse herd. Now Custer himself joined the two scouts at the lead as they cautiously advanced from hilltop to hilltop to reconnoiter ahead.

Finally one of the Osages returned to announce that there were "Heap Injuns" ahead. Crawling to the crest of a ridge, Custer could see the dark shapes of animals grazing. This, along with the tinkling of a bell such as Indian ponies sometimes wore, the yapping of a dog, and the crying of an infant, confirmed the presence of an Indian village somewhere near.

Retreating to a secluded position, Custer sent three white scouts forward to locate and size up the village. When they returned to report that they had found an Indian village of some fifty lodges nestled in a bend on the south bank of the Washita, Custer formed his command into four units. They would take up positions surrounding the village, and at dawn Custer would give the signal to attack. The ammunition wagons would be held back, ready to pick up the overcoats and haversacks laid aside by the troops, and would move forward when the fighting began.

Custer had no idea to what tribe this village belonged; he knew only that it was a Plains Indian encampment and that it offered him a chance for the victory he sought. As he waited impatiently for his moment of glory on November 27, 1868, he did not realize the historical coincidence—that this was the same camp of Cheyennes under Black Kettle that four years before, on the morning of November 29, 1864, Chivington had massacred at Sand Creek, Colorado Territory.

Only a few days before this cold morning of 1868, the Cheyenne peace chief had gone to Fort Cobb and talked with General Hazen, asking sanctuary. Hazen had refused, but he had warned Black Kettle that General Sheridan was in the field. When he offered to permit the Cheyenne chief to take refuge at Cobb, Black Kettle refused to leave his people. Before retiring on the night of November 26, the Cheyenne elders had decided that on the following day they would move their camp to a safer location.

It was a long, flesh-numbing four hours for the troops before the first light finally appeared on the eastern horizon. Custer was preparing to give his signal when a shot rang out on the northeast side of the camp. A Cheyenne man, who had come out to investigate his barking dog and spotted the movement of a trooper, had fired the shot alarming the village. Immediately Custer ordered his bugler to sound the call to attack, and the Seventh Cavalry band struck up the Scottish martial air "Garryowen." The pandemonium of battle exploded the serenity of the winter morning. All around the perimeter of the Cheyenne camp, Custer's troops jabbed spurs to their horses' flanks and yelled their huzzahs in a charge on the Indian camp, firing at the forms of frantic people as they fled from their lodges and scurried in every direction. Mingled in the overall thunder of the charge were the barking of orders by officers, the crack of gunfire, the defiant whoops of warriors, and the screams of women and children.

The troops poured into and through the camp, Indians fleeing before the soldiers. Many of the villagers gave their lives hopelessly trying to stymie the avalanche of horsemen that had fallen on them. Within a few minutes, perhaps ten, the occupants had been driven from the camp into gullies and the riverbed. The fight soon became a melee, and military order was lost. The cavalrymen, alone or in small squads, galloped in pursuit of escaping Cheyennes, giving no quarter.

Many of those villagers who managed to avoid the bullets or sabers of the cavalrymen were picked off by a platoon of forty dismounted sharpshooters. Among those killed were Chief Black Kettle and his wife, who were shot from the back of the chief's horse and fell into the ice-crusted channel of the Washita.

Custer claimed 103 Cheyenne warriors were slain at the Washita; however, that number may well be suspect, and it is certain they were not all warriors.[16] Four men of the Seventh Cavalry lay dead on the field, among them Capt. Louis McLane Hamilton, the grandson of Alexander Hamilton, who had been struck in the chest by a bullet and killed instantly.

When the fighting was done, Custer ordered the Indian ponies rounded up and shot and the village burned. Now it was realized that seventeen men were missing along with Major Elliott. An officer recalled to Custer that Elliott, with Sgt. Maj. Walter Kennedy, had headed off with a detachment of men in pursuit of a small band of Indians. As he left, Elliott had waved to his friend and yelled, "Here goes for a brevet or a coffin!"[17] That was the last he or the men with him had been seen, though heavy firing had been heard in that direction. Custer sent a scout with a detail of men to search for Elliott, but they returned to report they had found nothing.

By now the hills around the battle site were swarming with mounted Indians. They had come from large Cheyenne, Arapaho, and Kiowa camps that stretched for some distance eastward along the Washita valley. Realizing that the camp he had struck was merely the small tip of a much larger encampment and that a sizable force of warriors was still in the field, Custer became concerned about his situation.

His ammunition supply had been seriously depleted, and the Indians might well cut him off from his wagon train at the Antelope Hills. The darkness of the winter evening was closing in, and it would be dangerous, indeed, to remain at the battle site. He had easily overwhelmed the small Cheyenne village; he had the victory he desired. But Custer had no desire to engage a large force of forewarned Indians in open battle.

The problem now was how to get back safely to Camp Supply with his victory and the women and children he had taken captive. On the advice of his scouts, Custer drew his troops into formation and, with the band playing the Civil War air "Ain't I Glad to Get out of the Wilder-

Willam S. Soule was on hand at Camp Supply to photograph the Cheyenne women and children taken captive at the Battle of the Washita. (Archives and Manuscript Division, Oklahoma Historical Society)

ness," feinted a march downstream toward the Indian villages. As predicted, the warriors watching from the hills immediately flew to the protection of their families and homes. Then, when darkness had fallen, Custer ordered a countermarch, and the Seventh Regiment headed at a quick pace back toward the Antelope Hills, not stopping to rest until two in the morning.

Custer returned to Camp Supply on December 1 and reported to Sheridan with much fanfare, exultant at the great victory he had won over the Cheyennes. Sheridan was pleased with Custer's success, but he was determined to follow up on the victory. During Custer's absence, the Nineteenth Kansas Volunteer Cavalry Regiment had arrived at Camp Supply after a near disastrous march through the late November blizzard. Many of their horses were lost, and others in poor condition had been left behind. Sheridan and Custer set out for Fort Cobb at the head of the Seventh and Nineteenth regiments.[18]

The march was made via the Washita battlefield, largely because the question of Elliott and his detachment hung over Custer's hurried retreat. Custer—the dashing, long-haired Civil War hero—was receiving much criticism from officers for leaving the battlefield without knowing the fate of the missing men.

The answer was found on December 11 when the scene of Custer's massacre was revisited. A search party found the frozen, nude bodies of Elliott, Sergeant Major Kennedy, and fifteen other men, all chalky white in death, all with numerous bullet and arrow wounds, and all severely mutilated by beheading or throat slashing. One trooper was never found.

Also discovered on the battle site were the bodies of Clara Blinn and her two-year-old son, who had been taken prisoner in an attack on a wagon train in Colorado Territory the previous October. She had been shot in the head and her skull had been crushed; the dead child had a single bruise on his head. Mrs. Blinn's story was even more tragic in that an attempt to rescue her had been made a short time before by Cheyenne Jenny, the wife of the Indian trader Dutch Bill Greiffenstein. However, Jenny herself had died before the rescue could be made. All of the dead enlisted men were buried in a common grave on a knoll overlooking the Washita. The bodies of Elliott, Mrs. Blinn, and her child were taken with the expedition as it moved on down the winding Washita toward Fort Cobb.

En route there was an interesting confrontation between Custer and the famous Kiowa chief Satanta, who rode at the head of a large force of warriors. Refusing to shake hands with the chief, Custer issued Sheridan's demand that the Kiowa accompany the troops to Fort Cobb. Reluctantly Satanta consented and went along. At Cobb, Sheridan had him taken prisoner and put in leg-irons as a hostage to the surrender of his tribe. The tough-minded Sheridan threatened to hang the chief if he did not bring his tribe in to Fort Cobb. Other Kiowa chiefs, aware that their villages might well suffer the same fate as Black Kettle's, soon arrived with the majority of their people and went into camp near the fort.

A Cheyenne captive girl was also sent out with instruc-

These three Cheyennes, invited by Custer to his camp, were seized and held hostage against the return of two white women captives of the Cheyennes. (Archives and Manuscript Division, Oklahoma Historical Society)

Kiowa war chief Satanta (White Bear), one of the most refractory warriors on the southern plains, eventually died in the federal prison at Huntsville, Texas. (Western History Collections, University of Oklahoma)

Arapaho chief Big Mouth is said to have led the war party that killed Major Elliott and his men during Custer's attack on the Cheyennes at the Washita. (Photo by Alexander Gardner, Washington, D.C., 1872; Smithsonian Institution, Bureau of American Ethnology, neg. no. 68)

tions for the Cheyennes and Arapahos in the area to come in to the fort. On the night of December 31, 1868, in extremely cold weather, twenty-one Cheyenne and Arapaho chiefs arrived at Cobb. The freezing, destitute chiefs had come on foot, they said, because both their horses and their people were dying of starvation. There were no buffalo to be found, and all of their camp dogs had been eaten. They asked for food, agreeing to keep peaceful relations with the whites. Sheridan promised them safety and provisions if they came in. However, the fearful Cheyennes still had not arrived by January 6, when Sheridan relocated his command post from Fort Cobb to a newly established location forty miles south on Medicine Bluff Creek just east of the Wichita Mountains. The new post would become known as Fort Sill.

While Sheridan and Custer were dealing with the Indians at Fort Cobb, another of the prongs of Sheridan's Indian Territory campaign had been scouring the country west of the Wichitas. This was Evans's Fort Bascom command, which had been engaged in building a subdepot on Monument Creek in the Texas Panhandle at the time of the Washita fight.

On December 15, Evans headed down the Canadian River with a force consisting of 459 officers and men of the Third U.S. Cavalry Regiment and Thirty-seventh U.S. Infantry and nine scouts. Also in the group were thirty-three citizen packers and teamsters plus additional horses and pack mules, four six-mule wagons with forage and ammunition, four howitzers, and a herd of fifty beef cattle. Despite the cold weather, only one canvas tent was permitted, that for hospital purposes.[19]

Evans considered going north to Wolf Creek, where—Pueblo Indians had told scouts—a large number of Cheyennes, Arapahos, Kiowas, and others were camped. However, on December 18, while within twenty miles of the Antelope Hills, Evans struck the trail of an Indian village of fifty to sixty lodges. Following the trail south, he crossed the headwaters of the Washita and continued on to the North Fork of the Red River, moving with caution down the North Fork to the eastern foothills of the Wichita

Mountains. There the guides lost the Indian trail in the hard, granite-pocked country. Evans circled about in an effort to relocate it and to find a warm camping site on the bitterly cold day of December 25.

Before the day was done, Evans's command was engaged in a hard battle with Indians near the mouth of Devil's Canyon. The fracas began when two Indians were spotted. A detachment of thirty-four men under Maj. E. W. Tarlton was sent in pursuit while the rest of the command located a camp. Crossing the North Fork very near where the Wichita village had been visited by the Leavenworth-Dodge expedition in 1834, Tarlton proceeded eastward along the north bank. There he met a large force of mounted warriors.

These Indians were from a village directly ahead. They had been watching Evans's command as it wandered about, hoping their location would not be discovered. But when Tarlton had begun moving in their direction, a war party had rushed forth to head off the intruders. Who fired the first shot is not known. The Indians made a strong charge on the detachment with rifles, pistols, and lances. They were repulsed, leaving four of their dead on the ground. Among the Indian casualties was a Comanche chief named Arrow Point who was carried, mortally wounded, from the field, leaving behind an ancient Spanish lance he had taken into battle.

The Indians made two more charges, but the troops drove them back through a stand of timber in the canyon. Tarlton, whose horse had been shot from under him, sent a call to the main command for reinforcements and artillery. More troops and the two mountain howitzers were rushed forward, and the combined unit advanced down the river.

After pushing some two miles from the scene of the first action, the troops sighted the Indians' village located in a large, wooded bend of the river at the base of a mountain (in present Kiowa County some fifteen miles east of Mangum, Oklahoma). The howitzers were brought into action, and two shells were thrown into the village. Only one exploded, but it was enough to cause a hurried evacuation by the Indians. Now a cavalry charge was made, driving the villagers into the hills and capturing the camp.

The troops found the encampment to be a rich one. Its sixty or more lodges were mostly new and well made, their red-cedar poles long and straight and the covering skins neatly dressed. An ample supply of foodstuff for the winter was found—some 25,000 pounds of buffalo meat, 150 bushels of Mexican corn, 200 sacks of corn meal, and large quantities of sugar and coffee. There were also large supplies of tobacco (which the soldiers divided among themselves), brass kettles, iron pots, tin buckets, knives, axes, camp kettles, hammers, anvils, rifles, pistols, shields, and lances. Nearly 1,000 buffalo-hide panniers, used to transport goods, were discovered, along with some 200 lariats and the playthings of Indian children. The Indians had managed to escape with their best furs and ponies, thus preventing the troops from carrying off much of the goods. Everything except the meat, corn, and tobacco was torched and destroyed.

At first the soldiers thought the village was Cheyenne; later it was found to be Comanche under Chief Horse's Back, who had signed both the Treaty of the Little Arkansas and the Treaty of Medicine Lodge and was known to be friendly to whites. Once again an Indian camp had been attacked and demolished with no prior knowledge as to its tribe or whether the camp was hostile or friendly. It was later said that men of this band had recently raided Spanish Fort and Gainesville, Texas; however, the goods found in the camp smacked more of trade items than raiding loot.

The fighting was not yet done. Indian riflemen harassed the troops from positions behind the granite rocks of the ridges above, causing the soldiers to fall back to a grove of trees until Evans arrived with the main command. More Indians also appeared on the scene—fancy-decked warriors who poured down from the bluffs of the river's south bank. They displayed their horsemanship, riding about in circles and waving their shields. These turned out to be Kiowas from the village of Woman's Heart, who had heard the sound of the fighting and had come to support the Comanches.

When it appeared that the Kiowas would try to cross the river behind the command, Evans deployed the Thirty-seventh Infantry in a line along the riverbank and stifled the flanking movement. Meanwhile, the Indian sharp-shooters in the bluffs ahead at the mouth of Soldier Springs Creek were causing trouble for Evans's forward elements. When an infantryman was hit and mortally wounded, Evans ordered three companies of the Third Cavalry to dismount and push forward to flush out the sharpshooters. Several Indians fell and were carried away by comrades.

On another occasion a troop came onto the members of a large war party in a ravine and drove them off. Again the Indians left no dead behind, but the soldiers reported much blood left on the ground and a number of riderless ponies. During the night the Indians tried to burn the grass to the windward of the command and at daybreak shot at the pickets. However, they made no attempt to assault the command.

In total, Evans's loss was only the one man, with two others suffering slight wounds. The action, recorded in military records as Engagement on Salt Fork, Indian Terri-tory, is generally known now as the Battle of Soldier Springs.[20]

Evans turned back to the north, striking the Washita River west of Fort Cobb. He considered hunting out the Wolf Creek region before returning to the Monument Creek depot, but his horses were becoming weak from having to forage on grass alone. Many were dying and had to be abandoned. Also, rations for the troops were growing short, and the men were suffering badly in the intense cold.

On December 30 the Fort Bascom command met with four scouts from Fort Cobb twenty miles to the east. From them Evans learned that Custer had succeeded against Indians at the Washita and that Sheridan was at Cobb. Evans dispatched a detail to contact the general, report the events of his march, and request supplies. Sheridan responded with eight days' rations and directed Evans to proceed to his subdepot, which the troops reached on January 13 after a month in the field.

The third prong of Sheridan's campaign—Carr's incursion from Fort Lyon southward along Beaver Creek—was uneventful. Having failed to find any Indians in its march to Evans's supply depot on Monument Creek, the force turned back for Fort Lyon.

However, there was more action ahead for Custer. In early March 1869, he led his Seventh Cavalry and the Nineteenth Kansas on a trek into the Texas Panhandle in an effort to locate and rescue two white women whom the Cheyennes were known to be holding. After a grueling march west along the Red River and north to the Sweetwater River of the Texas Panhandle, Custer came onto a Cheyenne camp under Chief Medicine Arrow.[21]

The meeting was friendly, but later, when the Indians accepted Custer's invitation to his camp, he ordered his men to grab three and hold them as hostages against the release of the two captives. The women were brought in and turned over to the troops. Still Custer refused to release his three prisoners, taking them along as he marched his command back to Camp Supply and on to Fort Hays, Kansas.

Sheridan's winter campaign, though conducted largely to free Kansas from the warring of the prairie tribes, had resulted in the conquest of what is now the western portion of Oklahoma. Custer's massacre of the Cheyenne village and the establishment of new military posts had changed the balance of power in the region. The Plains Indians no longer dominated the vast prairies of the Comanchería.

Although the land had been conquered, the warring spirit of the prairie tribes was not yet dead. Additional bloody battles would have to be fought. But now Sheridan knew how to conquer the Plains Indians—strike them in their lodges without giving a warning or a chance to surrender, kill them at random, capture their horses, then burn their lodges and subsistence.

This, in hard truth, was the way the West was won.

CHAPTER 17

The Kiowa
Resistance

FOR years the Kiowas had played a secondary role in Comanchería. Although their warriors were
known to be among the fiercest of fighters on the plains,
the small, elusive tribe was viewed largely as an adjunct
to the allied Comanches. It was only after 1870 that the
Kiowas emerged as a major obstacle to the U.S. government's attempt to bring peace to Indian Territory. They
would prove to be difficult, implacable foes who would
not bend easily to the control of whites or willingly give
up their warring habits.

Sheridan had taken the Kiowa chiefs Satanta and Lone
Wolf as prisoners during his march with Custer to Fort
Cobb after the Washita fight in 1868, keeping them in leg-
irons and threatening to hang them if the remainder of the
Kiowas did not come in to the reservation. In a February
1869 meeting, the two Kiowa leaders promised to stop
their fighting. Sheridan relented and released them. Other
Kiowa chiefs made further pledges of good behavior in an
ensuing conference.[1]

But in February Sheridan returned to his Department of
Missouri headquarters, and shortly thereafter President
Grant assigned management of the Indian Territory tribes

to the benevolent, peace-seeking Quakers. It did not take long to discover that Sheridan was undoubtedly right—the Kiowas, Comanches, and other long-warring tribes would not give up their freedom and way of life unless forced to do so by military might.

Newly established Fort Sill became the center of the U.S. military presence in Indian Territory. After the departure of Custer and the Seventh Cavalry, it was garrisoned by four black companies of Tenth Cavalry and two white companies of Sixth Infantry under Col. B. H. Grierson. The Indians called the black troopers "buffalo soldiers" because of their black curly hair.

At first, the principal activity of the Fort Sill troops was to intercept horse thieves, both white and Indian, often pursuing them into Texas. But the stock of the agency and garrison soon became fair game for Indian predators. In May the Comanches ran off twenty horses and mules belonging to the Quaker agent, Lawrie Tatum. The next month the Kiowas garnered seventy-three mules from the post corrals. Two troops of cavalry pursued the Kiowas but lost the trail in the trampled wake of a buffalo herd.

This raid had been led by White Horse, whose self-acclaim over the feat incited Chief Big Tree to try to do one better. Big Tree set in action a crafty plan to steal the entire post herd and drive it far out onto the Llano Estacado where it could not be recovered. He almost succeeded. But Big Tree's scheme went awry when one of his warriors overzealously shot and scalped a white teamster, alerting the garrison.

These and other incidents clearly signaled that the peace plan effected by the Quakers was doing little to restrain their charges. One indication came in July when Kiowa chief White Horse raided into Texas, killed the settler Gottlieb Koozer, and took the man's wife and six children into captivity. After this, Chief Kicking Bird, goaded into action by other war chiefs, led a party into Texas looking for a fight.

He found it when, after some of the braves robbed a mail stage, troops from Fort Richardson, near present Jacks-

Chief Kicking Bird (Ton-a-en-ko) was a leading Kiowa peacemaker, playing a major role at the Little Arkansas and Medicine Lodge treaties. (Western History Collections, University of Oklahoma)

Lone Wolf (Queil-park), who signed the Treaty of the Little Arkansas in 1865, was nonetheless a much-feared Kiowa war chief. (Western History Collections, University of Oklahoma)

boro, engaged the Kiowa party. In retreating, Kicking Bird conducted a skillful military action against the soldiers, killing three.[2]

The Kiowas and Comanches both led attacks into Texas throughout the summer. When they attended a big pow-wow at Fort Sill in early August, they were severely scolded by authorities. The Kiowa chiefs, particularly Satanta and Lone Wolf, were disdainful of both Tatum and Grierson. They openly admitted to their raids and demanded more powder and lead as well as a dissolution of their reservation boundary lines. These demands were rejected, and Tatum refused to issue rations to the tribe until the agent's mules were returned and the Koozers were released. A ransom of one hundred dollars each was finally paid for the woman and children.[3]

Raids into Texas continued during the fall. In September a Comanche party fell on a homestead in present Montague County and killed a man, a young girl, and an infant child. A young boy was taken captive. White Horse and his braves attacked a stage on the road between Fort Griffin (northwest of present Breckenridge) and Fort Concho (near present San Angelo), murdering a soldier who was riding guard. Agent Tatum was besieged with claims submitted by Texans who had lost stock to the Indians.

Unusually cold weather kept the Indians to their lodges for most of the winter, though on January 24 a Kiowa party attacked four blacks who were hauling supplies near Fort Griffin. The Kiowas killed and scalped all the men, then drove back a Fort Richardson cavalry detachment that pursued them. A number of other depredations were committed in the Fort Richardson–Fort Griffin area during the spring of 1871, with a total of fourteen people being killed.

The bloodiest incident was the wagon train massacre on May 17, which took place on the Butterfield stagecoach route about halfway between Fort Richardson and the deserted Fort Belknap (near present Graham, Texas). The event occurred at the time that the general of the army, William T. Sherman, was touring the Texas forts in an army ambulance, guided by Gen. R. B. Marcy. Sherman's four-man inspection party was escorted by fifteen cavalry troopers as they journeyed from Fort Griffin to Fort Richardson on May 17. He and his party were at Fort Richardson that night when a survivor of the massacre staggered in to say that his wagon train had been attacked by a massive war party on the same trail that Sherman and his entourage had just traveled.[4]

The wagon train attack came as a result of a plan conceived by a Kiowa medicine man named Maman-ti, the Owl Prophet. Maman-ti called together a large following of Kiowa, Comanche, and Plains Apache warriors on the North Fork of the Red River to smoke the war pipe and hear how they would ride south into Texas and capture many horses. In the party that crossed the Red River were more than a hundred warriors, some riding double and some on foot holding on to horses' tails as they ran. Many carried bridles and ropes with them so that they could ride the stolen mounts on their return.

Satanta was there to give directions to the warriors. He carried with him an army bugle, which he had learned to blow. Posting themselves on a sandstone hilltop near Cox Mountain, the Indians prepared an ambush for the travelers that were certain to pass sooner or later. Finally, around noon, a small group of soldiers and a wagon with a canvas top—Sherman's party—appeared from the west. The impatient warriors wanted to attack, but Maman-ti refused to allow it. He insisted that a small advance party usually meant that a larger one would be coming along behind.

None appeared for some time, and many of the young men wanted to leave. But finally a train of ten wagons appeared. When they had reached an area of open plain where they were most vulnerable, Satanta sounded his bugle. The flood of warriors swept down the long slope of the hill toward the train. The teamsters attempted to circle their wagons, heavily loaded with corn, but it was too late. Desperately they tried to defend themselves as the whooping Indians engulfed them in a whirling carrousel of horses and spitting carbines.

Of the eleven men with the train, four were killed in the first rush. Realizing that their situation was hopeless, the other seven men made a dash for a line of woods some two miles away. Three of them were killed, but four escaped while the Indians competed with one another in claiming the mules, looting the wagons, and maiming the bodies.

When the attack was over, the Kiowas headed back north to Indian Territory, running into a torrential rainstorm. They left behind a gory scene of havoc and death for Col. Ranald Mackenzie's investigating party to find on May 19. The bodies of the dead men were riddled with bullet and arrow holes and were severely gashed, the skulls crushed. One teamster, his tongue cut out, had been tied face down over the pole of a wagon and a fire set below. All but one had been scalped.[5]

Sherman continued to Fort Sill on his inspection tour, carrying the news of the wagon train massacre. He was there when the Kiowas, including Satanta and his warriors, arrived at the agency on May 27 to draw their annuity rations. When Agent Tatum asked Satanta about the attack on the wagon train, the chief readily admitted that he had been a leader in it. The Kiowas, he said, were merely taking goods from the Texans, with whom they had been warring for years. It was a perfectly honorable thing to do. Besides, he had lost several men himself, making matters even.

Sheridan, however, did not see it in that light. He ordered the arrest of Satanta, Satank, and Big Tree and sent for Mackenzie to escort them, handcuffed and legs in chains, to Texas for trial. On the morning of June 8 two wagons, bedded with shelled corn for comfort, were brought to the guardhouse.

Satanta and Big Tree were submissive as the guards lifted them into the wagons, but Satank, the old patriarch chief of the Kiowas, resisted. His eldest son had recently been killed on a raid into Texas. Satank had gone there and retrieved his son's bones, washed them, and now sorrowfully carried them about on a packhorse wherever he went. Old timers at the fort knew that Satank was very dangerous, that he would rather die than leave his son's bones.

Tossed bodily into the lead wagon, Satank began singing his death song. Then, as the wagon lurched forward, the fierce old warrior stopped singing and grabbed his guard's carbine. The soldier was tossed tumbling out of the wagon as Satank worked with his manacled hands to throw a shell into the gun's chamber. Riding behind the wagon at the head of a company of troops, Lt. George A. Thurston saw the chief. Immediately he shouted for his men to fire and did the same with his revolver. The volley knocked the chief backward, but the Kiowa rose again, still trying to bring the carbine into action. This time a barrage of bullets brought Satank the death that he preferred over captivity.[6]

Satanta and Big Tree were taken to Fort Richardson and tried on charges stemming from the wagon train massacre. Both were quickly found guilty by a Texas jury and sentenced to be hanged. In response to public outcry in the East, the sentence was commuted to life imprisonment by the governor of Texas. The two Kiowas were sent to the Huntsville, Texas, state penitentiary.

In August 1871 a campaign against the Kiowas was conducted by Mackenzie, who led ten companies of Fourth Cavalry north from Fort Richardson, and by Grierson, who took his Tenth Cavalry from Fort Sill. Scouring the country west of the Wichita Mountains, the soldiers found that the Kiowas were, indeed, much as they had once been described—like wolves on the prairie, hard to find.

Grierson thought the Indians had been intimidated by this show of military strength. He was wrong. During September an attack against a patrol on Otter Creek and the murder of two civilian cattle herders not far from Fort Sill showed that the Kiowa warriors were still unrestrained.

The Comanches too were active. In October a band under Quanah Parker raided Mackenzie's camp in northern Texas and ran off seventy cavalry mounts. When a detachment went in pursuit, it was attacked by several hundred Comanches and barely escaped with the loss of only one trooper.[7]

The Kiowa chief White Horse was particularly troublesome. A Texas grand jury had indicted him for the Koozer murder. But catching him was another matter. On April 20, 1872, he helped assault a wagon train at Howard Wells on the desolate road between San Antonio and El Paso. The train was looted of its arms and ammunition cargo and then burned along with the bodies of seventeen Mexican teamsters. When two troops of cavalry on patrol appeared, the Kiowas attacked them, killing an officer and an enlisted man.

White Horse, who was shot in the arm during the fight, returned home to learn that while he was gone his younger brother had been killed on a separate raid into Texas. White Horse swore revenge, and on the quiet afternoon of June 9 he took it, in gory fashion. Leading a small war party south, he came onto an isolated homestead on the Clear Fork of the Brazos. A man, Abel Lee, sat on the porch in a rocking chair reading a newspaper.

White Horse shot from cover and killed Lee. He and his men then charged the house, killing and mutilating Mrs. Lee. One daughter, age fourteen, was killed with an arrow as she fled; three other Lee children—two girls, ages nine and seventeen, and a boy, age six—were taken prisoner. Other bloody revenge raids were conducted by the Kiowas while the Comanches were making still another raid on the Fort Sill horse herds.

The Quakers, though greatly alarmed by the mayhem, still hoped to settle the Indian-white differences peacefully. At a large council held on July 25 at abandoned Fort Cobb, the Quakers asked for peace. White Horse and others responded by boasting of their deeds. When demands were made for the return of 'the Lee children and stock that had been stolen, Lone Wolf replied with demands of his own. He wanted Fort Sill closed, all of the troops moved out of the country, and the Kiowa reservation extended south to the Rio Grande and north to the Missouri River. Raiding in Texas, the chiefs said, was their legitimate right.

Kicking Bird stood virtually alone as a Kiowa peacemaker. He apologized for the foolish talk of his fellow chiefs and agreed to work for the release of captive whites. However, nothing was settled by the conference, and it was now decided that matters could be resolved by taking a delegation of Kiowa and Comanche chiefs to the U.S. capital at Washington, D.C. This was done the next fall, the Indians (including Lone Wolf) being treated with presents and tours of the white man's capital city.

However, the sojourn did little to bring peace to the plains. The Kiowas and Comanches continued to roam and commit depredations at will, and the frontier military was convinced that punitive force was the only answer. In late September 1872, Mackenzie again invaded the Staked Plains, with a 222-man force guided by Tonkawa scouts. This time he surprised and wiped out a large Comanche village on the North Fork of the Red River, plus some smaller camps—262 lodges in all.

Mackenzie claimed to have killed 24 Indians. He also captured 120 to 130 women and children, 7 of whom died on the trail. Four of Mackenzie's troopers were killed, and several were wounded. In addition to destroying the Comanches' homes and property, the soldiers captured three thousand animals, among them some of the mules taken in the massacre at Howard Wells, Texas.

That night the Comanches returned and stampeded the captured herd by whooping and firing pistols. Nonetheless, some of the Comanche bands came in to Fort Sill, offering to trade white captives for the Indians Mackenzie had taken. They remained there through the winter.[8]

Kicking Bird and Lone Wolf kept their Kiowas quiet during the spring and summer of 1873 as the tribe waited for the release and return of Satanta and Big Tree. In August the two captive chiefs were sent from Huntsville to Fort Sill and were held in the guardhouse pending peace talks with the Kiowas and others. During a council held in October, the Kiowas agreed that if the two were released, they would stop their raiding and take up the white man's road.

But the commitments made by the chiefs failed to stymie the hot-blooded young warriors. In November a party of thirty Kiowas and Comanches headed south to steal horses and take scalps. Crossing the Rio Grande west of Laredo, they ravaged Mexican border settlements. Fourteen Mexicans were killed before the party headed back with two Mexican boys as captives and some 150 horses and mules. As they fled north with the stock, the Indians killed two American citizens.

Along the way, both of the boys managed to escape, carrying news of their capture to U.S. border troops at Fort

Clark (near present Uvalde, Texas). On December 7, a forty-one-man scouting patrol under Lt. Charles L. Hudson intercepted the war party. In a running fight, the patrol killed nine of the Indians and regained about a third of the stolen animals.

Of those killed, one was a favored son of Lone Wolf, another a nephew. The deaths were a severe blow to the chief. The Kiowa went into mourning. He cut his hair, killed his horses, and burned his lodges and other personal goods. From then on, he knew only hatred for whites.[9]

There would be other raids and other defeats at the hands of troops during the winter. The deaths of numerous Kiowa young men, plus the severe hunger the tribes were suffering because of the whites' decimation of the buffalo, added to the Kiowas' and the Comanches' anger and desire for vengeance. At the center was Lone Wolf, who had become determined to take a party south and recover the bones of his son and nephew. In March 1874 he began organizing a group to go with him.

Lone Wolf's intentions became known to the U.S. military, and an alert was sent out to the various army posts. The Kiowas managed to avoid detection and reached the site of the fight with Hudson. They had located the bones and were heading back with them when a cavalry unit found their trail and pursued.

The country was extremely hot, dry, and dusty. The cavalry mounts simply could not keep the pace of the fast-moving Indian ponies, and the troops eventually had to give up the chase. Though forced to bury the retrieved bones along the way, the band managed to take some horses from a post herd and kill one trooper. The Kiowas returned to the Wichita Mountains to celebrate their success and hold their sun dance.

In June the Kiowas and Comanches joined the Cheyennes and Arapahos in their resistance against the whites by taking part in the attack on Adobe Walls. On his release from prison, Satanta gave up his red medicine arrow—a Kiowa symbol of authority—and resigned as a Kiowa chief. The peaceable Kicking Bird, refusing to join in the forthcoming war, led a majority of the Kiowas back to Fort Sill.

But the young men who remained behind listened to the haranguing of Lone Wolf, who was still working to organize another raid into Texas to avenge the deaths of his son and nephew. The warriors paraded about the camp chanting war songs while the older men beat their rawhide drums and the young girls and women circled about in rhythmic tribal dances.

By the evening of July 11, a fifty-man party had been organized, each warrior carrying his own private medicine bag. Again Maman-ti, the prophet, was the leader. Moving south at a rapid pace, the Kiowas crossed the Red River close to the one hundredth meridian that marks the Texas Panhandle, then swung southeastward across the Big Wichita and followed along the general course of the Brazos to reach Cox Mountain near the site of the wagon train massacre.

They were also in the area of the Loving cattle ranch. Resting here, they followed Maman-ti's instructions and painted themselves and their horses for battle. After giving chase to four cowboys, who escaped, they killed some beef calves belonging to the Loving ranch. The Kiowas feasted on the meat, then used the hides to make shoes for the sore hooves of their ponies. They had returned to the high ground of the Cox escarpment when a group of some twenty-five horsemen rode up to where the calves had been killed. The men all wore tall white hats and were heavily armed.[10]

These men were Texas Rangers, some young and inexperienced, who were in the field to find a Comanche party that had recently raided a Loving corral and killed a cowboy. Maman-ti decided to set a trap. Two warriors were sent out as decoys, leading their horses as if they were too jaded to run. The ruse worked, bringing the rangers charging in pursuit. As they did so, the remainder of the Kiowas closed in from the east, forcing the rangers to dismount and take up a defensive position. The Kiowas surrounded and besieged them the rest of the day.

One ranger, who had been badly wounded early in the fight, died during the day; another was caught and killed while attempting to go for water at a creek a mile away. Finally, when night came, the wounded men were put aboard the few remaining horses, and the rangers made their escape back to the Loving ranch headquarters. The Kiowas, virtually unscathed, returned home singing their war songs, well satisfied with their encounter.[11]

Though the majority of the Kiowa and Comanche people were willing to draw their rations and reside in peace near Fort Sill, the small war faction of the two tribes kept the area in turmoil during the summer. A wood camp near the fort was attacked by a small band of Indians in mid-July, and a herder was killed during a raid on a herd of cattle. Other killings followed in August: a man at Signal Mountain, two others on Cache Creek, and two cowboys herding some Texas cattle near the fort.

Lt. Col. Davidson, following orders to separate the belligerents from the nonbelligerents, attempted to enroll the tribes, but with little success. Some of the troublesome Kiowas and Comanches camped near the Wichita Agency at Anadarko and raided the corn cribs and melon patches of the Wichitas and Caddos. The officer in charge of a small infantry detachment stationed at the agency, fearing trouble, sent a call to Davidson for help.

Davidson responded with four troops of the Tenth Cavalry. He found some sixty lodges of Comanches under Red Food camped near the Wichita Agency, as well as some Kiowas—all sharing in the agency beef rations, against regulations. When Davidson's troops attempted to disarm the Comanches, the Indians rebelled. There was much firing and whooping and dust raising but no major fight, though one young black bystander was killed.

The troops, much confused as to which Indians were hostile and which were friendly, finally drove the combatants from the field. However, on their retreat the hostiles caught a haying crew in the field and killed four men. Other Indians went to Shirley's trading post and looted it.

In retaliation for the outbreak, Davidson burned Red Food's camp and all of its paraphernalia.[12]

After the Anadarko fracas, most of the Comanche and Kiowa belligerents, knowing well enough that troops would soon be after them, moved west toward the Palo Duro Canyon of the Staked Plains. Among the Kiowas was a captive white boy called Tehan, now large and redheaded, who was winning a place as a warrior. When it was discovered that some horses had strayed from one camp, Tehan was sent to get them. In doing so, he met some soldiers who "rescued" him, despite his secret objections. He was shortly turned over to a thirty-six-wagon supply train, under Capt. Wyllys Lyman, that was on its way from Camp Supply with rations for General Miles, who was then in camp on the Sweetwater.[13]

When Tehan did not return to the Kiowas, they sent a party out in search of him. The searchers spotted Lyman's command and immediately sent word back to the main camp. A large force of warriors was soon on its way to intercept the soldiers and rescue Tehan. Kiowa sharpshooters engaged the wagon escort under Lt. Frank West early on the morning of September 9, 1874.

West's men were able to hold the Indians at a distance as the train moved ahead. The wagon train had reached the Washita near the mouth of Gageby Creek when the main Kiowa body appeared and forced the wagons and their military guard to take up a defensive circle. After an initial charge, the Kiowas settled for holding the train under siege, pot-shooting at any target that presented itself. During this time Tehan escaped by pretending he was going for water. He then informed the Kiowas that the whites were in bad shape from thirst. Though the whites had dug in, a number of men had been hit by Indian fire, and some were in serious condition.

On September 12 a cold rain set in, causing great discomfort to the shivering men in their wet trenches. Their situation was desperate when, on the following day, movement far to the west gave the hope of help. The soldiers fired their guns but received no response. What they had seen were the columns of Maj. William R. Price from New Mexico. The faint reports of firing had reached Price, but his scouts reported only a few Indians in the area. He went on his way.

However, the presence of the New Mexico force did cause the Kiowas to withdraw. Finally, on the fourteenth, troops from Camp Supply arrived to relieve the men in the beleaguered wagon train. The rescuers had been brought there by a German scout, William Schmalsle, who had made his way through the Indian lines to get help.[14]

The Kiowas had severely mauled the supply train and its escort, but they had gained no spoils of war. The fight, in fact, had used up their food and ammunition resources and worn their ponies badly. The women and children with the hostile band were suffering severely from hunger. In a tribal council, irreconcilables such as Lone Wolf and Maman-ti still refused to give up. They led their followers to the refuge of the Texas Panhandle's great Palo Duro Canyon, there joining Cheyenne and Comanche bands. This huge encampment of Plains Indians was attacked and routed by Colonel Ranald Mackenzie in late September.[15]

Meanwhile, Chief Woman's Heart and others decided to return to the reservation and hope for mercy from the soldiers. Among them was Satanta, who had taken part in the attack on the wagon train. Hoping to avoid being returned to prison, he went to the Darlington Agency rather than Fort Sill to turn himself in. It did him little good. He was placed in irons and escorted to Sill, then quickly shipped back to the Huntsville prison.

The loss of horses, food, and equipage at Palo Duro was critical to the Kiowas, but they would suffer more stinging blows from the overwhelming military forces put into the field by Sheridan. A Kiowa band was struck in what is now Greer County, Oklahoma, on October 9 and was driven north. Pursuing troops destroyed large numbers of their lodges. Still other camps were left in ashes on Gageby Creek in the Texas Panhandle, as was another village just north of the Washita in Indian Territory.

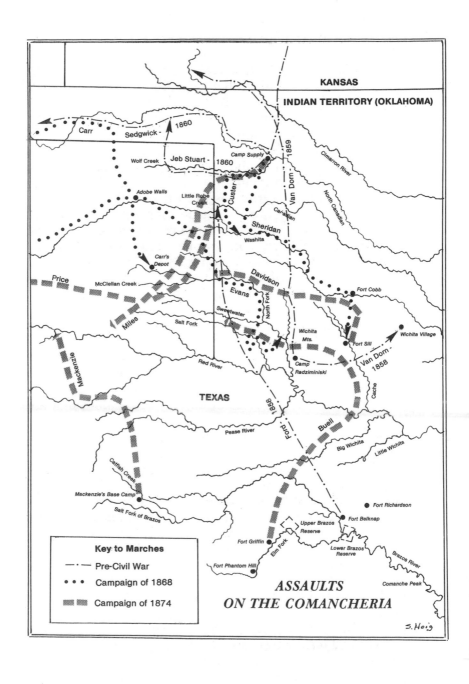

KANSAS

INDIAN TERRITORY (OKLAHOMA)

Carr · · · · Sedgwick - 1860

Cimarron River

Wolf Creek · Jeb Stuart - 1860 Camp Supply 1859

Adobe Walls Little Robe Creek Custer Van Dorn North Canadian

Canadian

Sheridan

Washita

Carr's Depot

Price McClellan Creek Davidson Fort Cobb

Evans North Fork

Miles Salt Fork Sweetwater

Wichita Mts. Fort Sill Wichita Village

Mackenzie Red River Camp Radziminiski Van Dorn 1858

TEXAS Ford - 1858 Cache

Pease River Buell

Big Wichita Little Wichita

Catfish Creek

Mackenzie's Base Camp Fort Richardson

Salt Fork of Brazos Upper Brazos Reserve Fort Belknap

Fort Griffin Lower Brazos Reserve Brazos River

Key to Marches

— · — · — Pre-Civil War Fort Phantom Hill Elm Fork

· · · Campaign of 1868

▨▨▨ Campaign of 1874

*ASSAULTS
ON THE COMANCHERIA*

Comanche Peak

S. Hoig

A command of Tenth Cavalry from Fort Sill, scouring the country to the north between the Washita River and Rainy Mountain, was met by a large, consolidated band of Comanches, who surrendered without resistance. However, on November 6 a troop of Eighth Cavalry ran into a group of some one hundred Kiowa hostiles on McClellan Creek and found more fight than they could handle. They were saved by two companies of Tenth Cavalry who arrived and drove the Kiowas from the field.

In mid-November, a severe norther with driving sleet and bitter cold blasted across the plains, making outdoor activity miserable for both troopers and Indians. Though actually few Indians had been killed, continued pressure by the army, lack of food, and numbing cold caused most of the lagging hostiles to finally give up their resistance. During December many of them surrendered at Fort Sill and Darlington.

Still out were Lone Wolf, Big Bow, Maman-ti, and other Kiowa die-hard leaders. Authorities persuaded the peaceful Kicking Bird to act as an emissary. First he arranged the surrender of Big Bow, and then, with Big Bow as a guide, he contacted the other Kiowa recalcitrants and persuaded them to come in as well.

The army placed many of the leading men in irons and took away the horses, mules, weapons, and even camping goods of the Indians. As they had done with the Cheyennes, government officials picked out the Kiowa chiefs considered most troublesome. Sent to Fort Marion, Florida, for imprisonment were eleven Comanches and twenty-six Kiowas, among them Lone Wolf, White Horse, and Maman-ti. Kicking Bird had been called on to help select the ones to be sent, and Maman-ti swore revenge against him. On May 4, 1875, Kicking Bird died after drinking coffee that the Fort Sill surgeon said had been laced with strychnine.[16]

Meanwhile, Satanta, still confined at Huntsville, dreamed of returning one day to his people. But in October 1878 he was told that it would never happen, that he would never be permitted to go home again. On the following day, Satanta leaped from a two-story balcony at the prison and killed himself.[17]

The warring efforts of the Kiowas and their tenacious effort to maintain their way of life had reached its end. They had fought hard and at times ruthlessly to keep the freedom they had once known. They had resisted the white man to their fullest measure, but the power of the U.S. military was too overwhelming. They now retired to their reservation, leaving the words spoken by Satank at the Treaty of Medicine Lodge to linger in history:

> We have warred against the white man, but never because it gave us pleasure. Before the day of oppression came, no white man came to our villages and went away hungry. It gave us more joy to share with him than it gave him to partake of our hospitality.
>
> In the far distant past there was no suspicion among us. The world seemed large enough for the red and white man: the broad plains seem now to contract, and the white man grows jealous of his red brother. He once came to trade; he now comes to fight. . . . He now covers his face with the cloud of jealousy and anger and tells us to be gone, as the offended master speaks to his dog. . . . We once gave you our hearts; you have them now.[18]

CHAPTER 18

Conquest of the Cheyennes

NO longer could the prairie Indians hope to successfully conduct an all-out war against the overwhelming military might of the United States. The network of military bases, the whites' advantage in manpower and firepower, the depletion of the buffalo by white hunters, and the dependency of the Indians on goods of the white man had made total tribal war virtually impossible. Yet the tradition and the spirit of warriorship were still deeply embedded in the fighting men of the tribes, who were ready to jump into action against unjust treatment and the increased occupation of their lands by whites.

In the aftermath of the Sheridan-Custer campaign in Indian Territory, leaders of the various Cheyenne bands were split over what path to follow. On April 7, 1869, Chiefs Little Robe, Minimic, Grey Eyes, and others brought their lodges in to Fort Sill. But when General Hazen asked them to go to Camp Supply, most returned to the plains. At a tribal council held on the Washita, a clash between Little Robe's peace faction and the Dog Soldiers took place. The Dog Soldiers, preferring war, decided they would go north, where they could remain free.[1]

Led by Tall Bull, some 165 lodges of Dog Soldier war-

Although he was one of the Cheyenne peace leaders, Chief Minimic was among the members of the tribe sent to the Fort Marion, Florida, prison. (Smithsonian Institution, National Anthropological Archives, Bureau of American Ethnology Collection, neg. no. 365-D)

Chiefs Little Robe and White Horse, shown here at Washington, D.C., in 1873, were deeply involved in Cheyenne affairs both as warriors and as peace chiefs. (Photo by W. H. Jackson, National Anthropological Archives, Smithsonian Institution, neg. no. 349)

riors and their families left for the Republican River in western Kansas. There they were assaulted by troops of a Fort Lyon expedition under Maj. Gen. Eugene A. Carr. The Dog Soldiers, numbering about five hundred warriors, put up savage resistance but were driven north, with a loss of twenty-five men. In retaliation they ravaged outlying settlements and transportation routes, killing thirteen people and taking two women captive.

In June, supported by 150 Pawnee scouts under Maj.

Cheyenne chief Whirlwind opposed going to war in 1872 and led his band to the agency. (Photo by William S. Soule, National Anthropological Archives, Bureau of American Ethnology Collection, Smithsonian Institution)

Although Arapaho chief Left Hand was a famed warrior in his earlier years, he led his people to accept the ways of whites. (Smithsonian Institution, Bureau of American Ethnology Collection, neg. no. 137)

Frank J. North, Carr set forth to clear out the Dog Soldiers. After a month of chase and minor clashes, he caught up with Tall Bull's band at Summit Springs near the Platte. In a standard maneuver, Carr's forces cut off the Cheyenne pony herd and charged the encampment. In a day-long fight, the cavalry and their Pawnee allies killed fifty-two Cheyennes, including Tall Bull, and destroyed their village. One of the white women was rescued, but one was killed by her captors. The Cheyennes who escaped fled farther north to join Cheyenne and Sioux camps there.

In Indian Territory, meanwhile, Cheyenne bands under Little Robe, Minimic, Medicine Arrows, and Buffalo Head moved to Camp Supply as requested. There they, like the Kiowas, found their fate was now under the direction of the Quaker Society of Friends, to whom Pres. Ulysses S.

This 1871 delegation to Washington included, *standing, left to right*, Edmund Guerrier, Kaw agent Mahlon Stubbs, John Simpson Smith, and Philip McCusker. Seated are, *left to right*, Arapaho chief Little Raven, Cheyenne chiefs Bird Chief and Little Robe, and Wichita chief Buffalo Goad. (Smithsonian Institution)

Grant had delegated the responsibility of caring for the Plains tribes. The new Cheyenne-Arapaho agent was the elderly Brinton Darlington.

Darlington first attempted to establish his agency at Pond Creek, Indian Territory, along the Cimarron River. However, because of the brackish water in the region and the close proximity of Kansas horse thieves, the Cheyennes would not go there. Darlington was forced to move his agency to Camp Supply. He remained at the fort until May 1870, when he relocated to a site on the North Canadian River near present El Reno. Here he established what became known as the Cheyenne and Arapaho, or Darlington, Agency.

Getting the Indians to follow him there was another matter. The Arapahos willingly complied, as did Chief Stone Calf and his band of Cheyennes and the Indian families of George Bent and John Simpson Smith. But most of the Cheyenne bands remained on the western prairie where they could hunt, trade, and live more freely. There, however, they were subject to the influences of both the whiskey peddlers and the taunting Kiowas and Comanches who led their young men off on horse-stealing raids into Texas. The Osages were also contributing to trouble by bringing contraband arms to the Cheyenne camps for trade.

Though the clouds of war loomed on the horizon of Indian Territory throughout 1870, matters remained relatively calm. New trouble was anticipated during the spring of 1871 when the Dog Soldiers began a return south from the Fort Laramie region. Many of them joined the Sioux in western Kansas. Those arriving at Camp Supply were starved and destitute. They were fed and warned against again leaving the reservation.

The Cheyenne chiefs restrained their young men fairly well. When one party slipped off to Texas and returned with some stolen horses, the chiefs willingly turned the animals over to authorities. However, an old intertribal conflict was reignited when the government moved the Cheyennes' hereditary enemies, the Pawnees of Nebraska, to a reservation in northern Indian Territory. The Cheyennes promptly killed several Pawnees who ventured too far out onto the prairie.[2]

The return of Chief Medicine Arrow and his band to Camp Supply from the north in December 1871 further indicated Cheyenne pacification. Most of the Southern Cheyennes were back together now. During that winter and spring, they enjoyed a bountiful buffalo hunt in the region between the Canadian and the Cimarron rivers, their women dressing over ten thousand robes for the trade. A few of the Cheyennes had begun planting vegetable gardens, but most still lived by the hunt and depended heavily on government rations.

The death of the well-liked Brinton Darlington in April 1872, however, signaled a change in the direction of Cheyenne relations. Although apprehensive army officers at first blamed the Cheyennes for an attack on a military train's mule herd between Supply and Dodge, it turned out the Kiowas were responsible. But the Cheyennes evidently did participate in the August 1872 murder of a white family in southern Kansas.[3]

Many factors contributed to the renewal of Cheyenne hostility. Unscrupulous whiskey peddlers from both Kansas and New Mexico Territory preyed on the Indians, and heavy drinking was common among the easily excited young men. White buffalo hunters were swarming onto Cheyenne lands, helping to decimate the great herds that had long been the Indians' livelihood. Texas cattlemen, military units, surveying parties, and others were invading the territory. The new agent, John D. Miles, sometimes withheld rations and annuity goods to force changes in tribal behavior.

In December 1872 a party of Cheyenne warriors gave blunt warning to a group of surveyors: stay off the Cheyenne reservation or lose your scalps. Though badly frightened, the surveyors had continued with their assignment. In March, they paid the price. A large Cheyenne war party struck their camp and killed and scalped four men, including the chief surveyor, E. N. Deming, whose hands they cut off as well.

The guilty warriors took refuge on the Washita with bands controlled by the Dog Soldiers. The old split between peace and war factions returned. Little Robe, Big Jake, and Stone Calf worked to keep their young men quiet, but the call to the warpath was strong. Even as a delegation of Cheyenne leaders was visiting Washington, D.C., in September 1873, a 160-man war party invaded Colorado Territory to battle their longtime enemy, the Utes. Nothing came of the venture except to create alarm among white citizens there. Horse-stealing raids across the Red River were also keeping the Texas frontier in turmoil.

The causes of Cheyenne discontent were growing daily. White horse thieves ravaged Cheyenne herds; hunters left rotting buffalo carcasses strewn over the prairie; whiskey traders took away Cheyenne robes and ponies by the score, leaving behind whole bands of besotted tribespeople. At one point, the Cheyenne women rebelled against working to scrape and produce robes that the men immediately sold for whiskey. By the spring of 1874 it was clear to all that the young men were out of control and that serious trouble lay ahead. With the warm days of summer, trouble came.

In retaliation for stock they had lost to white thieves, Cheyennes took some horses from the agency and defied Miles's request to return them. Later a sizable Cheyenne party murdered and scalped three settlers near Medicine Lodge, Kansas; not long afterward a military unit was attacked by Cheyennes and Kiowas between Supply and Dodge. Meanwhile, a standoff battle between the prairie tribes and a group of white buffalo hunters was shaping up in the Texas Panhandle.

In early June, several buffalo hunters were killed, some tortured to death, near the old Adobe Walls post on the Canadian River. These events preluded a much larger engagement on June 27 that has become known as the Battle of Adobe Walls. At a gathering of prairie tribes on the Washita, the Cheyennes and Arapahos were joined by the Comanches, Kiowas, and Plains Apaches in smoking the pipe of war against the white intruders of their hunting grounds.

A large force of warriors, estimated at nearly three hundred men, assembled to ride against the buffalo hunters and others who had erected a small town near the abandoned old Fort Adobe, where Kit Carson had fought the Kiowas. Added to the initial trading complex and stable of Myers and Leonard were the sod store and corral of Rath and Company and a picket-style blacksmith shop operated by James Hanrahan, who also ran a dirt-roofed, sod-walled saloon. The slapdash town was an isolated oasis where the hunters could find food, clothing, ammunition, whiskey, and wagon repairs. On the day of the battle, it was populated by twenty-eight men and one woman.[4]

This second battle at Adobe Fort is interesting not so much for its importance but for its being one of the few occasions on which the prairie Indians assaulted a fortified location. The Indians seemed to be caught up more in the military grandness of their effort—bugle calls were even used by the Indians to sound charges—than in the results. Their attempt to overrun the makeshift battlement, however, would prove even less successful than the charges against Forsyth's scouts on the Arikaree six years earlier.

A large part of the reason for the Indians' failure was the excellent field of fire that the location offered its defenders. Equally as important was the shooting ability of the buffalo hunters with their long-barreled buffalo guns and Sharps rifles. They were, after all, professional marksmen. However, the most important reason for the whites' survival was an extremely fortunate event that took place the morning of the attack.

Around 2:00 A.M., the men were awakened by a loud report. It turned out that a support pole for the roof of Hanrahan's saloon had snapped. The men spent the rest of the night repairing it. One hunter, Billy Dixon, decided not to return to his bed, thinking he would get an early start in heading out. He sent his helper to the creek for his horses while he rolled up his bedroll. He then took it out to his wagon, which was parked a short distance from the settlement. In doing so, he saved his life and those of most of his comrades. Observing a dark mass moving toward him, he at first thought it to be a herd of buffalo. But even as he looked, a single piercing war whoop broke the morning stillness.[5]

The mass was an Indian force, composed largely of Cheyennes and Comanches. Leading it into battle was a young Comanche warrior named Isatai, who claimed that his medicine would protect the Indians from the white man's guns. Arriving at the small settlement during the night, the Indians had waited until the first light of dawn rose up from the eastern horizon. When they saw Dixon and his man emerge from the settlement, the mounted Indians—their bronze bodies and their horses daubed with vermilion, their arms and bodies decorated with silver and brass ornaments, and their heads covered with gorgeously feathered warbonnets—surged forward. They had the rising sun directly to their back.

Jumping onto his riding pony, Dixon made it safely back to the adobes. There he joined the others in putting up a deadly counterfire. The men took up positions in three of the town's stores, their big buffalo .50s and their .44-caliber Sharps rifles effectively thwarting the Indian assault. All through the morning and into the afternoon, the Indians made charges, directed by bugle calls, against the barricaded frontiersmen. Each time, they were driven back farther and farther by the effective fire of the hunters.

Finally, after having shot every horse, mule, and ox in the settlement, the Indians gave up and, much to the relief of the beleaguered hunters, headed back to their camps in Indian Territory. They left behind six dead Cheyennes and three Comanches, with many others wounded. The buffalo hunters had lost two brothers who had been asleep in their wagons at the time of the attack. These men were later found shot and scalped. Also, one of the Adobe Walls defenders had been hit and killed by an Indian bullet during the fight.

Only a few days later there was more evidence of Cheyenne anger when a cattle herder was killed and scalped on the wagon road north of the Darlington Agency. When news of this and of the Adobe Walls fight reached the agency, there was alarm that a general outbreak was under way. On July 5, Miles gathered his family and agency force together to make a dash for Kansas. Near the stage station at Kingfisher Creek, the travelers came onto the bloated body of the scalped herder, still lying where the Cheyenne war party had left it.

But it was farther up the road, just past Baker's station

and near the site of present Hennessey, Oklahoma, that they made the most gruesome discovery. Among the still smoldering ruins of a charred wagon train were the bodies of four teamsters. Two of them had been scalped, but the worst had been done to the wagon master, Pat Hennessey. He had been tied to a wheel of one of the wagons and burned to death. Giving the men a hasty burial, as they had the herder, Miles and his party continued on. At the Buffalo Springs stage station, they found teamsters, ranchmen, and people from a stagecoach gathered together in fear of a Cheyenne attack.[6] No attack came, and Miles's party made it safely to Kansas.

More Cheyenne strikes followed, however. On August 26, 1874, a surveying party working forty miles south and twenty miles west of Fort Dodge, Kansas, was mauled. The head surveyor, O. F. Short, and five of his crew were murdered by a war party under Medicine Water. Less than a month later, the same Cheyennes attacked a party of immigrants near the border of Kansas and Colorado Territory. John German, his wife, his son, and his oldest daughter were slain, and his four other daughters were taken captive.[7]

There could be no doubt now that the Cheyenne war faction was in control of the tribe, that an Indian war was under way, and that the Cheyennes were the principal perpetrators. Sheridan was convinced that the peacemakers had had their chance and failed; the time had come to crush the resistance of the prairie tribes once and for all. Accordingly, he set in motion a five-pronged invasion of their home ranges—what is now western Oklahoma and the Texas Panhandle.

Col. Nelson A. Miles would strike southwestward from Camp Supply. Lt. Col. John W. Davidson would move west from Fort Sill. Filling the gap between the two in the westward drive would be a force under Lt. Col. George P. Buell. At the same time, Col. Ranald S. Mackenzie would push up from Fort Concho, Texas, and Maj. William R. Price would march east from Fort Union, New Mexico Territory.

The campaign was well organized and neatly arranged,

:en. Nelson A. Miles in 1874 con-
ucted the campaign against the
heyennes, Comanches, and Kio-
'as that is generally known as
ie Red River War. (Western His-
ry Collections, University of
klahoma)

Gen. Ranald Mackenzie dealt the
Plains tribes a deadly blow when
he struck their camps in the Palo
Duro Canyon, burning 400 lodges
and shooting some 1,400 horses.
(Western History Collections,
University of Oklahoma)

but the results were a series of independent, scattered
actions. The first contact was made by Miles's advance
cavalry unit and scouts under Lt. F. D. Baldwin. Baldwin
arrived at Adobe Walls just in time to help repulse another
attack, though the Indians were able to lance a buffalo
hunter as the troops watched, too far away to help. Driving
on down the Canadian, Baldwin surprised a small party
of Indians, killing one of them and sending the remainder
fleeing to the south.[8]

Miles now joined Baldwin and headed south in pursuit.
When his advance unit entered a narrow canyon early on
he morning of August 30, it was attacked by a large force of

Cheyennes. Miles brought the main portion of his cavalry, infantry, and artillery to bear, forcing the Indians to retreat farther south to the Red River. Putting up a hard rear-guard action, the Indians escaped, though Miles was able to capture and destroy one sizable village and some smaller ones before retiring to his supply depot on the Washita.[9]

Meanwhile, the determined Mackenzie was scouring the country northward from the Clear Fork of the Brazos. While resting on the evening of September 27, his command was attacked by mounted Indians who attempted to stampede the cavalry horses. At daybreak, the troops took to the field and chased the Indians away.[10] On the following morning, Mackenzie's scouts made a startling discovery. They found themselves looking down into the great chasm of the Texas Panhandle's Palo Duro Canyon, where bands of Cheyennes, Comanches, and Kiowas had taken refuge.

Below them, Indian tipis, in miniature, stretched for miles along the floor of the winding gorge. When the troops arrived, it took some time for them to find a point at which it would be possible to descend the precipitous wall of the gorge. Finally a place was located, and the men, leading their horses, worked their way single file down to the canyon floor.

The Indians, too confident of their security, were caught asleep. The troops quickly formed into attack formation and began their charge, driving the Indians before them down the huge defile. Only a few defenders resisted from behind the boulders and cedars along the sides of the canyon. Camp after camp, each hastily abandoned, was destroyed, along with all the sustaining material of Indian life—lodges, robes, food, camp equipment, clothes, saddles, weaponry. Additionally, some fourteen hundred horses were captured. An experienced Indian fighter, Mackenzie knew he could not herd the semiwild ponies; nor could he leave them behind. Regretfully, he ordered the animals shot.

Just how many Indians were killed in the attack is not known. But destroying their life-supporting paraphernalia and putting them afoot on the edge of winter was an extremely severe blow to all of the tribes. Nor was their misfortune over. On October 9 Buell's command destroyed a Kiowa encampment in present Greer County, Oklahoma, pursuing the Indians northwestward, where more camps were found and burned. In addition to the nearly five hundred lodges he burned, Buell captured a large number of Indian mounts.

At this same time, the New Mexico strike force under Price engaged and routed a band of Indians on Gageby Creek in the Texas Panhandle. Four days later a cavalry detachment of Miles's command surprised an Indian camp on the Washita. Though all of the villagers escaped, their homes and goods were destroyed by the soldiers.[11]

The relentless Sheridan was determined to continue his search-and-destroy campaign until all of the Cheyennes had submitted themselves to reservation life. White Horse, a Dog Soldier leader who had been in the Mackenzie fight, surrendered himself and twenty-five of his band on October 20. But other Dog Soldiers, such as Grey Beard and Medicine Water, were still unreconciled, even though the plight of their people was becoming more desperate by the day.

The Cheyenne bands were destitute of the necessities of life, and their horse herds were badly depleted and worn. The Indians had limited weapons and ammunition, scarcely a place where they felt safe to camp, and no allies who could offer them succor or refuge. Their situation defied hope. No matter how determined and brave their warriors might have been, they had no chance against the overwhelming numbers and might of Sheridan's army.

Still, they held out against the imprisonment of reservation life. In an effort to replace the animals they had lost to the army, a small party of Cheyennes attempted a raid on a Caddo herd near the Wichita Agency. They were discovered, and three of them were killed. Six surrendered, but the others escaped and returned to the Dog Soldier camps,

The war continued through the remainder of the year

into the harsh days of winter. On November 6 a one-hundred-man Cheyenne party ambushed a much smaller cavalry patrol on McClellan's Creek but inflicted little damage. Two days later in the same vicinity, a unit under Lieutenant Baldwin struck Grey Beard's village with artillery bombardment, cavalry charge, and infantry who rode through the village in mule-drawn wagons, firing as they went. Though once again the main portion of the Cheyennes escaped, the village was taken and destroyed. After this attack the youngest two of the German girls, Julia Arminda and Nancy Adelaide were rescued, having been left on a hillside by a member of Grey Beard's band.

On the same day as Lieutenant Baldwin's action, another army unit captured and destroyed fifty lodges along the Red River, pursuing the fleeing Cheyennes so hotly that the Indians were forced to discard the animals carrying their camping goods. One cavalry command pursued a band of Cheyennes for nearly four hundred miles along the Canadian River but failed to make contact. But other units of Sheridan's army made successful strikes against two Cheyenne camps in late November and early December.[12]

Winter had now come to the plains, adding its miseries to the suffering of the Cheyennes. The impossibility of finding food on the snowbound prairie and the hopelessness of defeating the army finally ended the resistance of many tribal leaders. Gradually, they began breaking away from the Dog Soldiers and bringing their people in to the Darlington Agency. In mid-December, Little Shield surrendered. He was followed later by Medicine Water and Sand Hill. Other Cheyennes attempted to slip unnoticed onto the agency to melt into Little Robe's band.

Despite all of the army's successes, they had killed surprisingly few Cheyenne warriors—seventeen, according to Agent Miles. He reported in early January 1875 that there were still some sixteen hundred warriors under the control of the Dog Soldiers. But the campaign was almost over. An expedition under Colonel Miles swept the country southwest of Camp Supply during January and found little resistance. The Cheyenne bands he met were painfully making their way to Darlington.

Stone Calf remained aloof until February, when he arrived at Darlington to surrender himself and the members of his band. They brought the two older German girls, Catherine and Sophia, who told their story of being traded among Cheyenne men who had used them sexually. They pointed out the guilty ones, plus the Cheyenne Buffalo Calf Woman, who they said had killed their mother with a battle-ax. And not all of the Cheyennes came in. Grey Beard, Medicine Arrows, and White Antelope still refused to do so, though on March 6, 1875, they finally surrendered themselves and 821 of their people.

The Southern Cheyenne war appeared to be over, but peace lasted only until April. The army had adopted a policy of rounding up those Cheyenne leaders and warriors guilty of crimes as well as those considered to be the most volatile. One of these was a young warrior named Black Hawk. When a post blacksmith was hammering leg-irons on him in early April, a Cheyenne women began taunting the warrior. Knocking the blacksmith down, Black Hawk made a dash for freedom, only to be shot down by soldiers.

The incident aroused a nearby group of Cheyennes to a fury. They sent a fusillade of bullets and arrows at the soldiers before retreating across the North Canadian River to the cover of some sand hills, where a supply of arms and ammunition had been hidden. Entrenching themselves in rifle pits, they put up a heavy fire against the troops until night came. Though the soldiers thought they had the Cheyennes successfully encircled and pinned down, when morning came the Indians were gone. They had left behind six dead. Nineteen soldiers were wounded, three seriously.

As a result of the sand hills fight, many of the Cheyennes deserted the agency in fear of retaliation, some fleeing to the Antelope Hills, others going to the upper Cimarron River, and some heading north. Troops were again sent out to retrieve the Indians, and by the end of April most of them were back on the reservation.

Now the army concluded that it was necessary to imprison the most dangerous Cheyenne leaders. However, it was almost by random choice that thirty-one men and one woman were selected. These Cheyennes were placed in chains and shipped off to Fort Marion, Florida. One of them was Grey Beard, who attempted to escape en route and was shot to death.

One group of those who fled north after the sand hills fight was intercepted by troops on Sappa Creek in western Kansas. Pinned down in the creek bed, the Cheyennes were picked off one by one by sharpshooting soldiers. When the firing stopped, nineteen warriors and eight women and children were found to have been killed. Other escapees from Darlington made it to the northern bands, but most voluntarily returned south that fall.[13]

Though this was the last of the Southern Cheyenne wars, the military still had to confront the Northern Cheyennes. In 1866, the Northerners had struck out against white intrusion of their country west of the Black Hills in northern Wyoming and southern Montana territories by helping the Sioux outwit and massacre the troops under Fetterman at Fort Phil Kearny, Wyoming. For ten years the Northern Cheyennes resisted efforts of the government to move them south. Their warriors fought alongside the Sioux in overwhelming Custer and the Seventh Cavalry at the Little Rosebud in 1876. This was a great Indian victory, but it only strengthened the government's determination to consolidate the Cheyennes in Indian Territory.

Led by Gen. Ranald Mackenzie, U.S. forces struck and severely mauled the Northern Cheyennes at the Crazy Woman's Fork of the Powder River in November 1876. Left in severely destitute condition during midwinter, the Cheyennes had no choice but to surrender and capitulate to going south.

The move was a further tragedy for the Northerners. The seventy-day march through the driving heat of August 1877 made many of them weak and ill. During the winter that followed, nearly two-thirds of them were stricken with fever and ague. With virtually no medical help, forty-

Northern Cheyenne chiefs Little Wolf (*standing*) and Dull Knife led their people on a historic retreat back to their homeland from the Indian Territory in September 1878, five years after this photo was made in Washington, D.C., in 1873. (Smithsonian Institution, National Anthropological Archives, neg. no. 270-A)

one died. Others were sick at heart in being away from their beloved north country; further, they were badly received by the Southern Cheyennes, who resented their presence and called them "Sioux Cheyenne."

The Northerners got little sympathy from Agent Miles, and their condition continued to deteriorate in 1878. Their chiefs had always contended that they had agreed to come south only on a trial basis. By fall, Chiefs Little Wolf, Dull Knife, and others had made up their minds to return to the north despite government objections and threats.

"I am going north to my own country," Little Wolf told

These Northern Cheyenne chiefs were involved in the famous Little Wolf–Dull Knife retreat. They were tried at Dodge City, Kansas, and acquitted of all charges. (Kansas State Historical Society, Topeka)

the agent. "I do not want to see blood spilt about this agency. If you are going to send your soldiers after me, I wish that you would first let me get a little distance away from this agency. Then if you want to fight, I will fight you, and we can make the ground bloody at that place."[14]

On the morning of September 9, 1878, a party of more than 350 Northern Cheyennes slipped away from Darlington Agency and headed north. With troops and Darlington Indian police in pursuit, the band moved rapidly northwestward for two days. On the thirteenth, at a place known as Turkey Springs, fifty miles northwest of Camp Supply, they were engaged by two troops of cavalry under Captain Joseph Rendlebrock. The Cheyenne fighting force of ninety-two men and sixty-nine boys stood off the soldiers, killing three troopers and an Arapaho scout before moving on.[15]

Another slight skirmish was held with a small detachment of soldiers from Camp Supply. Led by Little Wolf, the Cheyennes drove the guard away from the soldiers' wagons, capturing them and some ammunition. Moving at night, the Cheyennes reached the Arkansas River, there charging the camp of some buffalo hunters. They took eighteen slaughtered buffalo cows for food, but released the hunters without harm.

Soon after crossing the Arkansas above Fort Dodge, the refugees were again attacked by troops, whom they repulsed after a brief fight. From there they moved across western Kansas, dodging the U.S. Army and fighting when necessary. Eventually they reached the north country, only to be recaptured. Most of them were allowed to remain in the north country, but seven of their men were sent to Kansas to stand trial for killings that had occurred during their flight. All were eventually released and returned to the Darlington Agency.

The Cheyenne wars of Indian Territory were over. Now would begin the long and difficult task of adjusting to the new world of the whites. Today no one can justly deny the Plains tribes' right to resist. Homeland, freedom, way of life were just as dear to them as to the American revolutionists of 1776. It would be difficult to argue that the Indians' cause was not as just and worthy as that for which the minutemen at Concord and George Washington's men at Valley Forge once fought.

The Plains Indians' battle for justice is not over. After nearly a century of citizenship, they are still struggling to overcome the racial prejudice, poverty, and government mismanagement that have kept them in social bondage during the past century. But perhaps their greatest battle today is that of preserving and maintaining their unique heritage and tribal being, which is threatened by an ever-changing world.

Notes

Abbreviations

OHSL—   Oklahoma Historical Society Library
OHSA/M—Oklahoma Historical Society Archives and Manuscripts
BTHC—   Barker Texas History Center
TSL—   Texas State Library
WAMS— Western Americana Microfilm Series
NA—   National Archives American Indian Microfilm Publications
WHC—   Western History Collections, University of Oklahoma

Introduction

1. Utley, *Indian Frontier of the American West*, 30.
2. Ewers, "Intertribal Warfare," 409.
3. Pope to Sawyer, *Official Communications from General Pope*, 23, WAMS Reel 5646.
4. Personal conversation with Mike Haney, McCloud, Oklahoma.
5. Holm, "Fighting a White Man's War," *Journal of Ethnic Studies*, Summer 1981, 70.

Chapter 1. The Warrior Ethic

1. Wood and Liberty, *Anthropology on the Great Plains*, 232.
2. Ewers, "Intertribal Warfare," 397–98.
3. Ibid., 400–401; Kirkland and Newcomb, *Rock Art of Texas*, 35, 200–201.
4. Ewers, "Intertribal Warfare," 400.
5. Tyrrell, *David Thompson's Narrative*, 262–63.
6. Masson, *Les Bourgeois*, 386.
7. Margry, *Découvertes* 6: 307–18; Lewis, "La Harpe's First Expedition," 345–47; "The Missouri Reader," 505.
8. Margry, *Découvertes* 4: 343.
9. Price, "Comanches' Threat," 36.
10. *Washington National Republican*, March 27, 1863.
11. Margot Liberty, "The Sun Dance," in Wood and Liberty, *Anthropology on the Great Plains*, 164.
12. Utley, *The Indian Frontier*, 29.
13. Hyde, *George Bent*, 48.
14. Charles MacKenzie quoted in Masson, *Les Bourgeois*, 371.
15. Foreman, "The Cherokee War Path," 261–63.
16. Jones, "Diary of Assistant Surgeon Leonard McPhail," 288.
17. *Arkansas Intelligencer*, January 6, 1844.
18. Smith, *Sagebrush Soldier*, 78, citing Capt. John G. Bourke, *Mackenzie's Last Fight with the Cheyennes*, 33.
19. Harper, "Taovayas Indians," 287, citing Antonio Trevino, *Testimonio*, August 13, 1765, Bexar Archives, Library of the University of Texas.
20. Garrard, *Wah-to-Yah and the Taos Trail*, 58–59.
21. "The Journal of Elijah Hicks," 85.
22. *New York Tribune*, October 23, 1867.
23. Grinnell, *The Cheyenne Indians* 2: 130.
24. Ibid.; McDermott, *Tixier's Travels*, 181.
25. Masson, *Les Bourgeois*, 379.
26. *Report of the Commissioner of Indian Affairs, 1857*, 141.
27. Stanley, *Early Travels* 1: 37–38; Custer, *My Life on the Plains*, 33–34.
28. *New York Tribune*, November 8, 1867; see also Hoig, *Battle of the Washita*, 32–34.

Chapter 2. Warfare on the Plains

1. Lee, *Three Years among the Comanches*, 134–37.
2. Ibid., 136.

3. Gibson, The American Indian, 21.
4. White, Roots of Dependency, 149.
5. Bandelier and Bandelier, Journey of Alvara Nuñez Cabeza de Vaca, 119.
6. Winship, The Coronado Expedition, 364–67.
7. Ibid., 368.
8. Secoy, "A Functional-Historical View of Plains Indian Warfare," 1–10.
9. Ibid.
10. Ibid., 33–36.
11. Roe, The Indian and the Horse, 230.
12. Dodge, The Plains, 383.
13. Margry, Découvertes 4: 307–18.
14. Leckie, Military Conquest, 8–9.
15. Catlin, North American Indians 2: 65.
16. McDermott, Tixier's Travels, 168–69.
17. Ewers, "Intertribal Warfare," 399–401.
18. Berlandier, Indians of Texas, 140.
19. McDermott, Tixier's Travels, 221–25.
20. Niles' Weekly Register, September 27, 1817.
21. Catlin, North American Indians 1: 141.
22. Dodge, Our Wild Indians, 450.
23. Berlandier, Indians of Texas, 119.
24. Berthrong, The Southern Cheyennes, 138–40.
25. Ibid.; Hyde, George Bent, 171–73.
26. Downey, Indian-Fighting Army, 42–44.
27. Dodge, The Plains, 376–77.
28. Cherokee Advocate, November 5, 1870.
29. Ibid.
30. Clifton, Prairie People, 358–61.
31. Ibid., 377.
32. Gibson, The Kickapoos, 213–14.
33. Report of the Commissioner of Indian Affairs, 1868, 64–67; Kansas Daily Tribune, June 6, 7, 8, 11, 1868.
34. Berlandier, Indians of Texas, 115.
35. Coues, Journal of Alexander Henry . . . and David Thompson, 377.
36. Daily Missouri Republican, November 3, 1851.
37. Lee, Three Years among the Comanches, 97.
38. Pettis, Kit Carson's Battle, 48–54.
39. Leavenworth Daily Conservative, July 10, 1867.
40. Whirlwind quoted in Haley, Buffalo War, 136–37.
41. Hutton, Soldiers West, 6.
42. Bull Bear quoted in "Sand Creek Massacre," Report of the Secretary of War, 215–17.

Chapter 3. The Tattooed People of Kansas

1. Hammond and Rey, *Don Juan de Oñate* 2: 746-60, 836-77.

2. Bolton, *Spanish Exploration*, 225.

3. The Escanjaques have been variously identified by modern scholars as Kaws, Apaches, Osages, Tonkawas, or Tawakonis. Some believe that the Escanjaques were originally the tribe called Aguancanes, a Caddoan people who eventually merged with the Yscanis (Iscanis). Newcomb and Campbell, "Southern Plains Ethnohistory," 35-38.

4. A significant fact of Indian history, which has been generally overlooked and certainly went unrecognized during the U.S. treaty-making period with the tribes, is that the Wichitas, so far as we know, were the earliest of our modern Indian tribes to reside in the area now included in southern Kansas and Oklahoma. No known tribe of modern times predated the Wichitas in the region.

5. The French, Spanish, Americans, and other tribes used many variations of spelling in referring to the Pawnee Picts/Taovayas. See Harper, "Taovayas Indians," 271, n. 9.

6. Thomas, *After Coronado*, 8.

7. Ibid., 13-14.

8. Bell, Jelks, and Newcomb, *Wichita Indian Archaeology*, 246.

9. Margry, *Découvertes* 4: 307-18; Lewis, "La Harpe's First Expedition," 331-49; Lewis, "Du Tisné's First Expedition"; 319-23; Wedel, "Claude-Charles Dutisné:" 147-73. It is believed that the Lasley-Vore dig in eastern Oklahoma may well have been the site of the villages visited by La Harpe. Many French trade items have been uncovered there.

10. Lewis, "La Harpe's First Expedition," 331-49.

11. Lewis, "Du Tisné's First Expedition"; Margry, *Découvertes* 6: 307-18.

12. Folmer, "Étienne Véniard de Bourgmond." 279-98.

13. Further indication that these Indians were Wichitas lies in the fact that when Bourgmond sought to make peace between this tribe and others, no mention was made of the Wichitas, some of whom may well have been still in Kansas. Another clue lies in a speech of the Padouca chief, who indicated that with peace established between them and tribes to the east, it might be possible to retrieve "women and children whom they [eastern tribes] took and who are slaves with them." Ibid., 294. This extensive loss of slaves to eastern tribes would not apply well to either the Apaches or the Comanches, but it would to the Wichitas.

14. Andreas, *History of the State of Kansas* 1: 48-49.

15. Bell, Jelks, and Newcomb, *Wichita Indian Archaeology*, 255-56; Margry, *Découvertes* 6: 193-94; Nasatir, *Before Lewis and Clark* 2: 28.

16. Herbert E. Bolton, "French Intrusion into Mexico, 1749–1752," in Stephens and Bolton, *The Pacific Ocean,* 400–404.

17. Ibid., 396–98; Bolton, *Athanase de Mézières* 1: 47, n. 47.

18. Thoburn, "Oklahoma's First White Settlement," 34; Wedel, *Deer Creek Site,* 5–8.

19. Wedel, *Deer Creek Site,* 46.

20. Bolton, *Athanase de Mézières* 1: 167.

21. Emmet Starr Collection, Indian Documents, Microfilm Series, OHSL, 29–30: 141–42. Ni-as-tor stated that when they left the Arkansas, the Wichitas had never seen horses and other aspects of this tradition. It is difficult to reconcile this claim with known fact.

Chapter 4. The Norteños of Texas

1. Dunn, "The Apache Mission."

2. Allen, "The Parrilla Expedition." 53–71.

3. Bolton, 90; Harper, "Taovaya Indians," 278; Bell, Jelks, and Newcomb, *Wichita Indian Archaeology,* 261–65.

4. Bell, Jelks, and Newcomb, *Wichita Indian Archaeology,* 261–65.

5. Ibid., 272.

6. J. Gaignard, "Journal of an Expedition up the Red River, 1773–1774," in Bolton, *Athanase de Mézières* 2: 83–100.

7. Bolton, *Athanase de Mézières* 2: 204.

8. Ibid., 201–203.

9. Bell, Jelks, and Newcomb, *Wichita Indian Archaeology,* 277–78.

10. John, "Portrait of a Wichita Village," 414.

11. Ibid., 412–37.

12. Foreman, *Indians and Pioneers,* 53, quoting Jamison to Calhoun, January 20, 1819, AG.

13. James, *Three Years,* 123–37.

Chapter 5. Comanche Conquest in New Mexico

1. Quoted in Jackson, *Zebulon Montgomery Pike* 2: 354–58.

2. Pike, *Sources of the Mississippi,* appendix to part 2, 18.

3. Ibid., 143.

4. Flores, *Jefferson and Southwestern Exploration,* 125 n. 5.; Flores, *Journal of an Indian Trader,* 22, 106 n. 39.

5. Price, "Comanches' Threat," 38.

6. Richardson, *Comanche Barrier,* 55–57.

7. Quoted in Thomas, *After Coronado,* 211.

8. Bolton, *Athanase de Mézières* 1: 58–59.
9. Loomis and Nasatir, *Pedro Vial*, 16–27.
10. Thomas, *Forgotten Frontiers*, 60.
11. Richardson, *Comanche Barrier*, 56–57.
12. Thomas, *Forgotten Frontiers*, 62–63.
13. Ibid., 134.
14. Ibid., 135.
15. Ibid., 123–39.
16. Ibid., 73.
17. Richardson, *Comanche Barrier*, 62–63.

Chapter 6. Comanche Conquest in Texas

1. Bolton, *Texas*, 27–28.
2. Ibid., 29.
3. Ibid., 31.
4. Ibid., 432–33.
5. Ibid., 434.
6. The spelling of the Comanche band names, as is often the case in the interpretation of Indian language, varies from one source to another. There is also some disagreement over the Comanche tribal division, which evolved over time.
7. Bolton, *Athanase de Mézières* 2: 93–94.
8. Quoted in Fehrenbach, *Comanches*, 221.
9. Richardson, *Comanche Barrier*, 70: Thomas, *Forgotten Frontiers*, 72.
10. Bolton, *Texas*, 127.
11. John, "Nurturing the Peace." 345–69.
12. Richardson, *Comanche Barrier*, 70–73.
13. John, "Nurturing the Peace," 358–59. This is the same Chief Cordero whom the trader Thomas James met while en route to New Mexico in 1821. See chapter 4.
14. Berlandier, *Indians of Texas*, 31–32.
15. Molyneaux, *Romantic Story of Texas*, 22–24.
16. De Shields, *Border Wars of Texas*, 17.

Chapter 7. Challengers from the North

1. Mayhall, *Kiowas*, 14–15.
2. *Daily Missouri Republican*, November 10, 1851.

3. Wheelock as quoted in "Col. Henry Dodge Report of Leavenworth Expedition," *Senate Document No. 1,* 87.
4. *Daily National Intelligencer,* September 30, 1834.
5. Mayhall, *Kiowas,* 15.
6. Berlandier, *Indians of Texas,* 108, n. 136.
7. Jackson, *Zebulon Montgomery Pike* 2: 38, 174.
8. Mayhall, in *Kiowas,* identifies the Kaskaias as Kiowa-Apaches. Although there may have been some intermingling of the Plains Apaches and the Kiowas, it is apparent they were still separate tribes. The Long expedition secured a lengthy vocabulary of Kaskaia words but could understand little or nothing of the Kiowa language.
9. James, *Account of an Expedition* 2: 60–61.
10. Ibid., 185.
11. Ibid., 103–4.
12. Coues, *Jacob Fowler,* 58.
13. Ibid., 56.
14. Mayhall, *Kiowas,* 19.
15. Fehrenbach, *Comanches,* 248.
16. Bolton, *Athanase de Mézières* 1: 167.
17. Pike, *Sources of the Mississippi,* 124.
18. Characterish as quoted in "Extracts from the Diary of Major Sibley." 205.
19. Ibid.
20. Ibid.
21. Foreman, *Pioneer Days,* 74.
22. Nuttall, *Travels into the Arkansas Territory,* 228–32.
23. Ibid., 208–11.
24. Berlandier, *Indians of Texas,* 67 n. 67.
25. James, *Three Years,* 123–37.
26. Ibid., 190–231.
27. Berlandier, *Indians of Texas,* 73.
28. Ibid., 257–59; Foreman, *Pioneer Days,* 115–19.
29. Catlin noted this misnaming of the tribe during his visit in 1834. He stated: "'The Towayahs are the Indians who have been hitherto called by us *Pawnee Picts.* They are not known by this name to the Camanches or Kioways, and do not recognize it themselves, but answer to the name of *Towayah.*" *Daily National Intelligencer,* September 30, 1834.
30. Pike, *Sources of the Mississippi,* 15–17.
31. *Niles' Weekly Register,* August 1, 1818.
32. Hyde, *Pawnee Indians,* 170–71.
33. James, *Three Years,* 172–73.
34. *Niles' Weekly Register,* March 6, 1830; *Daily National Intelligencer,* March 8, 1830; *Cherokee Phoenix,* March 17, 1830.
35. *Niles' Weekly Register,* January 8, 1831.
36. McDermott, *Tixier's Travels,* 252.

Chapter 8. The Cheyennes and Arapahos Push South

1. Berlandier, *Indians of Texas*, 110–11.
2. Ibid., 185–87.
3. Ibid., 197.
4. Hyde, *George Bent*, 72.
5. Grinnell, *Fighting Cheyennes*, 72–73.
6. Ibid., 45–62.
7. *Daily National Intelligencer*, April 16, 1839.
8. Grinnell, *Fighting Cheyennes*, 64–69.
9. Berthrong, *Southern Cheyennes*, 110, citing Fitzpatrick to Harvey, December 18, 1847, June 24, Upper Platte Agency, Ltrs. Recd.
10. Ibid., 107.
11. Ibid., 116–17.
12. Berthrong, *Southern Cheyennes*, 134–35.
13. Grinnell, *Fighting Cheyennes*, 117–23.

Chapter 9. Wars of the Immigrant Nations

1. Sibley, "Historical Sketches," *American State Papers.*
2. Thoburn, *History of Oklahoma*, 71–72.
3. *Journal of Andrew Ellicott*, 113.
4. Bogy, *Senate Document No. 23.*
5. John, "Nurturing the Peace," 357.
6. Sibley, "Historical Sketches," *American State Papers*, 16.
7. Foreman, *Indians and Pioneers*, 33.
8. Carter, *Territorial Papers* 15: 304.
9. *Niles' Weekly Register*, September 27, 1817.
10. Foreman, *Indians and Pioneers*, 58.
11. *Niles' Weekly Register*, January 8, 1818.
12. Foreman, *Indians and Pioneers*, 59.
13. Ibid., 85–86.
14. Ibid., 111–12.
15. Ibid., 117.
16. *Arkansas Gazette*, December 29, 1821.
17. Foreman, *Indians and Pioneers*, 123–25.
18. Ibid., 126, n. 13.
19. Ibid., 147.
20. Ibid., 148.
21. Ibid., 238–39.
22. McLean, *Robertson's Colony in Texas* 2: 543–46, 565, 583, 624, 635.
23. A detailed narrative of the affair was related by a half-blood Cherokee war captain named John Smith to another Cherokee, John

Ridge, in 1836 while the two were in Washington. See Foreman, "Cherokee War Path," 233–35.

24. Houston to Arbuckle, July 8, 1829, cited by Foreman, *Indians and Pioneers,* 270.

25. Brown, *Indian Wars,* 10–14.

26. Foreman, "Cherokee War Path." See also Brown, *Indian Wars,* 10–14.

27. Wooten, *History of Texas* 1: 745.

28. Arbuckle ltr., July 24, 1830, Ltrs. Recd. by AGO, Main Series, 1822–60, NA.

29. *Daily National Intelligencer,* June 16, 1831.

30. Ibid., July 28, 1831.

31. Foreman, *Advancing the Frontier,* 20.

32. *Daily National Intelligencer,* July 16, 1832.

33. Ibid., March 12, 1833.

34. Ibid., April 13, 1833.

35. Chouteau reports, November 25, December 8, 1837, May 1, 1838, Ltrs. Recd., Western Superintendency, 1837–39, NA.

36. Logan to Crawford, May 30, 1842, Ltrs. Recd., Creek Agency, 1839–42, NA.

37. Foreman, "North Fork Town," 82.

38. Hyde, *Pawnee Indians,* 206–7.

39. Foreman, *Advancing the Frontier,* 215–16.

40. *New Orleans Picayune,* December 3, 1843.

41. *Cherokee Advocate,* March 15, 27, June 19, 1845.

42. Ibid., March 27, May 8, 22, 1845. A decade later, however, the Comanches would send word to the federal government that they greatly admired the prosperity of the Creeks and wished to be granted their own tract of land on which to settle down and live as farmers. Debo, *Road to Disappearance,* 137.

43. *Cherokee Advocate,* June 19, August 21, 1845.

44. Ibid., May 21, 1846.

45. Ibid., March 21, 1851.

46. McReynolds, *The Seminoles,* 161–63.

47. Ibid., 280–81.

48. Richardson, *Comanche Barrier,* 234, n. 457.

Chapter 10. The American Presence

1. Foreman, *Pioneer Days,* 103–4.
2. Morrison, "A Journey across Oklahoma," 33–37.
3. Irving, *Tour of the Prairies,* 152–53.
4. Ibid., 104–5.
5. Young, "Mounted Ranger Batallion," 468–69.

6. Foreman, *Pioneer Days*, 116–19.

7. Wheelock, Proceedings of a Council Held at Fort Gibson, September 1834, Record Group 75, NA.

8. Ibid.

9. Ibid.

10. Ibid.

11. Ibid.

12. Foreman, "Journal of the Proceedings," 394.

13. Mason letter of August 12, 1935, in *National Intelligencer*, September 23, 1835.

14. Jones, "Leonard McPhail," 285.

15. Foreman, "Journal of the Proceedings."

16. Ibid.

17. Ibid., 413.

18. Tiche-toche-cha as quoted in Kingsley, "Report on the Expedition of Dragoons." *American State Papers, Military Affairs*, 130–46.

19. Foreman, *Pioneer Days*, 225–26.

20. Maj. P. L. Chouteau report, September 8, 1837, Ltrs. Recd., Western Superintendency, 1837–39, NA.

21. Treaty with Kioway, Documents of Ratified Indian.

22. Chouteau letter, September 8, 1837, Ltrs. Recd., Western Superintendency, 1837–39, NA.

23. William Armstrong letter, June 8, 1839, Western Superintendency, 1837–39, NA.

24. *Daily National Intelligencer*, November 14, 1838.

Chapter 11. The Texas Frontier Wars

1. *Atkinson's Saturday Evening Post*, August 17, 1833. John Warren Hunter, in *Rise and Fall of the Mission of San Saba* (Mason, Texas, 1906), erroneously gives the date of the fight as 1834, but he is likely correct that the attackers were Lipan Apaches. Razin (or Rezin) was killed at Monterey during the Mexican War in 1846.)

2. See Hoig, "Diana, Tiana, or Talihina?" 64.

3. Clarke, *Chief Bowles*, 86.

4. Wooten, *History of Texas* 1: 344–46; Clarke, *Chief Bowles*, 94–111.

5. Fehrenbach, *Comanches*, 237–40.

6. Richardson, *Comanche Barrier*, 90–91.

7. Fehrenbach, *Comanches*, 293–304.

8. Webb, *The Texas Rangers*, 46–47.

9. Richardson, *Comanche Barrier*, 104–5.

10. Webb, *Texas Rangers*, 46–47.

11. *Cherokee Advocate*, May 22, 1845.

12. Webb, *Texas Rangers*, 45–46.

13. Ibid., 70–72.

14. Winfrey and Day, *Indian Papers of Texas* 1: 163.

15. Kakatish as quoted in *Portraits of North American Indians*, 32.

16. Winfrey and Day, *Indian Papers of Texas* 1: 161–62.

17. Eldridge Report to Houston, December 8, 1843, in ibid. 1: 251–75.

18. Ibid., 242–46. Thomas Torrey, who had been with the ill-fated Texas Expedition of 1841 and among those imprisoned in a Mexico City leper colony, died during the council. The block fort had been erected by Jonathan Bird on the West Elm Fork of the Trinity River in 1841.

19. Clift, "Warren's Trading Post," 128–40.

20. *Arkansas Intelligencer*, December 30, 1843.

21. Winfrey and Day, *Indian Papers of Texas* 2: 66–72.

22. Ibid., 103–19.

23. Ibid.

24. Kappler, ed., *Indian Treaties*, 554–57. During the treaty council, attempts were made to ransom Cynthia Ann Parker from the Comanches. She, however, refused to leave her Comanche husband. *Reports of Messrs. Butler and Lewis*, 13.

25. *Report of Messrs. Butler and Lewis*, 4–5; "Journal of Elijah Hicks"; Butler to Medill, June 28, 1846, Ltrs. Recd., 1838–48, Texas OIA Letter Book, I, BTHC; *Baltimore Sun*, June 16, 1848.

26. Galvin, 47–48.

27. Winfrey and Day, *Indian Papers of Texas, 1825–1916*, 3: 130–36; Articles of Treaty, December 10, 1850, Ltrs. Recd., Texas Agency, 1847–52, NA.

28. Mix to Drew, May 26, 1853, Ltrs, Recd., Southern Superintendency, 1853, NA.

29. Richardson, *Comanche Barrier*, 172; *Daily Missouri Democrat*, July 19, 1856.

Chapter 12. Invasion of the Comanchería

1. Richardson, *Comanche Barrier*, 234.

2. *Daily National Intelligencer*, June 10, 1858.

3. Ford to Runnels, May 22, 1858, *House Ex. Doc. 27*, 18–19.

4. Ibid.; John Ford Memoirs, BTHC, Collection, 4; 676 ff.

5. Sergeant Cotter to Governor Runnels, Governors' Letters File, TSL.

6. John S. Ford to Runnels, May 22, 1858, *House Ex. Doc. 27*, 19.

7. Richardson, *Comanche Barrier*, 237.

8. Foreman, "Journal Kept by Douglas Cooper," 381–90.

9. Thoburn, "Battle with Comanches," 22–23.

10. Ibid., 22–28; Van Dorn report, October 5, 1858, *House Exec. Doc. No. 27,* 50–53.

11. Milligan and Norris, "Keeping the Peace," 265, citing Western Americana Collection, Beinecke Rare Book and Manuscript Library, Yale University.

12. Ibid., January 25, 1859.

13. *St. Louis Daily Democrat,* March 21, 1859.

14. Thoburn, "Indian Fight in Ford County," 314–29.

15. Richardson, *Comanche Barrier,* 245–59.

16. Wright, "Fort Cobb," 54–55; Chapman, "Wichita Reservation," 1048.

17. Richardson, *Comanche Barrier,* 265; James T. De Shields, *Cynthia Ann Parker: The Story of Her Capture;* Brown, *Indian Wars and Pioneers,* 41–43.

13. The Immigrant Indians in the Civil War

1. Emory to Townsend, May 19, 1861, *Compilation of the Official Records,* Series I, 1: 648.

2. *Lawrence Republican,* June 13, 1861.

3. Trickett, "Civil War," 266.

4. "Report of Albert Pike on Mission to the Indian Nations," December 12, 1861, WAMS, Reel 1330.

5. Quoted in Debo, "Battle of Round Mountain," 191–92.

6. Trickett, "Civil War," 268.

7. Wright, Shirk, and Franks, *Mark of Heritage,* 15; Debo, "Battle of Round Mountain," 187–206.

8. *Compilation of the Official Records,* Series I, 8: 6.

9. Ibid., 8, 17.

10. Ibid., 23–29.

11. Abel, 13–36. *American Indian as a Participant,* 13–36.

12. Ibid., 102.

13. Ibid., 125.

14. Franks, *Stand Waite,* 126–28.

15. Reports of Col. Weer, July 4, 6, 1862, *Compilation of the Official Records,* Series I, 13: 137–38.

16. Abel, *American Indian as a Participant,* 130–36; Rampp and Rampp, *Civil War,* 12–14.

17. Abel, *American Indian as a Participant,* 164.

18. Ibid., 197–98.

19. Franks, *Stand Waite,* 135–36.

20. Rampp and Rampp, *Civil War,* 139–40; Abel, *American Indian as a Participant,* 284–85; Franks, *Stand Waite,* 140–41.

21. Cooper report, August 12, 1863, *Compilation of the Official Records*, Series I, 12, Pt. 1: 457–61.
22. Blunt Report, July 26, 1863, ibid., 448–50.
23. Rampp and Rampp, *Civil War*, 38–51.
24. Franks, *Stand Watie*, 152.
25. Rampp and Rampp, *Civil War*, 59–68.
26. Ibid., 85–90.
27. Ibid., 98–99.
28. Ibid., 105–6.
29. Ibid., 120–21.

Chapter 14. The Prairie Indians in the Civil War

1. "Report of Albert Pike."
2. *Compilation of the Official Records*, Series IV, 1: 542–54.
3. Wright, "Fort Cobb," 59.
4. M. Leeper to Albert Pike, April 13, 1862, cited by Abel, *American Indian as a Participant*, 348–50.
5. *Compilation of the Official Records*, Series I, 13: 918–21; Thoburn, "Horace P. Jones," 383–85.
6. S. S. Scott to Gen. Holmes, November 2, 1862, *Compilation of the Official Records*, Series I, 13: 919–21.
7. *Emporia News*, December 6, 1862; Abel, *American Indian as a Slaveholder*, 329.
8. This account is based on numerous sources, which contain some conflicting information. See *Report of Commissioner of Indian Affairs, 1863–64*, 324–25; "Massacre of Confederates by Osages Indians in 1863," 62–66; *Weekly Commonwealth and Republican*, June 18, 1863; *Independence Daily Reporter*, February 7, 1914; *Kansas City Times*, October 14, 1906; "Massacre of Confederate Officers."
9. *Weekly Commonwealth and Republican*, June 18, 1863.
10. Richardson, *Northwest Texas*, 246–48; Mayhall, *Indian Wars of Texas*, 124–59; Capps, *Wagontrain Raid*, 103–9.
11. Richardson, *Northwest Texas*, 249.
12. Pettis, *Kit Carson's Battle*, 28–29.
13. Ibid., 22.
14. Ibid., 32–38.
15. Hoig, *Sand Creek Massacre*, 50–51.
16. Ibid., 98.
17. "Sand Creek Massacre," *Report of the Secretary of War*, Sen. Exec. Doc. 26, 213–17; Hyde, *George Bent*, 248.
18. Hyde, *George Bent*, 155.

Chapter 15. War and Peace on the Kansas Plains

1. Grinnell, *Fighting Cheyennes*, 181.
2. Hyde, *George Bent*, 168.
3. Berthrong, *Southern Cheyennes*, 225–27.
4. Ibid., 248–49.
5. Kappler, ed. *Indian Treaties*, 892–95; "Diary of Samuel A. Kingman," 44–50.
6. *Report of Commissioner of Indian Affairs, 1866*, 704.
7. Ibid., 714.
8. Sanborn quoted ibid., 717.
9. Ibid., 718–19.
10. Kappler, *Indian Treaties*, 887–92.
11. Berthrong, *Southern Cheyennes*, 256.
12. Ibid., 258.
13. Ibid., 263.
14. Ibid., 264.
15. Hoig, *Battle of the Washita*, 3–4.
16. Stanley, *Early Travels*, 1: 29.
17. Ibid., 37–38.
18. Custer, *My Life on the Plains*, 49–52.
19. Berthrong, *Southern Cheyennes*, 280.
20. Ibid., 283.
21. Frost, *Courts-Martial*, 151–52.
22. Berthrong, *Southern Cheyennes*, 286–87; Hyde, *George Bent*, 274–75.
23. Frost, *Courts-Martial*, 265.
24. Hoig, *David L. Payne*, 12–20.
25. Berthrong, *Southern Cheyennes*, 287–88.
26. Jones, *Treaty of Medicine Lodge*, 18–19.
27. *Cincinnati Gazette*, October 26, 1867.
28. Kappler, *Indian Treaties*, 977–84.
29. *New York Tribune*, November 8, 1867.
30. *Chicago Tribune*, November 4, 1867.
31. *Kansas Weekly Tribune*, November 11, 1867.
32. *Report of the Commissioner of Indian Affairs, 1866*, 720.
33. "Diary of Samuel A. Kingman," 448.
34. Shanklin to Commissioner, July 6, 1866, Agents and Agency File, Kiowa Agency, OHSA/M.
35. Shanklin to Col. E. Sells, July 13, 1866, Depredations File, Kiowa Agency, OHSA/M.
36. Shanklin to Wortham, September 1, 1867, *Report of the Commissioner of Indian Affairs, 1867*, 321–23.
37. *Leavenworth Daily Conservative*, September 27, 1867.
38. McCusker to Murphy, November 15, 1867, Ltrs. Recd., Wichita Agency, 1867–75, NA.

39. *Report of the Commissioner of Indian Affairs, 1868,* 748–51.

Chapter 16. The Sheridan-Custer Campaign

1. Crawford, *Kansas in the Sixties,* 296.
2. Godfrey, "Some Reminiscences," 421.
3. Sully to McKeever, Report, September 16, 1868, Selected Ltrs., 1868–72, Records of U.S. Army Commands, Nebraska, NA.
4. *Army and Navy Journal,* October 9, 1868, 102.
5. Godfrey, "Some Reminiscences," 423–24.
6. Sully to McKeever, Report, September 16, 1868.
7. Ibid.; *Record of Engagements with Hostile Indians,* 13.
8. Forsyth, *Thrilling Days,* 12–13.
9. *New York Herald,* October 12, 1868.
10. Ibid.
11. Hyde, *George Bent,* 303.
12. Hurst, "Beecher Island Fight."
13. *Record of Engagements,* 17–19. For a detailed account of Sheridan's winter campaign, see Hoig, *Battle of the Washita.*
14. Keim, *Sheridan's Troopers,* 103.
15. Godfrey, "Some Reminiscences," 37; Chandler, *Garryowen in Glory;* Harvey, "Campaigning with Sheridan" *New York Herald,* December 8, 24, 1868; *New York Tribune,* December 29, 1868. See also Hoig, *Battle of the Washita,* 112–44.
16. Letters and Reports from Indian Territory prior to and following the Battle of the Washita, *Senate Ex. Doc. No. 18,* 28. Hutton, in *Phil Sheridan,* 99–100, states that Custer's Washita attack "was not a massacre." His arguments are (1) that Black Kettle's Cheyennes were not unarmed innocents, (2) that Hazen had told Black Kettle there could be no peace until he surrendered to Sheridan, and (3) that the soldiers were not under orders to kill everyone. In rebuttal, it can be effectively argued that having arms does not prevent anyone from being massacred; that Black Kettle and his people were given no chance whatever to surrender, even though they had tried to do so; and that, orders or not, the troops attacked without warning, offered no opportunity for surrender during the action, and killed people promiscuously. They did, in fact, *massacre,* precisely as the word is defined by Webster: "to kill indiscriminately and mercilessly and in large numbers." For a fuller discussion of this matter, see Hoig, *Battle of the Washita,* xiii–xv.
17. Godfrey, "Some Reminiscences," 493.
18. *New York Herald,* December 24, 26, 1868; Sheridan to Nichols, December 2, 3, 1868, Letters and Reports . . . Washita, *Senate Ex. Doc.*

No. 18, 40th Cong., 3d sess., 34, 43. See also Hoig, Battle of the Washita, 145–62.

19. Rister, "Evans' Christmas Day," 275–301.
20. Nye, Carbine and Lance, 78–83.
21. Custer, My Life on the Plains, 359.

Chapter 17. The Kiowa Resistance

1. Keim, Sheridan's Troopers, 275; Nye, Carbine and Lance, 89–95.
2. Nye, Carbine and Lance, 112–13; Carter, On the Border, 105–8.
3. Nye, Carbine and Lance, 116–17.
4. Capps, Wagontrain Raid, 19–46.
5. Report of J. H. Patzki, Asst. Surg., 4th Cavalry, as cited in ibid., 53.
6. Nye, Carbine and Lance, 132–47. Another son of Satank, Joshua Given, took up the ways of the whites and became an Episcopal minister. Satank's granddaughter, Ioleta Hunt, was the first Kiowa girl to receive a liberal arts degree and became a schoolteacher.
7. Carter, On the Border, 165–78.
8. Army and Navy Journal, November 16, 1872; Nye, Carbine and Lance, 160–63.
9. Nye, Carbine and Lance, 182–84.
10. Haley, Buffalo War, 79–93.
11. Carnal, "Reminiscences of a Texas Ranger," 20–24; "Lost Valley Fight," 100, 104; Nye, Carbine and Lance, 192–200.
12. Army and Navy Journal, September 5, 1874; Haley, Buffalo War, 107–23.
13. Haley, Buffalo War, 148–67.
14. Nye, Carbine and Lance, 215–19.
15. Haley, Buffalo War, 169–83.
16. Ibid., 213–34.
17. Ibid., 254–55.
18. Cincinnati Commercial, November 4, 1867.

Chapter 18. Conquest of the Cheyennes

1. Hyde, George Bent, 331 ff.; Berthrong, Southern Cheyennes, 338–44.
2. Darlington to Hoag, August 12, 21, 1871, Ltrs. Recd., Upper Arkansas Agency, Central Superintendency, NA; Report of the Commissioner of Indian Affairs, 1871.
3. Berthrong, Southern Cheyennes, 371.
4. Baker and Harrison, Adobe Walls, 14–22.

5. Barde, *"Billy" Dixon*, 176 ff.; Haley, *Buffalo War*, 67–78.
6. John D. Miles report, *Kansas Daily Tribune*, July 8, 1874.
7. *Wichita Eagle*, July 9, 1874; *Kansas Daily Tribune*, October 28, 1874.
8. *Record of Engagements*, 46–49.
9. *House Ex. Doc. No. 1*, 2: 78.
10. "Scouting on the 'Staked Plains,' " 532–43.
11. Nye, *Carbine and Lance*, 225.
12. Berthrong, *Southern Cheyennes*, 394–96.
13. Ibid., 397–400.
14. Grinnell, *Fighting Cheyennes*, 403.
15. Wright, "Pursuit of Dull Knife," 147–48.

Bibliography

Archival Materials

Agents and Agency File, Kiowa Agency, OHSA/M
Cheyenne and Arapaho Indian Depredation File, OHSA/M
Depredations File, Kiowa Agency, OHSA/M.
Emmet Starr Collection, Indian Documents, Microfilm Series, OHSL.
Governors' Letters File, TSL.
John Ford Memoirs, BTHC.
Letter Book, Vol. 1, BTHC.

Articles

Allen, Henry Easton. "The Parrilla Expedition to the Red River." *Southwestern Historical Quarterly* 43 (July 1939): 53–71.
Bartles, W. L. "Massacre of Confederates by Osage Indians in 1863." *Collections of the Kansas State Historical Society* 8 (1903–1904): 62–66.
Carnal, Ed. "Reminiscences of a Texas Ranger." *Frontier Times* 1: 20–24.

Chapman, Berlin B. "Establishment of Wichita Reservation." *Chronicles of Oklahoma* 11 (December 1933): 1044–53.

Clift, W. H. "Warren's Trading Post" *Chronicles of Oklahoma* 2 (June 1924): 128–40.

Debo, Angie. "The Site of the Battle of Round Mountain, 1861." *Chronicles of Oklahoma* 27 (Summer 1949): 187–207.

"Diary of Samuel A. Kingman at Indian Treaty in 1865." *Kansas State Historical Quarterly* 1 (November 1932): 442–50.

Dunn, William Edward. "The Apache Mission on the San Saba River: Its Founding and Failure." *Southwestern Historical Quarterly* 17 (April 1914): 379–414.

Ewers, John C. "Intertribal Warfare as the Precursor of Indian-White Warfare on the Northern Great Plains." *Western History Quarterly* 6 (October 1975): 397–410.

"Extracts from the Diary of Major Sibley." *Chronicles of Oklahoma* 5 (June 1927): 196–218.

Fischer, LeRoy, and Kenny A. Franks. "Confederate Victory at Chusto-Talasah." *Chronicles of Oklahoma* 49 (Winter 1971–72): 452–76.

Folmer, Henri. "Étienne Vèniard de Bourgmond in the Missouri Country." *Missouri Historical Review* 36 (April 1942): 279–98.

Foreman, Carolyn Thomas, annot. "The Cherokee War Path." *Chronicles of Oklahoma* 9 (September 1931): 233–63.

———. "North Fork Town." *Chronicles of Oklahoma* 29 (Spring 1951): 79–111.

Foreman, Grant, ed. "A Journal Kept by Douglas Cooper of an Expedition by a Company of Chickasaw in Quest of Comanche Indians." *Chronicles of Oklahoma* 5 (December 1927): 381–390.

———. "The Journal of the Proceedings at Our First Treaty with the Wild Indians, 1835." *Chronicles of Oklahoma* 14 (December 1936): 393–418.

Gibson, Arrell Morgan. "Prehistory in Oklahoma." *Chronicles of Oklahoma* 43 (Spring 1965): 2–8.

Godfrey, E. S. "Some Reminiscences, Including an Account of General Sully's Expedition against the Southern Plains Indians, 1868." *Cavalry Journal* 36 (July 1927): 417–25.

———. "Some Reminiscences, Including the Washita Battle, November 27, 1868." *Cavalry Journal* 37 (October 1928): 481–500.

Harper, Elizabeth Ann. "The Taovayas Indians in Frontier Trade and Diplomacy, 1719–1768." *Chronicles of Oklahoma* 31 (Autumn 1953): 268–89.

Harvey, Winfield Scott. "Campaigning with Sheridan: A Farrier's Diary." *Chronicles of Oklahoma* 37 (Spring 1959): 71–105.

Hoig, Stan. "Diana, Tiana, or Talihina?" *Chronicles of Oklahoma* 64 (Spring 1986): 53–59.

Holm, Tom. "Fighting a White Man's War: The Extent and Legacy of American Indian Participation in World War II." *Journal of Ethnic Studies* 9 (Summer 1981): 69–81.

Hurst, Scout John. "The Beecher Island Fight." *Collections of the Kansas State Historical Society* 15 (1923): 530–47.

John, Elizabeth A. H. "An Earlier Chapter of Kiowa History." *New Mexico Historical Review* 60 (October 1985): 379–97.

———. "Nurturing the Peace: Spanish and Comanche Cooperation in the Early Nineteenth Century." *New Mexico Historical Review* 59 (October, 1984): 345–69.

———. "Portrait of a Wichita Village, 1808." *Chronicles of Oklahoma* 60 (Winter 1982–83): 412–37.

Jones, Harold W., ed. "The Diary of Assistant Surgeon Leonard McPhail on His Journey to the Southwest in 1835." *Chronicles of Oklahoma* 18 (September 1940): 281–92.

"The Journal of Elijah Hicks." *Chronicles of Oklahoma* 13 (March 1935): 68–99.

Lewis, Anna. "Du Tisné's First Expedition into Oklahoma in 1719." *Chronicles of Oklahoma* 3 (December 1925), 319–23.

———. "La Harpe's First Expedition into Oklahoma, 1718–1719." *Chronicles of Oklahoma* 2 (December 1924): 331–49.

"The Lost Valley Fight: Reminiscences of Walter Robertson." *Frontier Times* 7: 100–104.

"Massacre of Confederate Officers," *Osage Magazine,* May 1910.

"Massacre of Confederates by Osage Indians in 1863." *Kansas State Historical Society Collections* 8 (1903–1904): 62–66.

Milligan, James C., and L. David Norris, "Keeping the Peace: William H. Emory and the Command at Fort Arbuckle." *Chronicles of Oklahoma* 69, no. 3 (Fall 1991): 256–81.

"The Missouri Reader—Explorers in the Valley," part 2. *Missouri Historical Review* 39 (July 1945): 505–43.

Morrison, W. B. "A Journey across Oklahoma Ninety Years Ago." *Chronicles of Oklahoma* 4 (December 1926): 33–37.

Newcomb, W. W., and T. N. Campbell. "Southern Plains Ethnohistory: A Re-examination of the Escanjaques, Ahijados, and
Cuitoas." In *Pathways to Plains Prehistory*, ed. Don G. Wyckoff and Jack L. Hofman. Oklahoma Anthropological Society
Memoir 3. Norman: Cross Timbers Heritage Association.

Price, Catherine. "The Comanches' Threat to Texas and New
Mexico in the Eighteenth Century and the Development of
Spanish Indian Policy." *Journal of the West* 24 (April 1985):
34–45.

Rister, C. C., ed. "Colonel A. W. Evans' Christmas Day Indian
Fight (1868)." *Chronicles of Oklahoma* 16 (September 1938):
275–301.

"Scouting on the 'Staked Plains' (Llano Estacado) with Mackenzie, in 1874." *United Service* 13 (October–November 1885):
400–412, 532–43.

Thoburn, Joseph B. "Battle with Comanches." *Sturm's Oklahoma Magazine* (August 1910): 22–28.

———. "A Campaign of the Texas Rangers against the Comanches." *Sturm's Oklahoma Magazine* (July 1910): 30–38.

———. "The Collection of Relics and Artifacts from Ferdinandina, Oklahoma's First White Settlement." *Chronicles of
Oklahoma* 34 (Autumn 1956): 353–56.

———. "Horace P. Jones, Scout." *Chronicles of Oklahoma* 2
(December 1924): 380–91.

———. "Indian Fight in Ford County in 1859." *Kansas State
Historical Collections* 12 (1912): 313–29.

Trickett, Dean. "The Civil War in the Indian Territory." *Chronicles of Oklahoma* 18 (September 1940): 266–80.

Webb, W. P. "The Last Treaty of the Republic of Texas." *Southwestern Historical Quarterly* 25 (January 1922): 151–73.

Wedel, Mildred Mott. "Claude-Charles Dutisné: A Review of
His 1719 Journeys," *Great Plains Journal* 12 (Fall 1972, Spring
1973): 4–25, 166–73.

Wright, Muriel. "A History of Fort Cobb." *Chronicles of Oklahoma* 34 (Spring 1956): 52–63.

Wright, Peter M. "The Pursuit of Dull Knife from Fort Reno in
1878–79." *Chronicles of Oklahoma* 46 (Summer 1968): 141–
54.

Young, Otis E. "The United States Mounted Ranger Batallion,
1832–33." *Mississippi Valley Historical Review* 41 (December 1954): 453–70.

Books

Abel, Annie Heloise. *The American Indian as a Participant in the Civil War*. Cleveland: Arthur H. Clark Co., 1919.

———. *The American Indian as a Slaveholder and Secessionist*. Cleveland: Arthur H. Clark Co., 1915.

Andreas, Alfred Theodore. *History of the State of Kansas*. Ed. William G. Cutler. 2 vols. Atchison: Atchison County Historical Society, 1883.

Baker, T. Lindsay, and Billy R. Harrison. *Adobe Walls: The History and Archeology of the 1874 Trading Post*. College Station: Texas A&M University Press, 1986.

Bandelier, Fanny, and Adolf F. Bandelier, trans. and eds. *The Journey of Alvara Nuñez Cabeza de Vaca and His Companions from Florida to the Pacific, 1528–1536*. Chicago: Rio Grande Press, 1964.

Barde, Frederick, S. *Life and Adventures of "Billy" Dixon*. Guthrie: Co-operative Publishing Co., 1914.

Bell, Robert E., Edward B. Jelks, and W. W. Newcomb. *Wichita Indian Archaeology and Ethnology: A Pilot Study*. New York: Garland Publishing Co., 1974.

Berlandier, Jean Louis. *The Indians of Texas in 1830*. Washington: Smithsonian Institution Press, 1969.

Berthrong, Donald J. *The Southern Cheyennes*. Norman: University of Oklahoma Press, 1963.

Bolton, Herbert Eugene. *Athanase de Mézières and the Louisiana-Texas Frontier, 1768–1780*. 2 vols. Cleveland: Arthur H. Clark Co., 1914.

———. *Spanish Exploration in the Southwest, 1542–1706*. New York: Charles Scribner's Sons, 1925.

———. *Texas in the Middle Eighteenth Century*. New York: Russell and Russell, 1962.

Brill, Charles J. *Conquest of the Southern Plains*. Oklahoma City: Golden Saga Publications, 1939.

Brown, John Henry. *History of Texas, from 1685 to 1892*. St. Louis: L. E. Daniel, 1893.

———. *Indian Wars and Pioneers of Texas*. Austin: L. E. Daniel, 189?.

Calloway, Colin G., ed. *New Directions in American Indian History*. Norman: University of Oklahoma Press, 1988.

Capps, Benjamin. *The Warren Wagontrain Raid*. New York: Dial Press, 1974.

Carter, Robert Goldthwaite. *Massacre at Salt Creek Prairie and the Cow-boys' Verdict*. Washington: Gibson Brothers, Printers, 1919.

————. *On the Border with Mackenzie*. Washington: Eynon Printing Co., 1935.

Catlin, George. *North American Indians*. 2 vols. Edinburgh: Oliver and Boyd, 1926.

Chalfant, William Y. *Cheyennes and Horse Soldiers: The 1857 Expedition and the Battle of Solomon's Fork*. Norman: University of Oklahoma Press, 1989.

Chandler, Melbourne C. *Of Garryowen in Glory: the History of the Seventh United States Cavalry Regiment*. Annandale: Turnpike Press, 1960.

Clarke, Mary Whatley. *Chief Bowles and the Texas Cherokees*. Norman: University of Oklahoma Press, 1971.

Clifton, James A. *The Prairie People*. Lawrence: Regents Press of Kansas, 1977.

Colton, Ray C. *The Civil War in the Western Territories*. Norman: University of Oklahoma Press, 1959.

Connell, Evan S. *Son of the Morning Star*. San Francisco: North Point Press, 1984.

Conover, George W. *Sixty Years in Southwest Oklahoma*. Anadarko: N. T. Plummer, 1927.

Coues, Elliott, ed. and annot. *The Journal of Jacob Fowler*. Minneapolis: Ross and Haines, 1965.

————, ed. *New Light on the Early History of the Greater Northwest, the Manuscript Journal of Alexander Henry, Fur Trader for the Northwest Company, and of David Thompson, Official Geographer and Explorer of the Same Company, 1799–1814*. New York: Francis P. Harper, 1897.

Crawford, Samuel J. *Kansas in the Sixties*. Chicago: A. G. McClurg and Co., 1911.

Custer, George Armstrong. *My Life on the Plains, or Personal Experience with Indians*. Norman: University of Oklahoma Press, 1962.

Davies, Henry E. *Ten Days on the Plains*. Ed. Paul Andrew Hutton. Dallas: Southern Methodist University Press, 1985.

Debo, Angie. *The Road to Disappearance*. Norman: University of Oklahoma Press, 1941.

De Shields, James T. *Border Wars of Texas*. Tioga, Tex.: Herald Company, 1912.

———. *Cynthia Ann Parker: The Story of Her Capture*. St. Louis: Chas. B. Woodward Co., 1886.

Din, Gilbert C., and A. P. Nasatir. *Imperial Osages*. Norman: University of Oklahoma Press, 1983.

Dodge, Richard Irving. *Our Wild Indians*. Chicago: A. D. Worthington and Co., 1882.

———. *The Plains of the Great West and Their Inhabitants*. New York: G. P. Putnam's Sons, 1877.

Downey, Fairfax. *Indian-Fighting Army*. New York: Bantam Books, 1941.

Everett, Dianna. *The Texas Cherokees: A People between Two Fires*. Norman: University of Oklahoma Press, 1990.

Fehrenbach, T. R. *Comanches: The Destruction of a People*. New York: Alfred A. Knopf, 1974.

Flores, Dan L., ed. *Jefferson and Southwestern Exploration: The Freeman Custis Accounts of the Red River Expedition of 1806*. Norman: University of Oklahoma Press, 1984.

———. *Journal of an Indian Trader: Anthony Glass and the Texas Trading Frontier*. College State: Texas A&M University Press, 1985.

Foreman, Grant. *Advancing the Frontier*. Norman: University of Oklahoma Press, 1933.

———. *Indians and Pioneers: The Story of the American Southwest before 1830*. New Haven: Yale University Press, 1930.

———. *Pioneer Days in the Early Southwest*. Cleveland: Arthur H. Clark Co., 1926.

Forsyth, George A. *Thrilling Days in Army Life*. New York: Harper and Brothers, 1901.

Franks, Kenny. *Stand Waite and the Agony of the Cherokee Nation*. Memphis: Memphis State University Press, 1979.

Frost, Lawrence A. *The Courts-Martial of General George Armstrong Custer*. Norman: University of Oklahoma Press, 1968.

Galvin, John, ed. *Lieutenant James W. Abert's March through the Country of the Comanche Indians in the Fall of the Year, 1845, the Journal of a U.S. Army Exploration*. San Francisco: J. Howell, 1970.

Garrard, Lewis H. *Wah-to-Yah and the Taos Trail*. Norman: University of Oklahoma Press, 1955.

Gibson, Arrell Morgan. *The American Indian, Prehistory to Present.* Lexington, Mass.: D.C. Health Co., 1980.

———. *The Kickapoos, Lords of the Middle Border.* Norman: University of Oklahoma Press, 1963.

Grinnell, George Bird. *The Cheyenne Indians.* 2 vols. Lincoln: University of Nebraska Press, 1972.

———. *The Fighting Cheyennes.* Norman: University of Oklahoma Press, 1956.

Haley, James L. *The Buffalo War: The History of the Red River Indian Uprising of 1874.* Norman: University of Oklahoma Press, 1976.

Hammond, George P., and Agapito Rey. *Don Juan de Oñate: Colonizer of New Mexico, 1595–1628.* 2 vols. Albuquerque: University of New Mexico Press, 1953.

Hoig, Stan. *The Battle of the Washita.* Garden City, N.Y.: Doubleday and Company, 1976.

———. *David L. Payne, the Oklahoma Boomer.* Oklahoma City: Western Heritage Books 1980.

———. *The Sand Creek Massacre.* Norman: University of Oklahoma, 1961.

Hutton, Paul Andrew. *Phil Sheridan and His Army.* Lincoln: University of Nebraska Press, 1985.

———, ed. *Soldiers West: Biographies from the Military Frontier.* Lincoln: University of Nebraska Press, 1987.

Hyde, George E. *Life of George Bent.* Ed. Savoie Lottinville. Norman: University of Oklahoma Press, 1968.

———. *The Pawnee Indians.* Norman: University of Oklahoma Press, 1951.

Irving, Washington. *A Tour of the Prairies.* Ed. John Francis McDermott. Norman: University of Oklahoma Press, 1956.

Iverson, Peter, ed. *The Plains Indians of the Twentieth Century.* Norman: University of Oklahoma Press, 1985.

Jackson, Donald, ed. and annot. *The Journals of Zebulon Montgomery Pike, with Letters and Related Documents.* 2 vols. Norman: University of Oklahoma Press, 1966.

James, Edwin. *Account of an Expedition from Pittsburgh to the Rocky Mountains.* 2 vols. Ann Arbor: University Microfilms, 1966.

James, Thomas. *Three Years among the Mexicans and the Indians.* Chicago: Rio Grande Press, 1962.

John, Elizabeth A. H. *Storms Brewed in Other Men's Worlds.* College Station: Texas A&M University Press, 1975.

Jones, Douglas C. *The Treaty of Medicine Lodge.* Norman: University of Oklahoma Press, 1966.

Journal of Andrew Ellicott. Philadelphia: Budd and Bartram, 1803.

Kappler, Charles J., ed. *Indian Treaties.* New York: Interland Publishing, 1972.

Keim, DeB. Randolph. *Sheridan's Troopers on the Borders: A Winter Campaign on the Plains.* Philadelphia: David McKay, 1885.

Kirkland, Forrest, and W. W. Newcomb, Jr. *The Rock Art of Texas.* Austin: University of Texas Press, 1967.

Leckie, William H. *The Military Conquest of the Southern Plains.* Norman: University of Oklahoma Press, 1963.

Lee, Nelson. *Three Years among the Comanches.* Albany: B. Taylor, 1859.

Loomis, Noel M., and Abraham P. Nasatir. *Pedro Vial and the Roads to Santa Fe.* Norman: University of Oklahoma Press, 1967.

McDermott, John Francis, ed. *Tixier's Travels on the Osage Prairies.* Norman: University of Oklahoma Press, 1940.

McLean, Malcom D., comp. and ed. *Papers Concerning Robertson's Colony in Texas.* 2 vols. Fort Worth: Texas Christian University Press: 1974.

McReynolds, Edwin C. *The Seminoles.* Norman: University of Oklahoma Press, 1957.

Mails, Thomas E. *The Mystic Warriors of the Plains.* Garden City, N.Y.: Doubleday and Company, 1972.

Margry, Pierre, ed. *Découvertes et Établissements des Français dans l'ouest et dans le sud de l'Amérique Septentrionale.* 6 vols. Paris: 1879–88.

Marshal, S.L.A. *Crimsoned Prairie.* New York: Scribner, 1972.

Masson, Louis François Rodrigue. *Les Bourgeois de la Compagne du Nord-Ouest.* Quebec: Impr. Generale A. Cote, 1889–90.

Mathews, John Joseph. *The Osages.* Norman: University of Oklahoma Press, 1961.

Mayhall, Mildred. *Indian Wars of Texas.* Waco: Texian Press, 1965.

———. *The Kiowas.* Norman: University of Oklahoma Press, 1962.

Miskin, Bernard. *Rank and Warfare among the Plains Indians.* Seattle: University of Washington Press, 1966.

Molyneaux, Peter. *The Romantic Story of Texas.* Dallas: Cordova Press, 1936.

Morfi, Fray Juan Agustín. *History of Texas, 1673–1779.* Albuquerque: Quivira Society, 1935.

Nasatir, A. P. *Before Lewis and Clark.* 2 vols. St. Louis: St. Louis Historical Documents Foundation, 1980.

Newcomb, W. W., Jr. *The Indians of Texas from Prehistoric to Modern Times.* Austin: University of Texas Press, 1961.

Nuttall, Thomas. *A Journal of Travels into the Arkansas Territory during the Year 1819.* Ed. Savoie Lottinville. Norman: University of Oklahoma Press, 1980.

Nye, W. S. *Carbine and Lance: The Story of Old Fort Sill.* Norman: University of Oklahoma Press, 1937.

Pettis, George W. *Kit Carson's Battle with the Comanche and Kiowa Indians at the Adobe Walls on the Canadian River, November 25th, 1864.* Providence: S. S. Rider, 1878.

Pike, Zebulon Montgomery. *Sources of the Mississippi and the Western Louisiana Territory.* Ann Arbor: University Microfilms, 1966.

Portraits of North American Indians with Sketches of Scenery, Etc., Painted by J. M. Stanley, Deposited with the Smithsonian Institution. Washington: Smithsonian Institution, 1852.

Rampp, Lary C., and Donald L. Rampp. *The Civil War in the Indian Territory.* Austin: Presidio Press, 1975.

Richardson, Rupert Norval. *The Comanche Barrier to South Plains Settlement.* Glendale: Arthur H. Clark Co., 1933.

———. *The Frontier of Northwest Texas, 1846 to 1876: Advance and Defense by the Pioneer Settlers of the Cross Timbers Prairies.* Glendale: Arthur H. Clark Co., 1963.

Roe, Frank Gilbert. *The Indian and the Horse.* Norman: University of Oklahoma Press, 1955.

Smith, Sherry L. *Sagebrush Soldier.* Norman: University of Oklahoma Press, 1989.

Stanley, Henry M. *My Early Travels and Adventures in America and Asia.* 2 vols. New York: Charles Scribner's Sons, 1905.

Stephens, Morse, and Herbert E. Bolton, eds. *The Pacific Ocean in History.*

Thoburn, Joseph. *A Standard History of Oklahoma.* Chicago: American Historical Society, 1916.

Thomas, Alfred Barnaby. *Forgotten Frontiers: A Study of the Spanish Indian Policy of Don Juan Bautista, Governor of New*

Mexico, 1777–1787. Norman: University of Oklahoma Press, 1932.

————, trans. and ed. *After Coronado: Spanish Exploration Northeast of New Mexico, 1696–1727*. Norman: University of Oklahoma Press, 1935.

Tyrrell, J. B., ed. *David Thompson's Narrative of His Explorations in Western America*. Toronto: Champlain Society, 1916.

Utley, Robert M. *Frontier Regulars: The U.S. Army and the Indian, 1866–91*. New York: Macmillan Publishing Company, 1973.

————. *The Indian Frontier of the American West, 1846–1890*. Albuquerque: University of New Mexico Press, 1984.

Wallace, Ernest, and E. Adamson Hoebel. *The Comanches: Lords of the South Plains*. Norman: University of Oklahoma Press, 1952.

Webb, Walter Prescott. *The Texas Rangers*. Austin: University of Texas Press, 1965.

Wedel, Mildred Mott. *The Deer Creek Site, Oklahoma: A Wichita Village Sometimes Called Ferdinandina, an Ethnohistorian's View*. Series in Anthropology No. 5. Oklahoma City: Oklahoma Historical Society, 1981.

Wedel, Waldo R. *Prehistoric Man on the Great Plains*. Norman: University of Oklahoma Press, 1961.

White, Richard. *The Roots of Dependency*. Lincoln: University of Nebraska Press, 1983.

Winfrey, Dorman H. *Texas Indian Papers, 1825–43*. Austin: Texas State Library, 1959.

Winfrey, Dorman H., and James M. Day, eds. *The Indian Papers of Texas and the Southwest, 1825–1916*. 4 vols. Austin: Pemberton Press, 1966.

Winship, George Parker. *The Coronado Expedition, 1540–1542*. Chicago: Rio Grande Press, 1964.

Wood, W. Raymond, and Margot Liberty, eds. *Anthropology on the Great Plains*. Lincoln: University of Nebraska Press, 1980.

Wooten, Dudley Goodall, ed. *A Comprehensive History of Texas*. 2 vols. Dallas: W. G. Scarff, 1898.

Wright, Muriel, George H. Shirk, and Kenny A. Franks. *Mark of Heritage: Oklahoma's Historic Sites*. The Oklahoma Series, vol. 2. Oklahoma City: Oklahoma Historical Society, 1976.

Wyckoff, Don G., and Robert L. Brooks. *Oklahoma Archeology*. Norman: Oklahoma Archaeological Survey, 1983.

Dissertations

Secoy, Frank R. "A Functional-Historical View of Plains Indian Warfare: The Process of Change from the Seventeenth Century to the Early Nineteenth Century." Ph.D. diss., Columbia University, 1950.

Government Documents, Published

American State Papers, Class 2, Indian Affairs, 1789–1815. Bogy, Joseph, Petition of. *Senate Document No. 23,* 24th Cong., 1st sess.

Butler, P. M., and M. G. Lewis. *Report of Messrs. Butler and Lewis,* September 13, 1846. Western Americana Microfilm Series, Reel 5687.

Carter, Clarence Edwin, ed. *The Territorial Papers of the United States.* 28 vols. Washington: GPO, 1934–48.

Compilation of the Official Records of the War of the Union and Confederate Armies, War of the Rebellion.

Dodge, Henry. "Colonel Henry Dodge Report of Leavenworth Expedition," *Senate Document No. 1,* 23rd Cong., 2d sess.

Ford, John S., Report to Gov. Runnels, May 22, 1858, *House Ex. Doc. 27,* 35th Cong., 2d sess.

House Ex. Doc. No. 1, 44th Cong., 1st sess.

Kingsley, G. P. "Report on the Expedition of Dragoons, under Colonel Henry Dodge, to the Rocky Mountains in 1835." *American State Papers, Military Affairs,* VI, 24th Cong., 1st sess.

Letters and Reports from Indian Territory prior to and following the Battle of the Washita. *Senate Ex. Doc. No. 18,* 40th Cong., 3d. sess.

Official Communications from General Pope. St. Louis: Missouri Democrat Printing Co., 1865. WAMS, Reel 5646.

Pike, Albert, Report. *Message to the Congress of the Confederate States from Jefferson Davis,* December 12, 1861.

Record of Engagements with Hostile Indians within the Military Division of the Missouri, from 1868 to 1882. Chicago: Military Division of the Missouri, 1882.

Reports of the Commissioner of Indian Affairs, 1824–1889.

"Sand Creek Massacre." *Report of the Secretary of War*, Sen. Exec. Doc. 26, 39th Cong., 2d sess.

Sibley, Dr. John. "Historical Sketches of the Several Indian Tribes in Louisiana South of the Arkansas River and between the Mississippi and River Grande." *American State Papers*, Class 2, Indian Affairs.

Van Dorn report, October 5, 1858, *House Ex. Doc. No. 27*, 35th Cong., 2d sess.

Government Documents, Unpublished

Ltrs. Recd., Creek Agency, 1839–42, NA.

Ltrs, Recd., Kiowa Agency, 1864–80, NA.

Ltrs. Recd., Office of Adjutant General, Main Series, 1822–60, NA.

Ltrs. Recd., Secretary of War Relating to Indian Affairs, 1800–1823, NA.

Ltrs. Recd., Southern Superintendency, 1853, NA.

Ltrs. Recd., Texas Agency, 1847–59, NA.

Ltrs. Recd., Texas OIA Letter Book, I, 1838–48, BTHC.

Ltrs. Recd., Upper Arkansas Agency, Central Superintendency, 1865–67, NA.

Ltrs. Recd., Western Superintendency, 1832–51, NA.

Ltrs. Recd., Wichita Agency, 1867–75, NA.

Ltrs. Sent, Department of Texas, District of Texas and 5th Military District, 1856–68, NA.

Ltrs. Sent, Southern Superintendency, 1853–70, NA.

Message of Jefferson Davis, December 12, 1861, Reel 1330, Western Americana Microfilm Series.

Records of the Southern Superintendency, 1832–70, NA.

Records of the Western Superintendency, 1832–51, NA.

"Report of Albert Pike on Mission to the Indian Nations," WAMS, Reel 1330. Selected Ltrs., 1868–72, Records of U.S. Army Commands, Nebraska, NA.

Treaty with Kioway, Documents of Ratified Indian Treaties, 1833–37, NA.

Wheelock, T. B. Proceedings of a Council Held at Fort Gibson, September 1834, Record Group 75, NA.

Newspapers and Periodicals

Arkansas Gazette (Little Rock)
Arkansas Intelligencer (Van Buren)
Army and Navy Journal
Baltimore Sun
Cherokee Advocate
Cherokee Phoenix
Chicago Tribune
Cincinnati Commercial
Cincinnati Gazette
Daily Missouri Republican (St. Louis)
Daily National Intelligencer
Emporia (Kansas) *News*
Independence (Missouri) *Daily Reporter*
Kansas City Times
Kansas Daily Tribune (Lawrence)
Kansas Weekly Tribune (Lawrence)
Lawrence (Kansas) *Republican*
Leavenworth (Kansas) *Daily Conservative*
New Orleans Picayune
New York Herald
New York Tribune
Niles' Weekly Register
Osage Magazine
St. Louis Daily Democrat (also *Daily Missouri Democrat*)
Washington National Republican
Weekly Commonwealth and Republican (Denver)
Wichita Eagle

Index